Church State Corporation

Church State Corporation

Construing Religion in US Law

WINNIFRED FALLERS SULLIVAN

THE UNIVERSITY OF CHICAGO PRESS CHICAGO AND LONDON

The University of Chicago Press, Chicago 60637
The University of Chicago Press, Ltd., London

Published 2020
Printed in the United States of America

29 28 27 26 25 24 23 22 21 20   1 2 3 4 5

ISBN-13: 978-0-226-45455-9 (cloth)
ISBN-13: 978-0-226-45469-6 (paper)
ISBN-13: 978-0-226-45472-6 (e-book)
DOI: https://doi.org/10.7208/chicago/9780226454726.001.0001

Library of Congress Cataloging-in-Publication Data

Names: Sullivan, Winnifred Fallers, 1950– author.
Title: Church state corporation : construing religion in US law / Winnifred Fallers Sullivan.
Description: Chicago : University of Chicago Press, 2020. | Includes bibliographical references and index.
Identifiers: LCCN 2019039016 | ISBN 9780226454559 (cloth) | ISBN 9780226454696 (paperback) | ISBN 9780226454726 (ebook)
Subjects: LCSH: Church and state—United States—Cases. | Religion and law—United States—Cases. | Christianity and politics—United States.
Classification: LCC KF4865 .S85 2020 | DDC 344.73/096—dc23
LC record available at https://lccn.loc.gov/2019039016

♾ This paper meets the requirements of ANSI/NISO Z39.48-1992 (Permanence of Paper).

IN MEMORY OF FRANK REYNOLDS

Contents

Note on Capitalization

In this book, I drop initial caps for religious groupings—"catholic," "protestant," "mennonite," "mormon," and so on—because they tend to support orthodox descriptions of these groups rather than descriptions based in historical behavior. For example, I talk about mennonites as a broad group that includes some who wouldn't be considered orthodox by those in charge. One can be catholic without being Catholic. This practice does not eliminate all ambiguity or recognize the desire of dissenters to define or at least to be included in the uppercase designation, but it does call attention to the issue. I retain the convention of capitalizing "Christianity," although "christian" is sometimes lowercase.

As is customary in US legal writing, I capitalize "Court" to indicate the US Supreme Court as opposed to other courts.

Note to European Readers

Alessandro Ferrari, law and religion scholar at the University of Como, after reading the manuscript for this book, suggested that I provide a note for European readers to alert them to the fact that what I describe in this book differs from what they often take to be the "American Model" of religious freedom. His suggested language was this:

> This is a footnote for a European reader. I've often noted that in Europe US nonestablishment is understood to indicate the absence of a state religion. The US is thus categorized as a "separatist" country, in the same composite box with France, Belgium, The Netherlands, Ireland, and all other countries without either a bilateral agreement between state and religion or a state-church. In this book I will demonstrate that US nonestablishment is not this. At the end of the book, maybe, the European reader will find another way to categorize US experience, now realizing how American "state" and American "religion" have shaped themselves in their "new world."

I would not presume to tell European readers how to read the book, but in the spirit of Ferrari's suggestion, and at the risk of further contributing to a smug exposition of US exceptionalism, I do hope that this book might contribute to a better comparative understanding of these matters—not just with Europe but with all those who are interested, here and abroad.

INTRODUCTION

The Definite Article

The law knows no heresy, and is committed to the support of no dogma, the establishment of no sect. The right to organize voluntary religious associations to assist in the expression and dissemination of any religious doctrine, and to create tribunals for the decision of controverted questions of faith within the association, and for the ecclesiastical government of all the individual members, congregations, and officers within the general association, is unquestioned. All who unite themselves to such a body do so with an implied consent to this government, and are bound to submit to it.—*Watson v. Jones*[1]

In January 2012 I sat down to read the US Supreme Court's latest religion decision, *Hosanna-Tabor Evangelical Lutheran Church & School v. EEOC*.[2] As with most religion cases, the issues had already been fairly well rehearsed by law professors and other commenters. I did not expect to be surprised, only irritated. A disabled fourth-grade teacher at a parochial school in Michigan had been fired; she had filed a complaint claiming that the dismissal was in violation of the Americans with Disabilities Act. The school had just won; the Court declared for the first time that the religion clauses of the first amendment to the US Constitution removed churches and church-related institutions from the purview of employment discrimination laws.

The *Hosanna-Tabor* decision was unanimous, the opinion for the Court

1. *Watson v. Jones*, 80 U.S. (13 Wall.) 679 (1871), 728–729.
2. *Hosanna-Tabor Evangelical Lutheran Church & School v. EEOC*, 565 U.S. 171 (2012).

written by Chief Justice John Roberts.[3] After the usual rehearsal of the facts and the procedural history of the case, I had come to Section IIA. Section IIA begins with the sentence, "Controversy between church and state over religious offices is hardly new."[4] This oddly un-American reference to religious offices, using a medieval formulation, was followed by a curious mash-up of English church-state history beginning with King John and Magna Carta—a history marshalled in support of the proposition that the church in the US has rights granted to it in medieval England. The last sentence of Chief Justice Roberts' opinion in *Hosanna-Tabor* declares that "[t]he church must be free to choose those who will guide it on its way."[5] I sat up. *The* church? What is the church in US law? And, I asked myself, is it constitutional for the US Supreme Court to use the definite article in referring to church?

This book attempts to answer those questions. Chapter one discusses the *Hosanna-Tabor* opinions at greater length. Here, in the introduction, I will set my initial questions in the context of a broader set of issues about religion in US law.

The First Amendment to the US Constitution provides, in part, that "Congress shall make no law respecting an establishment of religion or prohibiting the free exercise thereof[.]"[6] These words are known as the religion clauses. There is no mention of the church or of churches in the Constitution.

The First Amendment, like the rest of the Bill of Rights (the first ten amendments to the Constitution) is addressed to Congress. It limits the power of the federal government with respect to religion. All of the states eventually adopted their own versions and interpretations of the religion clauses. However, in the middle of the twentieth century, the reach of the federal religion clauses was extended to the states. This was accomplished through new readings of the Fourteenth Amendment, which had been adopted in 1865 as one of the Civil War or Reconstruction Amendments meant to secure due process and equal protection of the laws to newly emancipated slaves.[7] In 1940 and 1947, in the decisions in *Cantwell v.*

3. There are also two concurring opinions, one by Justice Clarence Thomas and one by Justice Samuel Alito.

4. 565 U.S. at 182.

5. 565 U.S. at 196.

6. U.S. Const. amend. I, § 1.

7. The Fourteenth Amendment provides in relevant part that "[n]o State shall make or enforce any law which shall abridge the privileges or immunities of citizens of the United States;

Connecticut[8] and *Everson v. Board of Education*,[9] the Court held that both the establishment clause and the free exercise clause of the First Amendment should thereafter be understood to have been incorporated into the Fourteenth Amendment, incorporation understood to provide detail by reference to the specific guarantees of the Bill of Rights to the more general wording of the Fourteenth Amendment.[10] The Court thus federalized the First Amendment; it now limits the power of the states, as well as that of the federal government, to regulate religion, providing a layer of federal constitutional oversight on top of that provided by state constitutions.[11]

The interpretive journey begun in *Cantwell* and *Everson* has been a rocky one for the Court. One enduring challenge, though, has been whether and how the religious exercise of groups or organizations, rather than just that of individuals, is given special constitutional protection. Religion is said to be disestablished—but what exactly does that mean? Does it mean that churches and other religious organizations are or should be of no special legal consequence? Is it only the individual's religion that matters? This book tries to think through the terms of this challenge by focusing on the church-in-law, evident in *Hosanna-Tabor* and in many other cases and statutes, as one corporate body among others, but one that has had a surprisingly specific endurance in the American legal imagination.[12] Collective religion—the church—remains alive in law

---

nor shall any State deprive any person of life, liberty, or property, without due process of law; nor deny to any person within its jurisdiction the equal protection of the laws." U.S. Const. amend. XIV § 1. For a historical account of the Fourteenth Amendment, see William E. Nelson, *The Fourteenth Amendment: From Political Principle to Judicial Doctrine* (Cambridge: Harvard University Press, 1998).

8. *Cantwell v. Connecticut*, 310 U.S. 296 (1940).

9. *Everson v. Board of Education*, 330 U.S. 1 (1947).

10. Other amendments in the Bill of Rights have likewise been incorporated piecemeal. See Erwin Chemerinsky, *Constitutional Law: Principles and Policies*, 4th ed. (New York: Wolters Kluwer, 2011), at §6.3.3.

11. One result of incorporation has been an intensification of states' rights politics in a number of areas, not just with respect to religion. Chemerinsky, *Constitutional Law* at §6.

12. This book will focus primarily on federal law with respect to the disestablishment of churches. The legal history of the regulation of religion by state law, both constitutional and statutory, is significantly under-studied and is critical to a full understanding the history of religion in the US. Furthermore, while *Everson*'s interpellation of the establishment clause into the Fourteenth Amendment remains the law of the land, influential dissent from this reading of the Fourteenth Amendment has been led by Justice Clarence Thomas, who argues that state action with respect to religion is limited only by state constitutions. See, e.g., *Zelman v. Simmons-Harris*, 536 U.S. 639 (2002), Thomas concurring. Steven Green has argued that nineteenth-century regulation of religion by the states should be understood to have resulted, in effect, in a second disestablishment. See Steven K. Green, *The Second Disestablishment:*

after disestablishment but in ways that are deeply ambiguous and often unacknowledged.

In using the slightly awkward locution, the church-in-law, I mean to draw attention to the particular legal fiction of the church that is operative in US law. I also mean to invoke a resonance with others-in-law. In-laws are kinship relations both indispensable and troublesome, as anthropologists have documented.[13] In other words, the church-in-law keeps company with a myriad of other ambiguous creatures-in-law.

The dominant narrative throughout US history has been one that centers religious liberty on the individual and the individual's conscience; that narrative frequently has been accompanied by the assumption, expressed in various ways, that to recognize the religious collective legally would be somehow to "establish" religion. To solve this problem, then, to the extent that religious collectives are acknowledged in law, they have been legally and politically imagined as properly and wholly voluntary, entered and exited without penalty, and without special legal consequence, as the quote from *Watson v. Jones* forming an epigraph to this chapter suggests.[14]

Church and State in Nineteenth-Century America (Oxford: Oxford University Press, 2010). The twentieth-century doctrine of incorporation in the *Everson* decision might then be understood to make a third moment in disestablishment. Already by the time of the Revolution, however, the versions of the European churches in the North American colonies that would become the US had undergone earlier disestablishments of a sort in their transatlantic replantings and in their submission to varied colonial legal regimes. (While religious establishments of a sort existed at various times in the colonies, they were fragmentary and short-lived, legally and religiously distinct in important ways from their Old World counterparts.) Disestablishment is a tangled story, not accomplished yet, even in the twenty-first century. For a sociological account of religious organizations in the US, see N. J. Demerath III, Peter Dobkin Hall, Terry Schmidt, and Rhys H. Williams, eds., *Sacred Companies: Organizational Aspects of Religion and Religious Aspects of Organizations* (Oxford: Oxford University Press, 1998.) For an excellent account of the general problem of disestablishment in law in the UK, see Julian Rivers, *The Law of Organized Religions: Between Establishment and Secularism* (Oxford: Oxford University Press, 2010), 322–327.

13. See, e.g., David Schneider, *American Kinship: A Cultural Account* (Chicago: University of Chicago Press, 1968).

14. Understanding American religion as primarily an individual matter has also been a dominant practice among historians. As Laurie Maffly-Kipp wrote in her presidential lecture for the American Society of Church History, "Seeing religious life as primarily a process of choosing individual identities . . . threatens to obscure the importance of religious institutions and doctrine in our [historical] studies." Laurie Maffly-Kipp, "The Burdens of Church History," *Church History* 82 (2013): 362. In both law and history this bias threatens to overemphasize, even falsify, the nature of choice in such matters, notwithstanding its correspondence with dominant American ideas about choice in matters of religion. For a new history of religious choice in the US, see Lincoln Mullen, *The Chance of Salvation: A History of Conversion in America* (Cambridge: Harvard University Press, 2017).

Haunting this dominant narrative, however, has been the mimetic presence in US law of *the* church and of her sovereign companions—the state and the corporation, collectives that have legal capacities of their own that exceed those of their members.[15] US law about religion has, notwithstanding the apparent command of the First Amendment, repeatedly acknowledged the distinctive legal personhood of the church, privileging that legal personhood over that of the individual. Disestablishment remains unfinished business. And the church is very much still with us. Indeed, one might say that *the* church has actually gained in legal personality over the course of US history.[16]

This book essays a phenomenological description of the church-in-law in the United States, displaying the unexpected and ongoing presence of what christians call the Body of Christ in its religious liberty regime. One can tell a longitudinal or a structural story of this haunting. On the one hand one can, as Mark DeWolfe Howe did, trace a shift over time from an early and almost exclusive restriction through state law to the formation only of small wholly local voluntary congregations (often known as religious societies) in the first half of the nineteenth century, to an increasingly robust privileging in law of churches (first of the national churches and then of the transnational ones) in the late nineteenth and twentieth centuries.[17] On the other hand, one can also see an always present, built-in, constitutional tension between individual and corporate religion; that is, one can see both the never–wholly enforced prohibition against "an establishment of" the church, and the uneven protection of "the free

15. Conventional use of the feminine pronoun in reference to church derives from the biblical metaphor that speaks of the church as the bride of Christ and underlines its theological meaning, as is discussed at the end of chapter one.

16. In US law, the religion that has been protected has mostly been Christianity. While that might be lamented, it is not disputable. There are interesting and important exceptions but they are few and far between. Those instances, referred to at times in this text, form a part of a story that deserves a book of its own. Here it is, for the most part, Christianity that is addressed. And Christianity implies the church, very broadly understood. Even if you do not formally participate in a church community, to be a christian means to be a part of the church, theologically speaking. The church is one of those persistent structural issues for Christianity in the sense elaborated by Matthew Engelke in *A Problem of Presence: Beyond Scripture in an African Church* (Berkeley: University of California Press, 2007).

17. Mark DeWolfe Howe, *The Garden and the Wilderness: Religion and Government in American Constitutional History* (Chicago: University of Chicago Press, 1967). See also Ira Mark Ellman, "Driven from the Tribunal: Judicial Resolution of Internal Church Disputes," *California Law Review* 69, no. 5 (1981): 1378–1444, complaining of the inconsistent treatment of congregational and hierarchical churches in American law.

exercise of" the individual separate *from* the church, with the religious individual almost always understood only to be properly formed in and disciplined by a religious community. This always-unresolved tension has manifested itself in different ways at different times and at different scales in US history. Together, the longitudinal and the structural stories, rooted as they are in deep-seated American realities, offer a way to begin to explain the surprising endurance of the bodily presence of *the* church—in law.

It is not just churches. The individual is never wholly free of the collective. Indeed, in my view, the current religion jurisprudence in the US reflects, among other things, a broader and tragic inability to find ways to come together for communal projects of various kinds—education, health care, environmental stewardship, and global citizenship. The church-in-law—the jurisprudence of disestablishment and the related doctrine of freedom of association, in US parlance—is one site for thinking these larger questions.

In his introduction to a book thinking through the necessity of the institution, French anthropologist Bruno Latour relates an encounter between French corporate executives and a distinguished climate scientist:

> They're sitting around a table, some fifteen French industrialists responsible for sustainable development in various companies, facing a professor of climatology, a researcher from the Collège de France. It's the fall of 2010; a battle is raging about whether the current climate disturbances are of human origin or not. One of the industrialists asks the professor a question I find a little cavalier: "But why should I believe you, any more than the others?" I'm astonished. Why does he put them on the same footing, as if it were a simple difference of opinion between this climate specialist and those who are called climate skeptics? . . . I wonder how the professor is going to respond. Will he put the meddler in his place by reminding him that it's not a matter of belief but of fact? . . . But no, to my great surprise he responds, after a long, drawn-out sigh: "If people don't trust the institution of science we're in serious trouble."[18]

18. Bruno Latour, *An Inquiry into Modes of Existence: An Anthropology of the Moderns*, trans. Catherine Porter (Cambridge, MA: Harvard University Press, 2013), 2–3. For Latour's riveting and hilarious ethnographic account of the institution of law, see *The Making of Law: An Ethnography of the Conseil d'État* (Cambridge, UK: Polity Press, 2010).

"It is," Latour continues, "a little as though, responding to a catechumen who doubts the existence of God, a priest were to sketch out the organizational chart of the Vatican, the bureaucratic history of the Councils, and the countless glosses on treatises of canon law."[19]

Latour tells this story to remind us of the priority of the collective acting across time—of the institution—as necessary to ground human action. Science will not always be right, he reminds us, just as the church has not always been right, but he argues that we cannot do without these institutions, indeed we are defined and protected by them. The story also illustrates the interestingly parallel crises of authority in both science and religion. Latour reflects on the church itself at greater length in a very personal book, *Rejoicing: Or the Torments of Religious Speech*.[20]

Philosopher of religion Nancy Levene too insists that "all human life takes place in collectivities." She adds, "The question is how to value them."[21] By "value" I take her to mean at once the need for cherishing and the need for evaluation. She embodies the complexity of this dual task in the story of Abraham, boldly claiming him as *the* exemplar of the modern:

> Modernity is Abram insofar as he leaves his kin and clan, his land for another land. This event makes him Abraham, father of a multitude. The call is not only that he leave his land, it is that he leave his land for another one. In leaving his land, he is going somewhere and not nowhere, not toward an abstraction or toward the empyrean or simply to wander the earth. But then the new land, the promised land, will be no less subject to the original call—that it not become yet another homeland.[22]

"Modernity is a reformation of the collective,"[23] Levene says. You must leave your family and your home. You must go somewhere. But that place must also be a place you value in both senses. You must evaluate it and

19. Latour, *An Inquiry into Modes of Existence*, 4.

20. Bruno Latour, *Rejoicing: Or the Torments of Religious Speech* (Cambridge, UK: Polity Press, 2013). See also Bruno Latour and Steve Woolgar, *Laboratory Life: The Construction of Scientific Facts* (Princeton, NJ: Princeton University Press, 1986).

21. In her new book, Nancy Levene devotes a chapter to setting forth the terms of this modern predicament. Nancy Levene, *Powers of Distinction: On Religion and Modernity* (Chicago: University of Chicago Press, 2017), chapter 4 at 99–140. Levene's book is in part an extended riff on Émile Durkheim, *The Elementary Forms of Religious Life* (Oxford: Oxford University Press, 2008).

22. Levene, *Powers of Distinction*, 100.

23. Levene, *Powers of Distinction*, 101.

you must cherish it. It is an active commitment. The new collective, she says, must not "become yet another homeland." Religious freedom, in her words, is both impossible and necessary.[24]

In the specific context of the US, reformation in Levene's sense, reformation of the collective, modernity's task, is articulated, among other places, through the ongoing work of realizing the constitutional commitment to nonestablishment of religion. More so than in its commitment to the free exercise of religion. US modernity is in this respect distinctive. No other country does the legal reformation of religious collectivity in quite the same way. Most countries today formally protect freedom of conscience and have legally deprivileged religious institutions in various ways, but nowhere else are the state and the church disabled in quite the way they are in the US. Nowhere has government been given over to the people so completely, government of both church and state.[25]

The churches and the states of Europe are mostly still speaking to one another, even collaborating, as are governments and religious institutions in most countries. One can see that in the various cooperative bureaucratic projects European countries have had over the centuries to cultivate good religion and suppress bad religion, including the presence of religious education in their schools—now morphing from the sectarian to the sociological. Separation of church and state can mean something in those countries because there are a church and a state to be separated. Under US-style disestablishment, by contrast, the state is ideologically prohibited from being seen to involve itself with church matters. The US constitutional order gives control of both religion and government to the people.[26] Disestablishment American style sets up a new problem of

24. Levene, *Powers of Distinction*, 251.

25. Different churches—different consolidations of religious life, both imagined and actual—as well as different iterations of national and corporate sovereignty can be traced in law across the space and time of human history over the last two millennia. The phenomenology of the lives of the church and the state in early modern Europe before and after the dissolution of the absolute monarchy are explored in Ernst H. Kantorowicz, *The King's Two Bodies: A Study in Medieval Political Theology* (Princeton, NJ: Princeton University Press, 1957), and the current fallout of that story in Eric L. Santner, *The Royal Remains: The People's Two Bodies and the Endgames of Sovereignty* (Chicago: University of Chicago Press, 2011). Each considers how sovereignty is transferred to the people. See also Paul Christopher Johnson, Pamela Klassen, and Winnifred Fallers Sullivan, *Ekklesia: Three Inquiries in Church and State* (Chicago: University of Chicago Press, 2018).

26. This arrangement might also be understood in the context of the distinctiveness of the churchstateness of the Americas more generally, not just of the US. For an effort to use the

government—of church and state—one of incomplete subordination, one that still holds out hope for the sacred, perhaps.[27]

As Americans, we believe that we have definitionally solved the problem of church and state, that we are exempt from the terrors of the mutual enabling of an economy of religion and politics, the lingering vestiges of the medieval that Giorgio Agamben calls glorification.[28] Ironically, though, religion appears to many people more established in law and in politics in the US today than in Europe. Understanding how and why this is so requires a careful description of the legal phenomenology of disestablishment in the US, what it enables and what it excludes.

What exactly was imagined would happen to the church/es in the US after disestablishment? What would it/they look like? Where would it/they exist? How would it/they be legally organized? It helps to back up and understand that disestablishment of the American churches had begun long before the drafting of the First Amendment, in the Atlantic crossings. The territorial churches of Europe, rooted in very particular and fraught histories and geographies, "chronotopes of the law" one might say, to borrow Mariana Valverde's words, were uprooted and transformed by their migration, resulting in a very distinctive new "game of jurisdiction."[29] The churches lost place.[30] They were no longer sited physically and politically, instead taking on the burden and the expectation of utopian societies. It is difficult to exaggerate the violence that can be attributed to this "free" religion.[31]

---

concept of churchstateness to describe the difference between Europe and the Americas with respect to church/state relations, see Johnson, Klassen, and Sullivan, *Ekklesia*.

27. This American-style resistance to secularization—to capture by democratic capitalism, might be analogized to that of literature, as described by Simon During in *Against Democracy: Literary Experience in the Era of Emancipation* (New York: Fordham Press, 2012). In other words, religion in the US might do some of the same work as the literary fiction he shows us, that of George Eliot and E. M. Forster. I am grateful to Constance Furey for calling my attention to this work. For an exhortation to return to the sacred in governance, see Robert A. Yelle, *Sovereignty and the Sacred: Secularism and the Political Economy of Religion* (Chicago: University of Chicago Press, 2018).

28. Giorgio Agamben, *The Kingdom and the Glory: For a Theological Genealogy of Economy and Government*, trans. Lorenzo Chiesa with Matteo Mandarini (Stanford: Stanford University Press, 2011).

29. Mariana Valverde, *Chronotopes of Law: Jurisdiction, Scale, and Governance* (Milton Park, UK: Routledge, 2015), 56. She urges feminists to reject the essentialisms underlying that game, 122.

30. See Jonathan Z. Smith on the distinction between locative and utopian religions in *Map Is Not Territory: Studies in the History of Religions* (Chicago: University of Chicago Press, 1993); *To Take Place: Toward Theory in Ritual* (Chicago: University of Chicago Press, 1987); and "The Wobbling Pivot," *Journal of Religion* 52:2 (April 1972): 134–149.

31. See essays in Johnson, Klassen, and Sullivan, *Ekklesia*.

And yet, religious collectivity is pervasively recognized in American law today. The church, although disestablished, is always also enabled by US law. Such enabling can be seen in obvious ways in laws permitting church incorporation, in the rules and regulations of the IRS, in zoning regulation, in statutory exemptions of various kinds—in the parsonage exemption. Churches appear and are given special consideration in countless laws at every level of government, national, state, and municipal, notwithstanding the promise of disestablishment. All of this mundane legal work conjures *the* church—what is known in theology as the *corpus mysticum* (the mystical body of Christ).

The thesis of this book is that American law has shown that it cannot think religion without the church—that the space for religion in US law is a church-shaped space. But that does not mean that the church is simply the template for what counts as religion in law; *the* church itself lives on in American law in a new and very particular way. The church has a logic—a law—of its own. The church is not wholly the creature of secular law, subject to its meta-jurisdictional power, as liberal political theory would have it.[32] The symbiotic relationship between *the* church and *the* law in the US, in this more expansive sense, is a churchstateness of its own, which is, as Paul Johnson, Pamela Klassen, and I have argued, a product of the Atlantic crossings.[33] Mine is a phenomenological, not a normative argument. Like Levene, I see the US collective—the church—as distinctively modern, the product of critique as well as of robust legal enabling of alternatives to the state in US law. What is termed by secularists the "institutional turn" in religion clause jurisprudence is actually, in my view, a way to euphemize and misunderstand the nature of what is a theologically based resistance to the consolidation of christian doctrine in law.[34] In other words, "the church" in law in the US is not simply another

32. For a doubling down on the meta-jurisdictional authority of the state over religion in liberal political theory in response to American legal arguments over church autonomy, see Cécile Laborde, *Liberalism's Religion* (Cambridge: Harvard University Press, 2017).

33. See essays in Johnson, Klassen, and Sullivan, *Ekklesia*.

34. The claim I make is distinct from that made by those who advocate today for greater rights for churches in the US, known variously as the church autonomy movement or the church sovereignty movement. See, e.g., Paul Horwitz, "Freedom of the Church Without Romance," *Journal of Contemporary Legal Issues* 21, no. 1 (2013): 59–132. It is also distinct from that of their adversaries. See, e.g., Richard Schragger and Micah Schwartzman, "Against Religious Institutionalism," *Virginia Law Review* 99, no. 5 (September 2013): 917–985. At its strongest, the church autonomy advocates make a claim to sovereign jurisdiction, one that is essentially modern. As Talal Asad says in *Formations of the Secular: Christianity, Islam,*

synonym for organized religion or for religious institutions in a flat positivist sense. Nor is it a recognizable object defined for all time in the first centuries of the common era. The church as a metaphor in the strong sense is an exercise in public theology, available for critique.

In all the varieties of church polity, *the* church is imagined in a very specific way in the US, independently, but not wholly independently, of the law that enables it. *The* church is a unifying metaphor. While church language migrates unevenly across legal and political domains and back, there is a kind of phenomenological exchange between how law imagines law and religion and their relationship and how religion imagines them.

US law about religion has changed. As many have observed, the former verities—the mid-twentieth-century separationist verities—are rapidly becoming outdated, both legally and politically. Individual free exercise has been seriously constricted, constitutionally speaking, and separation has given way to what many see as a troubling coziness between religion and government. Religion itself seems to be taking new and sometimes unfamiliar forms, resisting privatization. These changes are sending many back to the cases—and back to the history books. What went wrong? And what was the American project with respect to church and state after all? Why the disarray?

Even after much work by historians, sociologists, and legal scholars, we have yet fully to understand the peculiar legal phenomenology of religion produced by American-style disestablishment. That is, we do not know in what ways religion changed under the new legal regime and how precisely church-state relations have shifted over time. Understanding the life of religion in US law—understanding disestablishment—demands a return engagement with ecclesiology, that is, with the doctrine of the church. We cannot understand today's cases without thinking again carefully about the church and whether and how her appearance in *Hosanna-Tabor* should strike us as surprising.

"Church and state" is sometimes said to have become an outmoded expression these days. We commonly move quickly to "religion and law," that is, we move from church to religious groups or associations—or even religion more diffusely—and from state to law, in gestures of intended in-

---

Modernity (Stanford: Stanford University Press, 2003), 222, "In tradition the present is always at the center."

clusiveness. We think we are moving from the specific to the general, from the epiphenomenal to the fundamental—from old-school established Christianity to all forms of religion—and from the state to regulation at every level, local, national, and trans- or international, even global. We do see some important things differently with this shift of register, but I think we also miss an important story. We have perhaps too readily shaken off a church that is still with us. Church and state and their tangled histories haunt the structures of current regimes; traces of the older edifices remain. The current persistence of religious forms—indeed of church forms-in-law—requires further thinking.

What is a church and what work does church—*the* church—do today in American law? The church, I would argue, as it figures in US law today, and as an object of faith, is inescapably tied to a labile christian mystical political theology, a religious logic that naturalizes it and gives it potency in the American legal imagination, constraining US law's capacity to acknowledge religion more broadly. It is also inescapably tied to other fictive collectivities in law—the state and the corporation—collectivities that can also usefully be investigated ecclesiologically. The interchangeability of these collectives is enabled by a shared history, but also by the fact that one thing that law and religion have in common is a reliance on fictive personalities.

Why use the word church instead of religion in this book about religious collective in US law, thereby giving offense to nonchristians? This is not a work of normative legal doctrine. This is a work of phenomenological description. My argument is that the church is present in US law. I choose here to focus on the church because I think that not talking about it leaves in place structures that affect lives. We need to make these visible, in my view, in order to address issues of inclusion and justice. Furthermore, the church is a different kind of thing from religion, historically and semantically speaking.[35]

US constitutional disestablishment produced neither secularism on the French model (*laïcité*) nor the partner state church of the northern European countries, but an unstable church-state alliance founded in the

35. According to political philosopher Giorgio Agamben, the church continues to be relevant because the "government of men" "in the West" continues to depend on a christian economy of salvation and on the glory. The church as an idea addresses the difficult task of linking God and man: "The empty throne, the symbol of Glory, is what we need to profane in order to make room for . . . eternal life." Agamben, *The Kingdom and the Glory*, xiii.

fraying free church ecclesiology of the radical reformation and the emergence of populist politics.[36] The alliance importantly expanded eventually to include the American avatars of the sovereign churches of the nonevangelical world and beyond, yet the free or dissenting churches that, in their European incarnation, existed historically in the shadow of and dependent on the state churches of Europe for definition, arguably became in the US the exemplary form of church, local, biblically warranted, voluntary, lay-led, self-funded, and democratically governed. All US religious communities, christian and otherwise, have been and continue to be in some sense domesticated through legal, political, and social pressure toward adoption of such a free-church polity.[37]

The free church also became established as a necessary and naturally occurring phenomenon through its deployment in the academic fields of church history and the sociology of religion, with Tocqueville's prescient observations naturalizing and providing the stamp of approval to this New World religious form.[38] In 1963, Sidney Mead, in *The Lively Experiment*, gave an unparalleled description of the effect of disestablishment on the American churches—and of the invention of religious voluntarism.[39] Mead's book is in many ways a terrifying read. Freed from their embeddedness in the political and cultural webs of their homelands, US churches claim a distinctive freedom to define the debt they owe to society. The unofficial dean of First Amendment studies in the US, Kent Greenawalt, in his magisterial summary of the jurisprudence of the First Amendment, takes the free-church model as paradigmatic and as virtually constitutionally mandated.[40] Martin Marty and other guardians of US religious exceptionalism have celebrated the free protestant congregation as the exemplary mediator between the citizen and the state—as functionally

36. "Free church" refers to a congregational model of church polity that originated in the politics of the reformations in Europe.

37. The romance of the free church has appealed beyond christian communities. All immigrant American religious communities celebrate the unique American opportunity to be truer versions of themselves than was possible in the old world. See Courtney Bender, "The Power of Pluralist Thinking," in *The Politics of Religious Freedom*, ed. Winnifred Fallers Sullivan, Elizabeth Shakman Hurd, Saba Mahmood, and Peter Danchin (Chicago: University of Chicago Press, 2016).

38. Alexis de Tocqueville, *Democracy in America*, trans. George Lawrence (New York: Anchor Press, 1969), 292–293.

39. Sidney E. Mead, *The Lively Experiment* (Eugene, OR: Wipf & Stock Publishers, 2007).

40. Kent Greenawalt, *Religion and the Constitution*, vol. 2: *Establishment and Fairness* (Princeton: Princeton University Press, 2009).

necessary to American governance.[41] This view is also enshrined in US tax policy.[42]

Yet the free church model has never been free or uncontested if the entire field of American religion is considered, and it is being vigorously challenged today (and arguably has been for a much longer period) by the church autonomy movement on the one hand, representing the claims to apostolic governance of mormons, catholics, and other liturgical traditions, and on the other by those resistant to ecclesial hierarchy of any kind—those making their religious lives in other places, including in the marketplace. Today the church may seem to be standing in for more traditional claims to associational autonomy for religion, but its longer history would suggest that the theology of the church has played a role in facilitating quite a range of peculiar but shifting forms that what one might call free religion in the US. All of these versions of church—in law—arguably draw sustenance from the enduring charisma of *the* church—what is theologically understood to be the body of Christ.

Careful examination of the church-state forms endorsed in two recent US Supreme Court decisions, *Hosanna-Tabor* (arguably a return to a pre–Vatican II institutionalism in its endorsement of the subordination of the sacramental life of the church to a coordinated church-state discipline) and *Hobby Lobby* (the perhaps accidental recognition of a wilder form of religion—sometimes mistaken for neoliberalism—that is, the protestant religion of retail commerce) reveals the failure of the alliance of free church ecclesiology and separationist politics to solve the church/state conundrum. In each of these two decisions, one sees a simultaneous effort at collusion with the state and a refusal of state sovereignty. Radical pluralism, severance from places of origins, and resistance to "organized religion" have combined to produce a religious field in the US that is adaptive and restive, resisting bureaucratization and domestication in the European church-state sense, yet strangely still tied to the sacramental power of the church as a sovereign body. The Court's renewed interest in the corporateness of religious life, parallel to that of advocacy groups and

41. See, e.g., Martin E. Marty, *The Public Church: Mainline, Evangelical, Catholic* (Eugene, OR: Wipf & Stock Publishers, 1981). One might see this religious politics as a part of a broader accommodation between American protestantism and positivism. See also Mark A. Noll, *The Scandal of the Evangelical Mind* (Grand Rapids, MI: Eerdmans, 1994).

42. See "Tax Information for Churches and Religious Organizations" on IRS website, accessed October 20, 2018, https://www.irs.gov/charities-non-profits/churches-religious-organizations/.

theorists of religious freedom, brings to the fore enduring and unresolved questions concerning the nature of religion, as well as the interrelationship of the individual, the religious community, and the state—and of governance more broadly.

There is a rich conversation today about the nature of the modern state and of popular sovereignty—especially about the ways that unfinished theological business haunts modern would-be secular democracies. Less work has been done, beyond specialized academic and ecclesial enclaves, on what happened to the church as a public institution in the wake of the collapse of European monarchical governance—particularly in its diaspora appearances outside of Europe—and how law has enabled the church's persistence. Furthermore, much of what has been written on what religion is for modern law and politics has focused on the individual person even while we have much evidence that individual conscience or belief is an inadequate proxy for human religiosity. Accepting that religion is inevitably social and embodied and cannot accurately be reduced to individual beliefs and associated motivated practices, we are nevertheless reluctant to embrace the consequences of those observations; we do not really understand what role the church/churches continues/continue to play and what that should mean for law. What kind of legal entity is/are it/they? We need to return to ecclesiology—and to its many related ideas, among them incarnation, eucharist, and the *corpus mysticum* in the catholic traditions and covenant, regeneration, and the eschatological kingdom in the others—in order to understand the church-in-law better.

The Court's decisions in *Hosanna-Tabor* and *Hobby Lobby* can be seen to disclose the corporate nature of religion-in-law, and, beyond religion, corporateness generally in law. They also disclose an anxiety about the dominance of corporations in contemporary life. An increasingly common critique of the *Hobby Lobby* decision is that it reveals the triumph of neoliberalism and the capitalist colonization of our lives—seen, as it often is, to be of a piece with the corrupt reasoning of *Citizens United*.[43] Too great an emphasis on an economic reading of these opinions, however, reflects an impoverished understanding of christian theology and of the

43. *Citizens United v. Federal Election Commission*, 558 U.S. 310 (2010). See, e.g., chapters 9–11 in Kathryn Lofton, *Consuming Religion* (Chicago: University of Chicago Press, 2017). The same might be said of the decision in *Masterpiece Cakeshop, Ltd. v. Colorado Civil Rights Commission*, 584 US __(2018), discussed in the conclusion.

relationship between religion and the economy, as well as a misreading of US religious and legal history. It is one more effort to insist on liberal theology as the jurisprudence of the First Amendment—even by would-be secularists. The religious lives and claims of the plaintiffs in *Hobby Lobby* are simply dismissed as the inauthentic products of late capitalism run amok. (Interestingly, the unanimity of *Hosanna-Tabor*, although arguably more troubling from a constitutional perspective, is rarely criticized with the same vehemence or even seen to be a part of the same phenomenon, at least by many commenters, perhaps because of its more familiar churchiness.) Considering the legal phenomenology of religion employed in these two decisions—and in several others—is a useful diagnostic toward the knotty difficulty of further understanding the multiple ways in which the church persists in US law.

What is a church in the mind of a secular American today? Many view churches as alien, dogmatic and inflexible institutions, full of mumbo-jumbo and predatory male clergy. Yet, at the same time, the First Amendment is understood to protect your right to be a church member and churches are recognized as having a right to exist and to enforce their own rules. This is a free country. You have a right to be foolish. But few would understand or publicly defend their continued existence as a public good. How did the US get to such a patchwork ecclesiastical settlement?

One might describe the semi-sovereignty of the church-in-law in the US today, not as the result of a singular model of religious accommodation but as the contingent result of the sedimentation of legal institutions and arrangements inherited from colonial powers as they morphed over time in the course of an ongoing negotiation between American legal reformers, on the one hand, and churches of various kinds, often at a local or state level, as well as being shaped by opportunistic collaborations of various kinds between religion and government.[44] Historian Evan Haefeli argues that the vaunted religious freedom of religion in the US was the result not of the philosophical commitments of the founders, as is often implied, but a result of the contingencies of colonial history. He argues

44. See Christopher L. Tomlins and Bruce H. Mann, eds., *The Many Legalities of Early America* (Chapel Hill: University of North Carolina Press, 2001). See also James Boyd White's discussion of Richard Hooker's Preface to *Of the Lawes of Ecclesiasticall Politie* (London: Da Capo Press, 1594), a classic defense of authority in the Church of England. White, *Acts of Hope: Creating Authority in Literature, Law, and Politics* (Chicago: University of Chicago Press, 1995), 82–124.

that the ongoing upheaval in England over politics and religion distracted colonial authorities from developing a policy of religious conformity as the Spanish and the French did in their colonies:

> Th[e] peculiar condition of early American religious history reflects its unusual legacy as the abroad of a different home, namely England and the British Empire. Before 1783, the center of early American religion was there, outside the boundaries of the future United States. It was that empire, not the desires of the colonists, the frontier, or the demands of the American environment, that lay the foundations for American religious diversity—often over and against the wishes of colonial Anglo-Americans. Time and again, it was the executive authority at the center of the empire—usually, but not always, the monarch—that protected religious minorities, indeed at times projected them into Anglo-America for reasons rooted in England.[45]

After the Revolution, lack of a consistent policy had other sources, as Haefeli explains. "[E]xecutive capacity to intervene in religious life on a national scale disappeared between the American Revolution and Civil War, as a trend towards disestablishment strengthened the ability of locally-rooted religion (like Baptists) and regional religious institutions (like the Methodist circuit riders) to gain the ascendancy in many of the new states in the West and South."[46] Those same trends also allowed Roman Catholicism—the anathema of the original colonists—to gain a strong presence across the North. Indeed, Haefeli suggests that "a look at a modern map of American religion shows how tenuous the connection between the present-day situation and the colonial past is. Instead of, say, a predominantly 'puritan' Congregational North vs. a majority Anglican South, one sees a Roman Catholic North vs. a Baptist South. It is as if each region has turned into its colonial nightmare."[47] New American versions of church and state were produced in the process.

45. Evan Haefeli, "A Home, Made Abroad: American Religion from Colonies to Civil War," in *At Home and Abroad*, ed. Elizabeth Shakman Hurd and Winnifred Fallers Sullivan (forthcoming).

46. Haefeli, "A Home, Made Abroad."

47. Hurd and Sullivan, *At Home and Abroad*. See also Evan Haefeli, "The Problem with the History of Toleration," in *Politics of Religious Freedom*, ed. Winnifred Fallers Sullivan, Elizabeth Shakman Hurd, Saba Mahmood, and Peter Danchin (Chicago: University of Chicago Press, 2015); Evan Haefeli, *English Tolerance and Overseas Expansion Between Renaissance and Early Enlightenment, 1497–1688* (Chicago: University of Chicago Press, forthcoming).

In *The Garden and the Wilderness*, Mark DeWolfe Howe gives an account of the surprising and growing deference to corporate church sovereignty over the course of US legal history. This history, rather than reflecting a constitutional commitment to the protection of religion and of religious communities, as proponents of church autonomy argue, might better be understood to showcase the result of the unintended consequences of a complex and jerky disestablishment and remodeling of churches. These later transformations to the legal status of religious communal life intersect with other important transformations, to the state, to the economy, and to other sectors of American life, most importantly those resulting from manifold failures to acknowledge and deal with slavery.[48]

The chaos of colonial religion policy also had consequences for the racialization of the protestant churches, as Katharine Gerbner has recently argued.[49] In the absence of metropolitan control, local contestations over slave conversion led to new articulations of what it was to be christian. An early effort on the part of planters, who ran both the plantations and the churches, to prevent the conversion of slaves because of their anxiety that conversion might lead both to automatic manumission and to rebellion gave way over time to a wholesale effort to evangelize them. As will be discussed further in chapter four, that newfound zeal for evangelization depended on a new theology of conversion, one that understood christian conversion to be a means to social control and which newly distinguished planters and slaves not as christians and pagans, but as white and black. By becoming christian, slaves now also became black.[50]

African-American Christianity and the African-American churches in the United States have a complex and contested legal history. That history is also part of the long history of the US church-in-law. In the twentieth century, suppression of that history might be seen in a particular consolidation of what W. E. B. Du Bois called the Negro Church, as Curtis Evans has detailed. Among other things, Evans says, "[t]he construction of the Negro Church (and its now common appellation, the black church) has

48. Howe also discusses the interrelationship between First and Fourteenth Amendment jurisprudence. Howe, *The Garden and the Wilderness*.

49. Katharine Gerbner, *Christian Slavery: Conversion and Race in the Protestant Atlantic World* (Philadelphia: University of Pennsylvania Press, 2018).

50. As Gerbner details, racialization is not wholly new in the early modern settler societies, but is articulated in new ways. See also J. Kameron Carter, *Race: A Theological Account* (Oxford: Oxford University Press, 2008).

obscured the very real differences among African Americans that Du Bois himself detected, and it has rendered invisible or regressive those black groups and practices that do not fit into such categories as progressive or prophetic."[51] In a cruel irony, those promoting faith-based programs in prisons today now seek to mobilize what they call the black church in a reprisal of the embedded logics of christian slavery described by Gerbner and the invisibility described by Evans.

Chapter one offers a close reading of the opinions in *Hosanna-Tabor*, introducing the figure of the church and the troubled dynamic between the individual and the collective revealed in that decision. Chapter two rereads what are known as the church property cases with a view to watching the shift from the early republican volunteer religious society celebrated in the *Watson* decision (1870) to the robust sovereign independence of the churches of eastern orthodoxy in the twentieth-century cases. Returning to the present, chapter three considers the uncanny sovereign interchange among church, state, and corporation through an examination of the assumptions in the *Hobby Lobby* decision and the history of the corporation. The black church-in-law is the subject of chapter four, heir to the religio-legal logics of slavery and the ongoing creation of massive incarceration, a shared project, like the others, of church and state, such as they are in the US. Finally, in the conclusion, I will return to the questions raised in this introduction, asking, through a reworking of the facts of the 2018 *Masterpiece Cakeshop* decision, whether the church-in-law can ever be otherwise.

In terming my method phenomenological in the socio-legal context I mean to speak from within an academic conversation about religion that takes religion as a universal aspect of human society. Rejecting a story of declension or secularization, but assuming the careful critical work of the genealogy of the modern understanding of religion, this position assumes that there is always a religion story just as there is always a law story, and that the two are always related, but that the story is different in different times and places. Law, too, will be read not as a high modernist romantic genre but, with historian Joan Scott, as "a broken series of par-

51. Curtis Evans, *The Burden of Black Religion* (Oxford: Oxford University Press, 2008), 165. For an account of the rise of black catholicism, see Matthew Cressler, *Authentically Black and Truly Catholic: The Rise of Black Catholicism in the Great Migration* (New York: New York University Press, 2017).

adoxes and reversals in which human action is ever open to unaccountable contingencies"—as a tragic genre.[52] A phenomenological perspective does not aim to speak from outside history and theology but to enable a comparative inclusion of discursive registers across social contexts. A phenomenological perspective is also attentive to scale—to a chronotopic approach to law—that is, the recognition that "different legal processes are shaped and given meaning by particular spacetimes."[53] I see this work as an experiment, an experiment in taking religion seriously without establishing it, that is, in speaking back theologically to the law.

52. Joan W. Scott, *Sex and Secularism* (Princeton: Princeton University Press, 2017), 232.
53. Valverde, *Chronotopes of Law*, 11.

CHAPTER ONE

The Church Makes an Appearance: *Hosanna-Tabor v. EEOC*

Husbands, love your wives, as Christ loved the church and gave himself up for her, that he might sanctify her, having cleansed her by the washing of water with the word, so that he might present the church to himself in splendor, without spot or wrinkle or any such thing, that she might be holy and without blemish. In the same way husbands should love their wives as their own bodies. He who loves his wife loves himself. For no one ever hated his own flesh, but nourishes and cherishes it, just as Christ does the church, because we are members of his body. "Therefore a man shall leave his father and mother and hold fast to his wife, and the two shall become one flesh." This mystery is profound, and I am saying that it refers to Christ and the church. However, let each one of you love his wife as himself, and let the wife see that she respects her husband.—Eph. 5:25–33 (ESV)

Introduction

In 2012, in *Hosanna-Tabor v. EEOC*, the US Supreme Court, in a unanimous decision, held that "[t]he church must be free to choose those who will guide it on its way."[1] This book is about what "the" church means—in law—in the US, a radically diverse country, one in which religion is constitutionally disestablished. To what precisely do those words of the Court—*the* church—refer? How does the church come to be both object and subject in law in the US? And how precisely does a disestablished church still have a legal public existence? What kind of thing—in law—is the church

1. *Hosanna-Tabor Evangelical Lutheran Church & Sch. v. EEOC*, 565 U.S. 171, 196 (2012).

exactly? And how do those words provide a clue into the way in which US law imagines religion more broadly?

Focusing attention on the disestablished church in the US does beg some questions about the nature of an established church and the various views of the framers and ratifiers of the Constitution as to that nature. Paradoxically, it seems, the church only really comes into view in law when it is disestablished. It is through disestablishment that a church gains legal personality in a modern sense. Churches did not and do not have independent jural personality when they are established. Disestablishment then is always also a new establishment.[2]

This chapter combines what a friend calls a rabbinic reading of the *Hosanna-Tabor* opinions, that is, a reading in the voice of a licensed American lawyer who must accept the interpretive authority of the Court and the self-contained coherence of the text, alongside a concurrent commentary on the decision critically examining the historical account of the church and its rights offered by the Court in support of its decision in *Hosanna-Tabor* and the exclusions and erasures effected by that history. The chapter concludes with the suggestion that the Court has resurrected a christian heresy in order to support its view of the First Amendment.

The case

As a general matter, federal law prohibits employment discrimination on the grounds of race, color, religion, gender, national origin, disability, genetic information, or age. Discrimination is broadly defined to include not just primary acts of discrimination but also "retaliation against an

2. Recent work examining this paradox in other legal contexts include Helge Årsheim on the recent disestablishment of the Church of Norway, "Imagine There's No Religion—and No State Church Too?: The Curious Tale of How the State of Norway Left a Religion and Established a Church," *Religion Going Public* (blog), accessed August 25, 2018, http://religiongoingpublic.com/archive/2017/imagine-theres-no-religion-and-no-state-church-too/ and Rivers, *The Law of Organized Religions*, offering a comprehensive look at the changing legal nature of the Church of England. This process arguably begins with the new legal arrangements for the churches during the reformations. See Sara Ludin, "The Reformation Suits: Litigation as Constitution-Making in a German Imperial Court, 1521–1555" (Ph.D. dissertation, University of California at Berkeley, 2019). See also *The Canea Catholic Church v. Greece*, European Court of Human Rights (143/1996/762/963), recognizing the legal personality of the Roman Catholic Church under Greek law in the absence of formal registration; and, on the legal capacity of the Coptic Church in Egypt today compared with that of Al-Azhar, the seat of Islamic authority in Egypt, Mona Oraby, "The Difference That Affiliation Makes: Religious Conversion, Minorities, and the Rule of Law" (Ph.D. dissertation, Northwestern University, 2017).

individual for filing a charge of discrimination, participating in an investigation, or opposing discriminatory practices."[3] A limited exception is provided by statute allowing "a religious corporation, association, educational institution, or society" to give a preference in hiring to members of their own religion "with respect to the employment of individuals of a particular religion to perform work connected with the carrying on by such corporation, association, educational institution, or society of its activities."[4] No statutory exemption for religious organizations is provided for other aspects of the employment relationship, including termination, and no statutory exception is provided in the case of retaliation.[5] In most cases, an employee seeking a remedy under the law for discriminatory conduct by her employer must file an initial claim with the US Equal Employment Opportunity Commission (EEOC). The EEOC reviews the claim and will usually issue a "right to sue" letter, allowing the individual claimant to bring suit under the statute in federal court. If the EEOC finds a serious violation, it may file suit against the employer in federal court on the employee's behalf. That is what happened in this case.

In *Hosanna-Tabor*, the EEOC brought an action on behalf of a fourth-grade teacher, Cheryl Perich, against her employer, alleging that her firing had constituted a retaliatory dismissal in violation of the Americans with Disabilities Act.[6] Her employer, the Hosanna-Tabor Evangelical Lutheran

3. 42 USCS §§ 2000e et seq. (Civil Rights Act of 1964).

4. "This title [42 USCS §§ 2000e et seq.] shall not apply to an employer with respect to the employment of aliens outside any State, or to a religious corporation, association, educational institution, or society with respect to the employment of individuals of a particular religion to perform work connected with the carrying on by such corporation, association, educational institution, or society of its activities." 42 U.S.C. §§ 2000e-1(a).

5. As the US Court of Appeals for the Sixth Circuit explained in its decision in *Hosanna-Tabor*, "Religious organizations are not exempt from title I of the ADA . . . A religious [entity] may give a preference in employment to individuals of the particular religion, and may require that applicants and employees conform to the religious tenants [*sic*] of the organization. However, a religious organization may not discriminate against an individual who satisfies the permitted religious criteria because that individual is disabled. The religious entity, in other words, is required to consider qualified individuals with disabilities who satisfy the permitted religious criteria on an equal basis with qualified individuals without disabilities who similarly satisfy the religious criteria." *Hosanna-Tabor v. EEOC*, 565 U.S. 171 (2012).

6. The ADA, like the Civil Rights Act of 1964, provides a limited exemption for religious organizations:

> (d) Religious entities.
>
> (1) In general. This title shall not prohibit a religious corporation, association, educational institution, or society from giving preference in employment to individuals of a particular religion to perform work connected with the carrying on by such corporation, association, educational institution, or society of its activities.

School, a parochial school in Redford, Michigan, moved to dismiss the EEOC action on the ground that the federal court lacked jurisdiction over the matter. The school argued that its employment relationship with Perich presented an ecclesiastical question, one that was entirely exempt from secular legal oversight, claiming immunity under a relatively recent judicially created ministerial exception to laws protecting employee rights. The ministerial exception goes beyond the statutory exceptions for religious employers, by barring all "employment-discrimination claims brought by ministers against the religious groups that employ or formerly employed them."[7]

Perich was not ordained and had no position of formal religious lead-

---

> (2) Religious tenets requirement. Under this title, a religious organization may require that all applicants and employees conform to the religious tenets of such organization. 42 U.S.C. § 12113(d).

But as the Court of Appeals made clear in its decision in *Hosanna-Tabor*, Congress intended the ADA to broadly protect employees of religious entities from retaliation on the job, subject only to a narrowly drawn religious exemption. The House Report provides the following illustrative hypothetical example:

> [A]ssume that a Mormon organization wishes to hire only Mormons to perform certain jobs. If a person with a disability applies for the job, but is not a Mormon, the organization can refuse to hire him or her. However, if two Mormons apply for a job, one with a disability and one without a disability, the organization cannot discriminate against the applicant with the disability because of that person's disability. H.R. Rep. No. 485 part 2, 101st Cong., 2d Sess. 76–77 (1990).

EEOC v. Hosanna-Tabor Evangelical Lutheran Church, 597 F.3d 769, 777 (2011). In the tautological language of this area of the law, the Court of Appeals goes on to say that "[t]o qualify as a religious institution under the first prong, the employer need not be a traditional religious organization, such as a church, diocese, or synagogue, nor must it be an entity operated by a traditional religious organization. Rather, a religiously affiliated entity is considered a religious institution if its 'mission is marked by clear or obvious religious characteristics.'" 597 F. 3d at 776.

7. Cases applying the ministerial exception cited by the Court included: *Fratello v. Archdiocese of N.Y.*, 863 F.3d 190, 198 (2017). See also, e.g., *Natal v. Christian & Missionary Alliance*, 878 F.2d 1575, 1578 (1st Cir. 1989); *Petruska v. Gannon Univ.*, 462 F.3d 294, 303–07 (3d. Cir. 2006), cert. denied, 550 U.S. 903, 127 S. Ct. 2098, 167 L. Ed. 2d 813 (2007); *EEOC v. Roman Catholic Diocese*, 213 F.3d 795, 800–01 (4th Cir. 2000); *Combs v. Cent. Tex. Annual Conference*, 173 F.3d 343, 345–50 (5th Cir. 1999); *Hollins v. Methodist Healthcare*, Inc., 474 F.3d 223, 225–27 (6th Cir. 2007), cert. denied, 552 U.S. 857, 128 S. Ct. 134, 169 L. Ed. 2d 92 (2007); *Schleicher v. Salvation Army*, 518 F.3d 472, 475–76 (7th Cir. 2008); *Scharon v. St. Luke's Episcopal Presbyterian Hosp.*, 929 F.2d 360, 362–63 (8th Cir. 1991); *Werft v. Desert Sw. Annual Conference*, 377 F.3d 1099, 1100–04 (9th Cir. 2004) (per curiam); *Bryce v. Episcopal Church*, 289 F.3d 648, 655–57 (10th Cir. 2002); *Gellington v. Christian Methodist Episcopal Church, Inc.*, 203 F.3d 1299, 1301–04 (11th Cir. 2000); *EEOC v. Catholic Univ. of Am.*, 83 F.3d 455, 460–63, 317 U.S. App. D.C. 343 (D.C. Cir. 1996).

ership in the church or school. She taught state-mandated secular subjects to fourth graders. She had qualified, however, after her first year at the school, to be a "called" teacher, a designation that led the school, in their pleadings, to designate her a minister under the law.[8] Being "called" for these Lutherans requires completion of a colloquy (a theological course), as well as election by a church congregation, and provides a sort of tenure.[9] Those termed "lay" teachers at the school are hired on year-to-year con-

8. Deciding who is a minister in law for purposes of the ministerial exception is largely left to religious organizations themselves. In its amicus brief in the case, the Lutheran Church–Missouri Synod explained that the church has two classes of ministers, ordained ministers and commissioned ministers, both church offices understood to be authorized by the book of Acts in the New Testament. Ordained ministers have the power to preach the word and administer the sacraments. Commissioned ministers serve in an auxiliary capacity, such as directing music or teaching in schools. Only men may serve as ordained ministers. Brief of the Lutheran Church–Missouri Synod at 4–6.

9. Called teachers have also been found to qualify for a tax-free housing allowance under the IRS parsonage exemption—an exemption limited by the IRS to a "minister of the gospel." The Internal Revenue Code provides (26 USC § 107) that

> In the case of a minister of the gospel, gross income does not include—
>
> (1) the rental value of a home furnished to him as part of his compensation; or
>
> (2) the rental allowance paid to him as part of his compensation, to the extent used by him to rent or provide a home and to the extent such allowance does not exceed the fair rental value of the home, including furnishings and appurtenances such as a garage, plus the cost of utilities.

See https://www.irs.gov/help-resources/tools-faqs/faqs-for-individuals/frequently-asked-tax-questions-answers/interest-dividends-other-types-of-income/ministers-compensation-housing-allowance/ministers-compensation-housing-allowance. The parsonage exemption is controversial, attacked by law professors and litigated against by the Freedom from Religion Foundation (FFRF), among others. Section 107 of the Internal Revenue Code was declared unconstitutional in *Freedom from Religion Foundation v. Lew*, 983 F. Supp 2d 1051 (2013), but was reversed on appeal for a want of standing. *Freedom from Religion Foundation v. Lew*, 773 F.3d 815 (2014). A more recent effort by FFRF was also successful in the district court but reversed on appeal, this time on the merits, the US Court of Appeals for the Seventh Circuit finding section 107 to be constitutional. *Gaylor v. Mnuchin*, Nos. 18-1277 & 18-1280 (2019). See also Erwin Chemerinsky, "The Parsonage Exemption Violates the Establishment Clause and Should Be Declared Unconstitutional," *Whittier Law Review* 24 (2003): 707; Meridith Satz, "Comment: Re-interpreting the Parsonage Exclusion: Constitutional Challenges and the Agency Response in the Wake of *Freedom From Religion Foundation, Inc. v. Lew*," *Administrative Law Review* 67, no. 4 (2016): 751; and Adam Chodorow, "The Parsonage Exemption," *UC Davis Law Review* 51 (2018): 849–910.

The IRS broadly interprets "minister" and "church," words that historically have referred to christian institutions and offices, to include functions they take to be present in all religions and understands this interpretive breadth to be necessary to prevent "entanglement" or excessive inquiry into church governance, an issue to be considered under the Court's current establishment clause jurisprudence.

tracts. Both called and lay fourth-grade teachers at the Hosanna-Tabor school have the same teaching duties, including leading brief daily prayers and teaching weekly religion classes, but they have different contractual relationships with the school and with the church community. Importantly, the school does not require either lay or called teachers to be Lutherans and more than half of the students in the school were not Lutherans at the time of the lawsuit.[10]

After five years teaching at the school, Perich had fallen ill over the summer of 2004 from an undiagnosed chronic illness and had taken a disability leave from her position at the beginning of that fall. When she sought to return to her classroom in January with her doctor's letter in hand declaring that she was being effectively treated, the school refused to accept her return, asking her to seek a "peaceful release from her call" under a church dispute resolution process.[11] She asserted her right to nondiscrimination on the basis of disability under the ADA and was subsequently fired for insubordination. The school faulted her for "going to law," as they said, citing the First Letter of Paul to the Corinthians: "When one of you has a grievance against another, does he dare go to law before the unrighteous instead of the saints?"[12]

After an investigation, the EEOC brought suit against the school on Perich's behalf in the US District Court for the Eastern District of Michigan. The district court granted summary judgment for the school, finding that it had no subject matter jurisdiction in the case because ministerial employment is a matter reserved to the church.[13] In its order dismissing the suit, the district court described the school and Perich's work as follows:

> Hosanna-Tabor's website indicates that it provides a "Christ-centered education" that helps parents by "reinforcing biblical principals [sic] and standards." Hosanna-Tabor also characterizes its staff members as "fine Christian role

10. 597 F.3d at 773.

11. Brief for the Petitioner at 9.

12. I Corinthians 6:1. See Brief of the Lutheran Church–Missouri Synod at 16.

13. *EEOC v. Hosanna-Tabor Evangelical Lutheran Church & Sch.*, 582 F. Supp. 2d 881 (2008). The district court cited *Hollins v. Methodist Healthcare, Inc.*, 474 F.3d 223 (6th Cir. 2007), subsequently abrogated by the Supreme Court in its decision in *Hosanna-Tabor*, for the proposition that the ministerial exception actually deprives federal courts of their jurisdiction over the employment relationship between a religious institution and a minister, a kind of separation of powers doctrine. The Supreme Court in *Hosanna-Tabor* held that the ministerial exception creates a defense, not a jurisdictional bar. 565 U.S. at 195, n. 4. This is an important distinction.

> models who integrate their faith into all subjects." Perich notes, however, that secular school subjects were taught with textbooks commonly used in public education and that she can only recall twice in her career when she introduced the topic of religion during otherwise secular discussion.[14]

The district court also found that the school qualified as a religious institution for purposes of the ministerial exception and that Perich qualified as a minister.

The district court's decision in the *Hosanna-Tabor* case was reversed in the US Court of Appeals for the Sixth Circuit, which both rejected the district court's ruling that the ministerial exception effected a jurisdictional bar and found that she was not a minister within the meaning of the ministerial exception because her work was predominantly secular. "As a general rule," the court of appeals said, "an employee is considered a minister if 'the employee's primary duties consist of teaching, spreading the faith, church governance, supervision of a religious order, or supervision or participation in religious ritual and worship.'" "[It] is clear," they said "that Perich's primary function was teaching secular subjects, not 'spreading the faith, church governance, supervision of a religious order, or supervision or participation in religious ritual and worship.'"[15] In a concurring opinion, Judge Helene White added that "Hosanna-Tabor's teachers are not required to be called or even Lutheran to teach or to lead daily religious activities. The fact that the duties of the contract teachers are the same as the duties of the called teachers is telling. This presence (or lack) of a predominantly religious yardstick for qualification as a teacher is a key factor in decisions finding the ministerial exception applicable and those finding it inapplicable alike."[16] The US Supreme Court granted certiorari to consider for the first time whether the religion clauses of the First Amendment require a ministerial exception.

While the Supreme Court justices stopped short of endorsing the school's strong assertion of the kind of exclusive sovereignty over its employees recognized as jurisdictional in the district court, they did reverse the court of appeals and find for the school in a unanimous decision, announcing that "both Religion Clauses bar the government from interfer-

14. 582 F. Supp. 2d at 884.

15. *EEOC v. Hosanna-Tabor*, 597 F.3d 769, 780. This court's definition of a minister only underscores the default christian assumptions courts use in describing religion.

16. 597 F.3d at 784.

ing with the decision of a religious group to fire one of its ministers."[17] They further found that Perich qualified as a minister for purposes of the ministerial exception: "Hosanna-Tabor held Perich out as a minister, with a role distinct from that of most of its members . . . Perich's title as a minister reflected a significant degree of religious training followed by a formal process of commissioning . . . Perich held herself out as a minister of the Church by accepting the formal call to religious service . . . Perich's job duties reflected a role in conveying the Church's message and carrying out its mission."[18] In other words, the Court of Appeals looked at Perich's job and saw the job of a fourth-grade teacher substantially like that of her counterpart in a public school; the district court and the Supreme Court looked at her and saw a minister, largely accepting the church's own characterization of her role.

How should US courts resolve these two positions? Was Perich a minister? Was her job religious or secular? How would they know? The incommensurability between the findings of the Court of Appeals and those of the Supreme Court reflects a deep ambiguity in US law about what counts as religious, particularly perhaps when religious institutions are licensed to provide education under state law.[19] Much First Amendment jurisprudence derives its incoherence from this ambiguity.[20] How does a court know who is a minister under secular law? "Minister" is used in different ways by different christian groups and not at all by some. Some congregations have no one with such a title. Some only one. Some use minister to title all service work for a church, including such work as providing music, hospitality, financial advice, etc.[21]

One could also view the ministerial exception, as the district court apparently did, as a formal recognition of the church's sovereignty and what socio-legal studies understands to be an always everywhere layered

17. 565 US at 181.

18. 565 US at 191–92.

19. See also murky law finessing the precise nature of the assistance given to church-related schools in cases concerning voucher schools and school choice, beginning with *Zelman v. Simmons-Harris*, 536 U.S. 639 (2002). Also see *In re JFS* in British Supreme Court. *R(E) v. The Governing Body of JFS* [2009], UKSC 15.

20. See Winnifred Fallers Sullivan, *The Impossibility of Religious Freedom* (Princeton: Princeton University Press, 2005), and *Prison Religion: Faith-Based Reform and the Constitution* (Princeton: Princeton University Press, 2009).

21. "Minister" is, of course, a common designation also of government representatives to parliament in many countries. Michel Foucault makes much of that linguistic overlap in *Security, Territory, Population: Lectures at the College de France, 1977–1978*, ed. Michel Sennelart, trans. Graham Burchell (New York: Picador, 2007).

legal pluralism; on this reading the *de facto* jurisdiction of the church was being formally acknowledged. This possibility will be further considered in chapter three.[22]

The opinions by the Supreme Court in *Hosanna-Tabor* showcase the predicament in which US law finds itself with respect to religion and religious collectivities in particular. While both courts and commentators have long sought neutral secular principles that would permit courts to rule on legal disputes within religious organizations without getting them entangled in theological disputes or taking sides between religious factions, *Hosanna-Tabor* strongly affirms the strain in these cases that mandates a privileged lawlessness for church governance.[23] One can understand the Court's deference to church authority in such cases to be motivated variously, sometimes founded in the often-expressed feeling of incompetence on the part of judges, at others in a genuine effort to acknowledge a rival sovereign. The carefully customized history lesson offered by the chief justice in his opinion for the Court in this case effects a naturalization of the church in US law that only intensifies the lack of resolution in these cases.

History

The last sentence of Chief Justice Roberts' opinion in *Hosanna-Tabor* announces the dogma that binds the Court. Affirming for the first time the constitutional status of the ministerial exception, the chief justice declares that "[t]he church must be free to choose those who will guide it on its way."[24] Those are startling words from a US court. Where is this mandate to be found? The church does not appear in the US Constitution. Is it even constitutional for the US Supreme Court to use the definite article when speaking of church? To what can the chief justice possibly be referring

22. On legal pluralism and overlapping jurisdiction see, among others, Lauren Benton and Richard J. Ross, eds., *Legal Pluralism and Empires: 1500–1850* (New York: New York University Press, 2013); J. B. Richland, "Jurisdiction: Grounding Law in Language," *Annual Review of Anthropology* 42 (2013): 209–226; and Valverde, *Chronotopes of Law*.

23. As one of the anonymous reviewers of this book manuscript noted, and as we will see as this book unfolds, "It is not only that the law has a church-shaped space in which it places religion, but also that religion has state- and law-like aspects within the unfolding life of the church. . . . So this is a matter of 'privileged lawlessness' from the perspective of government, but it is also a matter of lawful organization and governance from the perspective of the church."

24. 565 U.S. at 196.

when he says *the* church? By what authority does the Court speak of *the* church? Which church?

Linguists understand the definite article to operate as an intensifier. In the simplest sense, the definite article can be used to refer back to a concept that has already entered into the discourse. Once you and I have spoken of "a" particular movie, we can later in the conversation refer to "the" movie. The definite article can also be used more strongly to signal singularity, as, for example, when using "the president" as shorthand for the president of the United States. "The church" offers another layer of complexity, linguistically speaking. There is not just a temporary singularity as in the case of the president. There is a transcendent or metaphysical singularity. In legal contexts, use of the definite article can have effects in the world, such that abstract fictive concepts such as church are enabled to gain legal personality without doing the necessary political work of definition, changing relationships between people and between people and objects. US courts are arguably using the definite article to smuggle in and boost the sovereign claims and powers of an entity that was ostensibly constitutionally banned by the First Amendment.[25]

If one goes back and rereads Chief Justice Roberts' opinion in light of its final sentence it becomes clear that when he speaks of *the* church and its prerogatives, the Court is not speaking only of the Hosanna-Tabor Missouri Synod Evangelical Church in Redford, Michigan. Or even of the Missouri Synod Lutheran church more generally. Earlier in the opinion, while describing the purpose of the ministerial exception, Roberts says that "[t]he exception . . . ensures that the authority to select and control who will minister to the faithful—a matter 'strictly ecclesiastical'—is the church's alone."[26] Again, not the Hosanna-Tabor Missouri Synod Evangel-

25. Thank you to my colleague, Damir Cavar, professor of linguistics at Indiana University, Bloomington, for introducing me to these distinctions. See also Irene Heim, *The Semantics of Definite and Indefinite Noun Phrases* (New York: Garland Publishers, 1988). There is also the issue of capitalization. I have learned from a journalist friend, Elaine Monaghan, professor of practice at Indiana University Bloomington Media School, that the AP style guide has an entry on when to capitalize "church." It reads:

> Capitalize as part of the formal name of a building, a congregation or a denomination; lowercase in other uses: *St. Mary's Church, the Roman Catholic Church, the Catholic and Episcopal churches, a Roman Catholic church, a church*. Lowercase in phrases where the church is used in an institutional sense: *She believes in the separation of church and state. The pope said the church opposes abortion.*

26. 565 U.S. at 194–95.

ical Church in Redford, Michigan. Not "a church" or a religious group or association, but *the* church. Given the historical argument that the Court mobilizes to support this rule, as we will see, it is not too far-fetched to say that the Court is speaking here of what is known to christians as the Body of Christ. Indeed, the church figures throughout the opinion for the Court in *Hosanna-Tabor* as an opaque but necessary metaphor for the trans-historical permanence and significance of the right kind of religion and of its God-given right to select its own ministers, "a matter," as it insists, "'strictly ecclesiastical.'"[27]

Chief Justice Roberts' assertion concerning "the" church's right to choose its ministers is supported in his opinion for the Court with a curious mash-up of religious and political history, as well as a sprinkling of its prior decisions.[28] He begins oracularly: "Controversy between church

27. How does the Court understand what qualifies as "strictly ecclesiastical"? Is there such a thing under the US Constitution as a matter "strictly ecclesiastical"? What theology would be used to define such a matter? These words, "strictly ecclesiastical," are arguably from a different time and place—a time and place before disestablishment. In an article analyzing the *Hosanna-Tabor* decision, Ira Lupu and Robert Tuttle argue that the rare unanimity of the *Hosanna-Tabor* opinion, wondered at by many, can be accounted for by its invocation of the descriptive words "strictly ecclesiastical." They argue that these words and their origins in the church property cases (discussed in chapter two) reveal a Court concerned to draw a line between what is secular and what is religious, not one concerned to recognize church autonomy, as many advocates had hoped. Lupu and Tuttle argue further that such line-drawing is a necessary and not an impossibly difficult task. Ira C. Lupu and Robert W. Tuttle, "The Mystery of Unanimity in *Hosanna-Tabor Evangelical Lutheran Church & School v. EEOC*," *Lewis & Clark Law Review* 20 (2017): 1265–1315. Ira Mark Ellman argues to the contrary that virtually any activity performed by church personnel could be described in theological terms; neutral principles derived from contract theory, he further argues, suffice to decide these cases. No special line between what is religious and what is secular is needed. Ellman, "Driven from the Tribunal." Neutrality has proved an elusive goal in the religion cases, as many have observed. For more on neutrality, see *Zelman v. Simmons-Harris*, 536 U.S. 639 (2002), and Douglas Laycock, "Formal, Substantive, and Disaggregated Neutrality Toward Religion," *DePaul Law Review* 39 (1990): 993–1018.

28. The account that Roberts gives of the history of the ministerial exception is what is known as "law office history," historical accounts tailored to support a particular outcome in a case and constructed in this case by lawyers and law professors advocating for church autonomy. For critiques of the uses of history by the courts, see Howe, *The Garden and the Wilderness*; Lewis LaRue, *Constitutional Law as Fiction: Narrative in the Rhetoric of Authority* (University Park: Pennsylvania State University Press, 1995); and Farah Peterson, "Monuments and Memory: How the Law Writes American History" (lecture, 2018 Sherman Emerging Scholar Lecture Series, Warwick Center, University of North Carolina, Wilmington, October 17, 2018). See also Elizabeth Dale, "Spelunking, or, Some Meditations on the New Presentism" in *The Oxford Handbook of Legal History*, ed. Christopher Tomlins and Marcus Dubber (Oxford: Oxford University Press, 2018).

and state over religious offices is hardly new."[29] Wait, I want to say: is this a controversy between church and state? Do we have a church and state in the US? Didn't the founding fathers reject that history? A strong argument can be made that the US has neither a church nor a state in a medieval sense. But Roberts needs both in order to tell a story of continuity that will underwrite what he apparently understands to be the semi-sovereignty of the church.

Roberts begins his story in 1215, invoking the high medieval European struggle between popes and kings over the selection of bishops and other high church officials. Before the Act of Supremacy, we are told, passed by the English Parliament in 1534, making Henry VIII Supreme Head of the Church, the church in England had been free, at least since 1215, thanks to an earlier English king, King John, and Magna Carta. The church was free during those three intervening centuries, Roberts says, because King John had affirmed in Magna Carta that the church had the freedom of election to church offices.[30] Henry VIII, with his break from Rome, had interrupted the freedom granted to the church by King John. The church was not free again then, according to the Supreme Court, until the Puritans and the Quakers arrived in the New World. There, far from the control of the national church of England, whose head was the monarch, Americans adopted the First Amendment and ensured the restoration of King John's promise. The result, the chief justice announces, is that "[b]y forbidding the 'establishment of religion' and guaranteeing the 'free exercise thereof,' the Religion Clauses ensured that the new Federal Government—unlike the English Crown—would have no role in filling ecclesiastical offices. The Establishment Clause prevents the Government from appointing ministers, and the Free Exercise Clause prevents it from interfering with the freedom of religious groups to select their own."[31]

The Religion Clauses together are made in this gesture to be essentially about reversing Henry VIII's presumption. And notwithstanding the shift in this sentence to "religious groups," it is clear that the chief justice is still speaking of *the* church, as his reference to the English Crown signals.

What does Roberts' history lesson accomplish? There are many sleights of hand in this account.[32] Perhaps none is as important as the work done by

29. 565 U.S. at 182.
30. 565 U.S. at 182.
31. 565 U.S. at 184.
32. For a fascinating and meticulous account of Henry VIII's activities with respect to the English church, see Diarmaid MacCulloch, *Thomas Cromwell: A Revolutionary Life* (New York: Viking, 2018).

the definite article in the locution "the church." Hosanna-Tabor Evangelical Lutheran Church is said to have rights granted to *the* church by King John. But that was a different church. That was the medieval church. That was the church in Rome. The followers of Martin Luther and John Calvin stripped the altars. The lutherans and the puritans and the quakers had different understandings of church from that of the medieval church. Not to mention the rationalists among the American revolutionaries. Cheryl Perich would not have been termed a minister of any kind in the medieval church, the reformed churches of early modern Europe, or in any of the churches of North America until very recently. And it was a different state as well. Subsequent English political history saw the Glorious Revolution and the Act of Toleration.

What does it mean in the context of US constitutional interpretation to go back to the Holy Roman Emperor Henry IV kneeling to the pope at Canossa as some of the amicus briefs did?[33] Or perhaps even further back—to Constantine—or to the apostle Paul—in order to address the claims made by Perich? The Court's history invokes a church—*the* church—that is arguably foreign to the constitutional world envisioned by the religion clauses.

What Roberts calls "the freedom of the church," both in England during the time between King John and King Henry VIII, and after 1607 in the English colonies, but particularly since ratification of the First Amendment, can be summed up, he says, in the legally guaranteed capacity of *the* church to select its own ministers, free of political interference, a matter that is "strictly ecclesiastical." Two thousand years of church history and profound differences in Roman Catholic, reformation, and anabaptist ecclesiologies—as well as in understandings of the freedom of christians—are finessed in this breezy historical account. Not to mention the relationship between these various churches and shifting political authorities of various kinds. King John, Henry VIII, James Madison, and William Penn—members of very different churches with radically different understandings of church governance, as well as of political authority—are all mobilized on behalf of the same special freedom for "the church." The church appears in this opinion as an apparently mystical and trans-historical entity but it is also one that has touched down—been incarnated in local instantiations or avatars—always insisting on its right to select its own ministers. This church is figured as radically independent

33. See Brief Amici Curiae of Professor Eugene Volokh et al. at 10.

of the political authorities of societies in which it has always been deeply enmeshed.

In his article on church and empire, Sylvester Johnson comments on the curious capacity of the church to scale up and down and be simultaneously present in different geographical locations:

> Because it is conceived as the mystical body under the divine government of a universal, divine sovereign, the church—and this includes national churches like the Church of England—is impervious to the more parochial imaginaries of demographic constitution that characterize nations. This does not mean that nationalism does not directly shape and influence churches. It does mean, however, that the simultaneous presence of the Anglican Church in Cape Coast, the New Jersey colony, and the London metropole is not an anomaly but a paradigmatic manifestation of ecclesiastical formation.[34]

The church has the capacity to be both local and to be everywhere, Johnson says. It is also strangely embedded in US law, providing a structural logic for the First Amendment. *Hosanna-Tabor* stabilizes one version of the long, long debate among christians about the relationship between the invisible and the visible church, the invisible church (or true christians) being known only to God, a debate importantly inflected by local histories, giving that version a constitutional imprimatur.

Roberts begins with the claim that King John in Magna Carta had "agreed that 'the English church shall be free, and shall have its rights undiminished and its liberties unimpaired.'"[35] Magna Carta was an agreement between King John and his lords. It touched on many matters and has been a legal and political touchstone in both England and its colonies for centuries but the history and interpretation of Magna Carta and its effects in law are not simple. With respect to its effects on the church in particular, political historian Cary Nederman importantly emphasizes that "the ecclesiastical liberty" guaranteed by King John "pertained to the body of the Church as a mystical union, not to individual churches or their leaders." It "possessed specific liberties because it enjoyed a general form of liberty that did not depend on any grant from a secular dominion . . . the Magna Carta's statement of ecclesiastical liberty reflects a simple recog-

34. Sylvester Johnson, "Divine Imperium and the Ecclesiastical Imaginary: Church History, Transnationalism, and the Rationality of Empire," *Church History* 83, no. 4 (2014): 1005.

35. 565 U.S. at 182.

nition of a form of freedom that already exists independently, rather than a concession that the king might rightfully withhold or revoke."[36] In other words, King John could be understood to have been affirming a theological truth, not granting a right in law. The medieval argument between kings and popes about the selection of church officers depended on a shared political theology, albeit one that could be argued about. Henry VIII and the pope had different ecclesiologies but not different gods. Thomas More was executed for siding with the pope about the nature of the relationship between crown and church. But they were all catholics. There was, in a sense, no outside of the church in England in the sixteenth century. *The* church occupied all of the space.

That is not our history.[37] The selection of ministers was a focus of concern in the colonies as new and different churches struggled to establish themselves in law.[38] Freeing churches first from colonial and then from state governmental interference in the selection of ministers was one motive in disestablishment.[39] This history precedes, however, the postrevolutionary radical fragmentation and diversification of American religious life, the rise of capitalism, and the development of modern labor law. In the *Hosanna-Tabor* opinion, history mostly stops for the chief justice in 1791 with ratification of the Bill of Rights. After his loose account of English church history, what is most striking is the entire lack of acknowledgment of the remarkable changes to religion—and to churches—that occurred in the US after the Revolution. Division, revivalism, populism, innovation, and immigration profoundly changed the American religious landscape over the course of the nineteenth century. Churches became at once multiple and varied, but also gradually fixed into a new object—an object in law, an object that did not exist before the Revolution. American officials, when speaking of American religion, can no longer descriptively—or even, arguably, constitutionally—speak, as the Court does in *Hosanna-*

36. Cary Nederman, "The Liberty of the Church and the Road to Runnymede: John of Salisbury and the Intellectual Foundations of the Magna Carta," *Political Science and Politics* 43, no. 3 (July 2010): 458.

37. To be sure, Magna Carta became a talisman for American statesman and legal thinkers. See, e.g., A. E. Dick Howard, *Magna Carta: Text and Commentary* (Charlottesville: University Press of Virginia, 1998), and *The Road from Runnymede: Magna Carta and Constitutionalism in America* (Charlottesville: University of Virginia Press, 1968); and Ellis Sandoz, ed., *The Roots of Liberty: Magna Carta, Ancient Constitution, and the Anglo-American Tradition of Rule of Law* (Indianapolis: Liberty Fund, 2008). But its ecclesiastical assumptions are foreign to US legal culture.

38. Lupu and Tuttle, "The Mystery of Unanimity," 1281.

39. Michael W. McConnell, "Reflections on *Hosanna-Tabor*," *Harvard Journal of Law & Public Policy* 35, no. 3 (June 2012): 827–832.

Tabor, of "the church" and her rights. That church was left behind in the Old World. Whatever rights she may have enjoyed under Magna Carta no longer have purchase today. In the long struggle between the church and the state, the state has won.[40] That is one of the victories that was arguably affirmed in the Constitution.

No American government official is attempting to appoint men to church offices today in the sense meant during the investiture controversy. But the line between religious and secular authority is very blurry nonetheless—in new ways. For example, as various tasks of the welfare state devolve to private groups, and some of those private groups are religious organizations contracting with the state, the strength of the churches' argument for autonomy from regulation necessarily lessens. That is one of the ironic results of disestablishment. One person's minister is another person's worker entitled to the protection of the law. When the ministry is professionalized and religious professionals work in secular employment, their dual allegiance challenges separation.[41] Some churches have deliberately avoided a professional paid ministry in part for this very reason—to avoid government oversight.

Having finished with his history lesson, Roberts underlined the independent authority of "ecclesiastical tribunals" with a discussion of the church property cases, to be discussed in the next chapter. He then turned to deal with the most important precedent for the position claimed by Perich and the EEOC, the Court's 1990 decision in *Employment Division v. Smith*, the "peyote case," declaring religious exemptions not to be constitutionally mandated.[42]

Distinguishing *Smith*

Employment Division v. Smith concerned the then-illegal use of peyote in the Native American Church in Oregon.[43] Alfred Leo Smith and Galen

40. Andrew Koppelman, "The Freedom of the Church in the Modern Era: 'Freedom of the Church' and the Authority of the State," *Journal of Contemporary Legal Issues* 21 (2013): 145–164.

41. See discussion in Winnifred Fallers Sullivan, *A Ministry of Presence: Chaplaincy, Spiritual Care, and the Law* (Chicago: University of Chicago Press, 2014).

42. *Employment Division v. Smith*, 494 U.S. 872 (1990).

43. The Native American Church was first incorporated in 1918 in Oklahoma. Emerging out of a long history of Indian practice, including ritual ingestion of the fruit of the peyote cactus, the church was formed specifically to stabilize its legal identity. It has no specifically

Black had been fired from their jobs for ingesting peyote during church ceremonies. After being denied unemployment compensation, they sued, claiming that their right to the free exercise of religion under the First Amendment had been violated by the Oregon unemployment office. The Supreme Court, citing *Reynolds v. US*[44] (a nineteenth-century case refusing to recognize a constitutional exemption from laws criminalizing bigamy for mormon plural marriage practices), held in *Smith* that the free exercise clause of the First Amendment protects only opinions, not acts. No constitutional exemption from neutral laws of general application exists, the *Smith* court said, for the illegal actions of religiously motivated persons. To require such an exemption—or accommodation—would mean, as Justice Antonin Scalia explained in his opinion for the majority in *Smith*, that each person would be "a law unto himself," free to assert the bar of religious conscience for any refusal to observe the law.[45]

The *Smith* precedent had been considered by many Court observers in advance of the decision to be the most serious legal obstacle for the Court in getting to the result it reached in *Hosanna-Tabor*.[46] The Americans with Disabilities Act's protection of the rights of disabled employees is surely a neutral law of general application, one that was not designed to target or disadvantage any particular religious community, and thus, under *Smith*, there seemed to be no free exercise clause defense available to the Michigan school. Not so, said Roberts. The *Smith* rule does not apply in *Hosanna-Tabor*, he said, because the issue before the Court was not a claim by religious individuals to a special religious exemption from neutrally worded laws, as was the case in *Smith*; it was instead a claim by the church itself to the right to bar the application of those laws to its employees. The church's right in this regard—its jurisdiction as an independent sovereign with respect to all aspects of its relationship with those whom it deems to be ministers—was understood in the Court's unanimous opinion to be in effect pre- or extra-constitutional, trumping the rule in *Smith*.

christian identity or affiliation. https://nativeamericanchurches.org/native-american-church-first-nation-history/ (accessed October 20, 2018).

44. *Reynolds v. United States*, 98 U.S. 145 (1879).

45. 494 U.S. at 885, citing 98 U.S. at 167.

46. Lupu and Tuttle, in contrast, argue that the Court did not need to reach the *Smith* decision at all because what they take to be the ecclesiastical matters doctrine, developed in the church property cases, effects a jurisdictional bar under the establishment clause, precluding the necessity to consider the case under the free exercise clause. They argue that the jurisdictional bar derives from a recognition of a lack of judicial competence in matters of religion. "The Mystery of Unanimity," 1282.

Roberts arrived at this position in a short section of the *Hosanna-Tabor* opinion that has baffled many readers. He explained in a single short paragraph why *Smith* did not control the outcome in *Hosanna-Tabor*:

> It is true that the ADA's prohibition on retaliation, like Oregon's prohibition on peyote use, is a valid and neutral law of general applicability. But a church's selection of its ministers is unlike an individual's ingestion of peyote. *Smith* involved government regulation of only outward physical acts. The present case, in contrast, concerns government interference with an internal church decision that affects the faith and mission of the church itself.[47]

This paragraph warrants a very close reading. What the Court says here is that while, after the *Smith* decision, the free exercise clause of the First Amendment is no longer understood to provide constitutional exemption from laws of general application for individual believers who engage in "outward physical acts" consistent with their religious beliefs—even an act that in the case of Smith and Black, the plaintiffs in the *Smith* case, could be described in religious terms as a sacrament—a composite history running from Magna Carta through the US Constitution does provide such an exemption for the church because government interference with internal church governance is a threat to "the faith and mission of the church itself." Government interference with the acts of individuals apparently poses no such threat. *The* church requires protection that individuals do not.

The distinction the Court is making here between the individual and the church is not entirely clear. An individual's religious acts are characterized by the Court as "*only* outward" while the church's acts in this case, effectively casting someone from the church's employment, perhaps from the church altogether, are understood by Chief Justice Roberts to be internal, and therefore, more essential to the church's very essence, than are the sacraments to the individual. Indeed, in a semantic shift from speaking of "a" church in the second sentence of the paragraph to speaking of "the" church in the third, it is, on the Court's reading, the universal church in the person of the local visible church, rather than in the person of the individual believer, that seems to be recognized as having an internal religious life of consequence.

47. 565 U.S. at 190.

For the Court to make this distinction is for it to do theology. The distinction between the church and the individual christian made here is intelligible only in the context of what has been a very long and contentious theological conversation about the nature of the church and its relationship to its members, one that goes back to the early years of the christian community, one that has divided the historical churches ever since. Douglas Laycock, a distinguished First Amendment scholar representing the Hosanna-Tabor school in the Supreme Court, undertook to explain the theology of the First Amendment for the Court. The church's sovereignty, he explained to the justices at oral argument, should be understood as taking priority in law over an individual's right of access to the sacraments because the church forms the consciences of individuals.[48] Individuals have no independent constitutional right to act in accordance with their own consciences under US law. Churches do have such rights. The Constitution recognizes, in other words, according to the Court in *Hosanna-Tabor*, that the church, unlike an individual, is "a law unto itself."[49]

Justice Roberts' paragraph in the *Hosanna-Tabor* decision distinguishing *Smith* is a staggeringly dense piece of political-theological obfuscation, one enabled by Laycock's willingness to serve as a front man for Missouri Synod Lutheran orthodoxy. Laycock further insisted at oral argument that church and state are by nature separate and equal jurisdictions:

> The churches do not set the criteria for selecting or removing the officers of government, and government does not set the criteria for selecting and removing officers of the church . . . These decisions are committed to churches by separation of church and state . . . The position of minister is categorically special because that has been committed to the church in the system of separation of church and state . . . It's not that institutions are different from individuals. It is that the institutional governance of the church is at a prior step.[50]

The right of the church is at "a prior step" to the individual. Preserving the hierarchical discipline and right to autonomy of *the* church—what Roberts terms "the faith and mission of the church itself"—is constitutionally mandated, he says, further evident in the priority that disestablishment has

48. Oral argument transcript *Hosanna-Tabor*, No. 10-553 at 57.
49. 494 U.S. at 885, citing 98 U.S. at 167.
50. Oral argument transcript *Hosanna-Tabor*, No. 10-553 at 57.

to free exercise in the ordering of the religion clauses in the language of the First Amendment itself.

Laycock and Roberts speak authoritatively of the church as if its sovereign self-understanding has been and must be acknowledged in US law, echoing King John at Runnymede. The mystical unity of the church here serves to mask differences among christian churches and among religious communities more broadly, all in service of the recognition of an independent jurisdictional power. Laycock refers to "the system of separation of church and state" in the US, although no such separation formally exists in law.[51] The church in the US is disestablished, not separated. Church and state were never in need of separation in the US because they were never together.[52] By distinguishing *Smith* in this way, the Court recognized and located Laycock's understanding of the church in relationship to the First Amendment in a way parallel to that of the church and Magna Carta. But this is an anachronism. As historian Cary Nederman has said, "The Church [in the thirteenth century] possessed specific liberties because it enjoyed a general form of liberty that did not depend on any grant from a secular dominion."[53] King John recognized what was a transhistorical mystical entity made visible in existing historical church institutions but not exhausted by them.

By adopting English church history as its own, disestablishment is here understood by the Court to guarantee the pre- or extra-constitutional right of *the* church to select its ministers specifically refused by Henry VIII. The individual has no part in the version of that history imported into US constitutional law by the Court. What are termed "individually motivated religious acts" by the Court are simply outside of, perhaps threatening to, the very order of the faith and mission of the church itself, as well as that of the state, because the sovereignty of each depends on the subordination of the individual. Acts understood by the Court to be performed in obedience to the religious conscience of the individual must bow to secular law because they are subversive of the authority of the church. The US consti-

51. The "separation of church and state" in a US context is not a constitutional principle but a political one. See Philip Hamburger, *Separation of Church and State* (Cambridge: Harvard University Press, 2002). Indeed, there is a certain irony in a doctrine largely pioneered by baptists being adopted as a banner by the liturgical churches.

52. The church in France was, for example, separated from the state in a 1905 law, separated but arguably not disestablished, entangled as its administration remains in French law. Historic church buildings in France are, for example, maintained at taxpayer expense.

53. Nederman, "The Liberty of the Church and the Road to Runnymede," 458.

tutional doctrine supporting the subordination of Perich is thus a classic example of a church/state partnership regulating membership through the naming of heretics, a regular practice of the premodern church.

The *Hosanna-Tabor* Court's peculiar solicitude for *the* church's faith and mission over the conscience of the individual, and its move, in effect, in distinguishing *Smith*, to put church order before sacrament, thrusts it into age-old theological debates within and among christian churches about the relationship of the sacrament to the church—and of the church to the state, as well as of individual conscience to the church's magisterium. Although political and economic explanations can be offered for the emergence today of the church autonomy movement in the context of neoliberal corporatism, as will be discussed in chapter three, it is astonishing really that the US Supreme Court would take such a strong theological position in such an overt way in the twenty-first century—and to do so unanimously.

Those within the US legal academy advocating constitutional deference to church autonomy, or what is sometimes called the freedom of the church, have struggled to find a theory of the church to serve contemporary US law, often relying on compressed and oversimplified accounts of church history such as the one used by the Court in *Hosanna-Tabor*. Paul Horwitz attempts a more complex story in a recent article, although he too acknowledges the staggeringly difficult task that it is. As an alternative, he suggests using economic theories of the flourishing of religion under conditions of competition.[54] Horwitz asserts that the church is so diminished from its medieval heyday that its claims to freedom are more pitiable than threatening.

This book suggests that rather than viewing today's churches as faint and harmless shadows of their former selves, one might see the US church as a metastasis, potentially more deadly than the high medieval version. On what grounds can Horwitz value the harm to Perich and the others on the losing end of these cases as less significant than the harm done to those he sees as medieval victims of the church? As with many arguments from history in First Amendment law, his assertion is merely stated rather than argued. No historical evidence is offered. Just the usual slurring reference to premodern barbarity and primitivism.

54. Horwitz, "Freedom of the Church Without Romance." This competition theory of American religion has been criticized by sociologists. See, e.g., Bender, "The Power of Pluralist Thinking."

The church and the sacrament

There are a number of ways to critique the political theology in the paragraph from the *Hosanna-Tabor* decision distinguishing *Smith*. In this section I will suggest one possible critique from within the theology of the Roman Catholic Church, the church of Chief Justice Roberts and several other justices. The theologies and ecclesiologies of other churches will appear in other chapters of the book, although a truly comprehensive historical and theological critique of the church and its various legal personalities would be exceedingly complicated and require another book. Indeed, it is perhaps the very complexity and fluidity of the metaphor of the church that has enabled its survival.[55]

Sometimes there have been dark warnings by Court watchers about the possible anti-American consequences of the Court's now having a majority of Catholic justices.[56] (One of the current justices is protestant and three are jewish.) But if that fact is a threat to the Court's jurisprudence, these particular catholics do not seem to have read the catechism of the church (the summation of Catholic doctrine for laypersons)—or to be up on current Catholic theology. If the Court is going to undertake a Theodosian definition of orthodoxy, it might start by getting its theology right.

The church since at least the apostle Paul has been described by many different kinds of christians as the body of Christ—among other metaphors. In the christian theology of the high liturgical traditions, Christ is

55. The difficulty, in part, is that in its petition to the state for recognition, the church is secularized; it relinquishes its claim to the role of critic, to being, as some would say on its behalf, in this world but not of this world. For a recent critical theology of the church from within conservative evangelical theology, see James K. A. Smith, *Awaiting the King: Reforming Public Theology* (Grand Rapids, MI: Baker Academic, 2017).

56. See various blog posts by law professor Geoffrey Stone, e.g., "Our Faith-based Justices" https://www.chicagotribune.com/news/ct-xpm-2007-04-30-0704290277-story.html/. What *Hosanna-Tabor* and other cases like it show is that US law cannot think religion without the church. The mystical church shapes its imagination. Yet to call the majority opinion in *Hosanna-Tabor* catholic seems too simple. After all, Hosanna-Tabor was a lutheran school. Chapter two will consider cases brought by two eastern orthodox churches. And the plaintiffs in *Hobby Lobby*, discussed in chapter three, were pentecostal and mennonite. We may be seeing a renewed interest in corporate religious rights but it would be wrong to term this interest catholic in the narrow sectarian sense. Or to suggest that the noncatholic justices are not also faith-based, whatever exactly it is that Stone means by that. See Winnifred Fallers Sullivan, review of Christopher J. Scalia and Edward Whelan, eds., *Scalia Speaks: Reflections on Law, Faith, and Life Well Lived*, *Commonweal* 145 (2018): 33–34.

understood to be indivisibly and interdependently present in at least three bodies: in his own historical first-century body, in the Eucharist, and in the church. The current catechism of the Catholic Church—available on the Vatican website in twenty-three languages—announces, in somewhat awkward English, that this last meaning should be understood as follows:

> In Christian usage, the word "church" designates the liturgical assembly, but also the local community or the whole universal community of believers. These three meanings are inseparable. "The Church" is the People that God gathers in the whole world. She exists in local communities and is made real as a liturgical, above all a Eucharistic, assembly. She draws her life from the word and the Body of Christ and so herself becomes Christ's Body.[57]

This is a short excerpt from a much longer description of the nature of the church in Catholic teaching. The sacrament and the church, on this account, cannot be separated or ordered. They are co-present. This is the teaching of the church fathers and of Henri de Lubac, the great twentieth-century theologian who was one of the principal influences in the drafting of the new "Constitution of the Church" published by the Second Vatican Council in 1964.[58]

The theology of the church and its relationship to the political order has been a matter of intense interest since the early councils, but as the story goes for the Roberts Court, it was particularly so during the investiture struggles of the Middle Ages and the early modern periods, affecting politics as well as religion. This is a far more complex history than the Court acknowledges. Ernst Kantorowicz famously described the transformation of theories of divine kingship over the course of the Middle Ages in *The King's Two Bodies*, showing how European political regimes can be seen to have made powerful use of Christ's multiple natures and bodies as the mystical bodies of the church were juridified and transferred to successive monarchies as the modern nation-state was born.[59] A key turning point for Kantorowicz came with the invention of the Tudor legal

57. http://www.vatican.va/archive/ENG0015/__P27.HTM/.

58. Henri de Lubac, *Corpus Mysticum: The Eucharist and the Church in the Middle Ages*, trans. Gemma Simmonds with Richard Price and Christopher Stephens (Notre Dame, IN: University of Notre Dame Press, 2006). Original edition 1944. Vatican II documents are available on the Vatican website: http://www.vatican.va/archive/hist_councils/ii_vatican_council/index.htm (accessed October 22, 2018).

59. Kantorowicz, *The King's Two Bodies*, 19.

fiction of the king's two bodies, the king now having replaced Christ as the metaphorical center of political power. It was the productive discursive mutability of these bodies in the birthing of the modern state that so interested Kantorowicz. He argued that it was the reduction of the three bodies to two and the eventual violent separation of the king's earthly and divine bodies that made secular democratic government possible.

Kantorowicz offers a political and aesthetic account of the relationship between church and state. Lubac saw this same process of linguistic migration and separation over the course of the Middle Ages as having had a pernicious effect on the church, not because the church was deprived of influence on or surpassed by the state but because, ironically perhaps, the church was secularized through its centuries of rivalry with the state. It had lost its way.[60] In a kind of mimesis, its body too was juridified, but it was also desacralized.[61] Lubac—and the bishops of the Second Vatican Council—sought to reclaim the unity and sacrality of Christ's three bodies in their redefinition of the nature of the church and its relationship to the political order.[62]

This is not an uncomplicated or uncontested history—and I am, of course, here leaving out ongoing differences within the Roman Catholic Church, the strikingly different political theologies of the churches of the East and of the protestant reformations—and the further bodily transformations of all of them in the Atlantic crossing and across US history. (We will come back to some of these transformations and these churches when we discuss the church property cases, the *Hobby Lobby* decision, and the black church-in-law in subsequent chapters.) But reading *Hosanna-Tabor* by way of Lubac and Kantorowicz can help us to see, that in the particular way in which the Court distinguishes *Smith*, the Court is enacting yet one more transformation of the *corpus mysticum*. In recognizing a kind of sovereignty in the church, and by separating church and sacrament, the church is once more being recognized as a secular political entity, just as Lubac feared, one with its own exclusive jurisdiction. One might even go so far as to say that the *Hosanna-Tabor* Court was not only endangering its own precedents in its treatment of *Smith*, it could also be seen to have been re-

60. For another important theological account of this history, see William T. Cavanaugh, *Migrations of the Holy: God, State, and the Political Meaning of the Church* (Grand Rapids, MI: Eerdmans, 2011).

61. See Samera Esmeir, *Juridical Humanity: A Colonial History* (Stanford: Stanford University Press, 2012).

62. It was Vatican II as well that issued *Dignitatis Humanae*, the Declaration on Religious Freedom. http://www.vatican.va/archive/hist_councils/ii_vatican_council/documents/vat-ii_decl_19651207_dignitatis-humanae_en.html/ (accessed October 22, 2018).

versing Vatican II's theology of the church, returning to an earlier scholastic political theology, one that underwrote a church seeking worldly power as a rival to the state. This scholasticism is now favored by the conservatives in the church—and apparently on the bench—both Catholic and noncatholic.

By reading its version of church history into the First Amendment—by returning to what it takes to have been the church of King John—the *Hosanna-Tabor* Court has given priority to the rights of some christians over others. It has also prioritized the church over that of the individual. But what of those who do not belong to churches? While other religious communities speak of collective identity in various equally complex ways, the Court's opinion would seem to suggest that its First Amendment doctrine is tightly and very specifically bound to a history and theology of "the" christian church. While the Court in *Hosanna-Tabor* acknowledges that it might occasionally prove difficult to decide who qualifies as a minister for these purposes, it nowhere acknowledges its political theological debts or even the possibility of non-christians.

The church, in its claim to universality, is arguably by nature a supersessionist institution. Its very creation in the mission to the Gentiles is said to have resulted from the refusal of the jews to recognize Jesus as Messiah. Its continuing indispensability to the Court and to American religious life more generally draws power from this same well.[63]

It is the argument of this book that simplifying ecclesiology and church history in the way performed by Laycock and the justices further contributes to the impossibility of religious freedom. There is theological work to be done that such cheap and shallow appropriations of convenient proof texts inhibits.

Who is a minister?

At issue in *Hosanna-Tabor* was whether judicial expansion of the Americans with Disabilities Act's existing deference to religiously based discrimination beyond the narrow statutory exception for pastoral hiring deci-

63. The church was not founded by Jesus. Jesus preached the Kingdom. It was, according to German theologian Erik Peterson, the rejection of Christ by the jews and the resulting eschatological postponement that made the church necessary. Erik Peterson, *Theological Tractates*, trans. Michael J. Hollerich (Stanford: Stanford University Press, 2011). A fuller account of the relationship of the church to the jewish community would require, among other things, an account of the long history of the figure of synagoga in Western Christianity. See, e.g., Nina Rowe, *The Jew, the Cathedral, and the Medieval City: Synagoga and Ecclesia in the Thirteenth Century* (Cambridge: Cambridge University Press, 2011).

sions to the entire employment relationship of a broader set of employees by the lower federal courts was constitutionally mandated. Even if one accepts the practical advisability of such an extension in many situations, one that might be defended on traditional employment law grounds as a BFOQ (bona-fide occupational qualification), it is not at all clear that Perich herself should be considered a minister in the sense invoked by the Court and its defenders.[64] Furthermore, the alleged discrimination was on the basis of disability not religion. If she is a minister for the purposes of the ministerial exemption, does that mean that religious groups can name anyone a minister and thereby evade all employment discrimination laws with respect to those employees? In many American churches and other religious organizations virtually all employees are understood to be engaged in some form of ministry.

Perich's job, as the court of appeals opinion in the case insisted, was basically the same as that of any other fourth-grade teacher in the country. She just happened to perform those duties at a parochial school. Was she deprived of all of her rights by a reading of history that sees "the church" as having a kind of mystical sovereignty acknowledged by a medieval king, and further that disputes over the conditions of her employment should properly be kept in house, following a parochial reading of Paul's injunction against "going to law," as Missouri Synod leaders averred? Should we understand her to have consented to such an abridgment of her rights under US law, as many would argue?

One of the most startling aspects of the *Hosanna-Tabor* decision is that it was unanimous. The three women justices, each of whom might be thought to be sensitive to discrimination against women in the workforce,[65] all signed on to an opinion judicially depriving a disabled woman employee of her statutory rights on the ground that an avowedly patriarchal institution had a virtually unreviewable right to exclude her. As Ira Lupu and Robert Tuttle acknowledge in their article analyzing the decision, "the most common categorical exclusions from the clergy are based on sex . . . ministerial exception cases in U.S. courts frequently involve claims of covert discrimination based on sex. To put it bluntly, in operation the ministerial exception tends to be detrimental to women who are clergy, or teachers in religious schools."[66]

64. See, e.g., McConnell, "Reflections on *Hosanna-Tabor*," 821–835.

65. See, e.g., *Ledbetter v. Goodyear Tire & Rubber*, 550 U.S. 618 (2007), Ginsburg, J., dissenting.

66. Lupu and Tuttle, "The Mystery of Unanimity," 1310.

The gender discrimination embedded within the ministerial exemption of this situation is not mere accident—or only "in operation." The church defended by Laycock and recognized by the Court is an almost exclusively male-led institution, one whose dominant metaphors for self-understanding are male. That there are alternative versions of church and of ordained ministry is not acknowledged by Laycock or by the government.[67]

Oddly, at oral argument in *Hosanna-Tabor*, the justices and the lawyers on all sides repeatedly returned to the example of the Catholic priest, all of them seemingly assuming the necessary exclusivity of the male Catholic priesthood as the limit case in the regulation of churches by secular law.[68] This assumption is also common in academic legal commentary. The nonnegotiability of this religious doctrine *in secular law* is accepted by legal scholars across the spectrum. Lawrence Sager, a leading liberal First Amendment scholar, has argued that "[a]s a matter of political morality, the Catholic Church is entitled to insist that its priests be male without interference from the state."[69] Michael McConnell, a leading evangelical protestant conservative scholar, states that "[i]t is intuitively obvious to anyone with an understanding of American constitutional values that the Roman Catholic Church (and others including Orthodox Judaism, Eastern Orthodoxy, Islam, and many conservative Protestant denominations) must have a right to hire as clergy only men, just as other religious traditions [may] enforce other requirements seemingly at odds with secular law."[70] The closed circle of the male priesthood and the church—and the legal academy—all entitled to priority over the female schoolteacher, appears unbreachable by the end of the unanimous opinion in *Hosanna-Tabor*.

The strategy in Roberts' opinion seems to be to incorporate Perich into the male priesthood in order to make her disappear.[71] She is a min-

67. There are, of course, feminist theologies of the body of Christ and of the church. See, e.g., Elizabeth Johnson, *She Who Is: The Mystery of God in Feminist Theological Discourse* (New York: Crossroad Publishing, 1992).

68. Law arguably needs a fixed dogmatic object in order to think about religion. See oral argument transcript *Hosanna-Tabor*, No. 10-553 at 22, 38, 50, https://www.supremecourt.gov/oral_arguments/argument_transcripts/2011/10-553.pdf/.

69. Lawrence G. Sager, "Why Churches (and Possibly, the Tarpon Bay Women's Blue Water Fishing Club) Can Discriminate," in *The Rise of Corporate Religious Liberty*, ed. Micah Schwartzman, Chad Flanders, and Zoe Robinson (New York: Oxford University Press, 2016), 77. See also Laborde, *Liberalism's Religion*, 177.

70. McConnell, "Reflections on *Hosanna-Tabor*," 821.

71. See Françoise Meltzer, *For Fear of the Fire: Joan of Arc and the Limits of Subjectivity* (Chicago: University of Chicago Press, 2001), on similar moves made with respect to Joan of Arc during her trial.

ister when it is convenient for enhancing the power of the church but not a minister when it comes to the power of the ordained ministry to wield sacramental power and disciplinary authority. Her church excludes women from sacramental ministry.[72] This second-class citizen status is the pivot point that enables her scapegoating, René Girard–style, in order to preserve the sovereign intactness of the church.[73] The charge against her is insubordination. Aligned against her are the originalist constitutional historians (McConnell et al.) retailing a long story about the right of the church to select her ministers, the Lutheran theologians and their lawyers (Laycock et al.) describing a biblical and doctrine-laden orthodoxy dripping with gendered piety and condescension, and the liberal separationists (Lupu and Tuttle and Sager) protecting a religion-shaped space of "strictly ecclesiastical" matters for the church to enact its sovereignty. She is a minister when it is useful to them and she is not a minister when it is not.

Laycock's brief for the Missouri Synod Lutheran Church begins with a hierarchy also founded in class distinctions: "The courts of appeals agree that there is a ministerial exception to employment-law litigation. They agree that it extends beyond pastors, priests, and rabbis, but not as far as janitors or secretaries. The question is where to draw the line."[74] He characterizes Perich's work as follows: "[S]he was important to the religious mission of the Church because she taught religion classes, led worship, and led prayer. She was expected to, and did, integrate faith into the secular curriculum . . . And she was the Church's primary means for communicating the faith to her students."[75] And then he described her offense:

> She violated church teaching, was found unfit for ministry by a vote of the Church congregation, and was removed from ecclesiastical office. Instead of challenging that ruling within the church, she filed a claim in civil court seeking reinstatement as a commissioned minister and "called" teacher. Such a claim would run roughshod over the Lutheran system for resolving internal religious disputes.[76]

72. A. L. Barry, *What about the Ordination of Women to the Pastoral Office?* Office of the President, Lutheran Church–Missouri Synod, 1997, http://lcms.org/Document.fdoc?src=lcm&id=1099&dialogFeatures=protocol=http/.

73. René Girard, *Violence and the Sacred* (New York: W. W. Norton, 1979). See also Meltzer, *For Fear of the Fire*.

74. Brief for the Petitioner at 2.

75. Brief for the Petitioner at 14–15.

76. Brief for the Petitioner at 2.

Explaining further the Lutheran Church's relationship with Perich, Laycock referred to her calling, citing the Augsburg Confession, the Lutheran Church–Missouri Synod (LCMS) website, and the Amicus Brief for the Lutheran Church: "The call is a rich theological concept within Lutheranism, dating to the Augsburg Confession of 1530, which states that 'no one should publicly teach in the Church or administer the Sacraments unless *he* be regularly called'" [emphasis supplied].[77]

The LCMS brief further explains the richness of their theology of the ministry, those "chosen by God":

> . . . the Synod fervently believes in a divinely established ministerium in which individual ministers are first called by God and then ordained by the church to do God's work. The biblical basis for a divinely established ministerium goes back to Jesus selecting his disciples, impressing them into service, and conferring on St. Peter the keys to the kingdom. See, e.g., Matthew 4:18–21, 10:1–41, 16:13–20. In this view, ministers are not chosen by human beings. Rather, they are chosen by God; human beings merely recognize that certain individuals have already been selected for the ministry by God. See, e.g., Acts 20:28 ("Pay careful attention to yourselves and to all the flock, in which *the Holy Spirit* has made you overseers . . .") [emphasis added]; Galatians 1:1 ("[N]ot from men nor through man, but through Jesus Christ and God the Father.").[78]

Authoritatively enclosed within a fervent church and state, Perich did not have a chance. Whether and how these theological claims are or are not contested within the Missouri Synod Lutheran Church, and without, one might ask how an American court can recognize these kinds of claims as limiting right after disestablishment?

Justice Samuel Alito's concurring opinion in *Hosanna-Tabor* does, at least, begin the project of expanding the discussion beyond christian churches. "Minister," the catholic Alito announces, apparently without irony, is a term that is mostly limited to protestant churches.[79] His solution to this problem of specificity is to define "minister" functionally and universally, apparently easily assuming—via sociological thinking—that

77. Brief for the Petitioner at 12. Cited authorities include Martin Luther, *On the Councils and the Church* (1539), in *Luther's Works*, ed. Eric W. Gritsch (Minneapolis: Fortress Press, 1966), vol. 41; Augsburg Confession (1530); 1 Corinthians 6:1–11.

78. Brief of the Lutheran Church–Missouri Synod at 2.

79. *Hosanna-Tabor*, Alito, J., concurring. 565 U.S. at 198.

such a role can be found in all religious traditions—and beyond. Alito writes that

> [t]he term "minister" is commonly used by many Protestant denominations to refer to members of their clergy, but the term is rarely if ever used in this way by Catholics, Jews, Muslims, Hindus, or Buddhists. In addition, the concept of ordination as understood by most Christian churches and by Judaism has no clear counterpart in some Christian denominations and some other religions. Because virtually every religion in the world is represented in the population of the United States, it would be a mistake if the term "minister" or the concept of ordination were viewed as central to the important issue of religious autonomy that is presented in cases like this one. Instead, courts should focus on the function performed by persons who work for religious bodies.[80]

He goes on to describe the ministerial function as "the conducting of worship services and other religious ceremonies and rituals, as well as the critical process of communicating the faith."[81] In other words, he solved his problem by generalizing from the role of the protestant pastor, assuming that that role is universal, an assumption that once more inscribes a very particular protestant standard for what it means to be religiously privileged under US law.

The exclusions effected by the common default to a stereotyped view of religious ministry can be seen from the following interchange in a 1981 case challenging payment of federal unemployment taxes for employees of church schools.[82] The assistant solicitor general representing the US as an amicus curiae in the case, Barry Sullivan, sought to clarify which church employees were covered from those who were not by reference to whether or not they worked in a church building. He analogized to a

80. *Hosanna-Tabor*, Alito, J., concurring. 565 U.S. at 198.

81. *Hosanna-Tabor*, Alito, J., concurring. 565 U.S. at 199.

82. *St. Martin Evangelical Lutheran Church v. South Dakota*, 451 U.S. 772 (1981), concerned the liability of churches to pay unemployment tax. The Federal Unemployment Tax Act (FUTA) had a special exemption for church employees: "This section shall not apply to service performed—(1) in the employ of (A) a church or convention or association of churches, or (B) an organization which is operated primarily for religious purposes and which is operated, supervised, controlled, or principally supported by a church or convention or association of churches; (2) by a duly ordained, commissioned, or licensed minister of a church in the exercise of his ministry or by a member of a religious order in the exercise of duties required by such order; (3) in the employ of a school which is not an institution of higher education." 451 U.S. at 777.

distinction made in the corporate context based on the location where the employee worked. Justice Thurgood Marshall rejected the analogy:

THURGOOD MARSHALL: Don't get too carried away with this building, please. Because I know of a church in Washington that up to a few years ago met in Hogate's restaurant. So don't get too hooked up on that building.

BARRY SULLIVAN: Well, I would assume in that case, Mr. Justice Marshall, that Hogate's restaurant paid the janitor, and that consequently we wouldn't have a problem for purposes of this statute.

THURGOOD MARSHALL: Except in our church we called him a sexton, and you'd better not call him a janitor.[83]

In responding to the attorney, Justice Marshall called attention here to the existence of different protestant models of church and to different models of ministry, models not encompassed by the *Hosanna-Tabor* Court's ecclesiology.[84] Such variations could be multiplied almost endlessly.

Shortly after the exchange with Marshall, Chief Justice Warren Burger, in a further exchange with the attorney, gave his own opinion about how religious ministry worked:

WARREN E. BURGER: You don't have any paid teachers in Sunday Schools, do you?

BARRY SULLIVAN: Again, I cannot speak authoritatively to that. I wouldn't know the answer to that.

WARREN E. BURGER: If you can't answer that I think I can take judicial notice of the fact that generally speaking in this country, in all faiths, Sunday School teachers are volunteers.[85]

Here again, the deeply accidental and amateur nature of the justices' religious knowledge is well illustrated. No evidence having been taken on this question, the Court just generalizes from its own limited experience or defers to the parties. And efforts to define religious offices functionally for purposes of secular law proved elusive. In a recent ministerial exception

83. See oral argument transcript, *St. Martin Evangelical Lutheran Church v. South Dakota*, No. 80–120 at 58–59. https://www.supremecourt.gov/pdfs/transcripts/1980/80-120_03-03-1981.pdf/.

84. Justice Marshall himself was an Episcopalian. The Episcopal Church recognized him as a saint in 2006. It celebrates the Feast of Thurgood Marshall on May 17.

85. *St. Martin Evangelical Lutheran Church v. South Dakota* oral argument transcript, No. 80-120 at 62–63.

case, a court of appeals, following *Hosanna-Tabor*, declined to investigate a charge of employee discrimination; the judge deferred to the church's assertion that an organist is a minister, citing the precedent of Mozart's firing by the Archbishop of Salzburg in 1777.[86]

Alito's functional approach to understanding religious life is also evident in the assumption in his *Hosanna-Tabor* opinion that religious communities are to be legally regarded as the same as other kinds of voluntary associations. He, with the EEOC, sees the rights of religious organizations with respect to ideological control of their members as similar to that of all other voluntary associations, a right founded not in church autonomy or sovereignty over strictly ecclesiastical matters, but in "the right of the people peaceably to assemble" recognized in the First Amendment. "Religious groups," Alito says, comparing them to the Boy Scouts, "are the archetype of associations formed for expressive purposes, and their fundamental rights surely include the freedom to choose who is qualified to serve as a voice for their faith."[87] The First Amendment right to free association is, at its core, a right to discriminate.

While it is in some ways deeply odd—indeed heterodox—for a Roman Catholic like Justice Alito to describe the church as an "association formed for expressive purposes," his secularizing turn to the voluntariness of American associational life corresponds much more closely to the ways in which disestablished religion is understood in the US today. Most Americans understand their relationship to their religious communities as one not of top-down hierarchy but one of bottom-up participation. It

86. *Stanislaw Sterlinksi v. Catholic Bishop of Chicago*. No. 18-2844 (decided August 8, 2019). Judge Frank Easterbrook announced the rule in such cases when deciding whether an employee is a minister for purpose of the ministerial exception:

> The answer lies in separating pretextual justifications from honest ones. In normal Title VII litigation a court does not start with the question whether the discharge or other adverse action was caused by prejudice. It waits for the employer to articulate a reason for the discharge and then asks whether that reason is pretextual—in other words, whether it is honest. If the court finds that the reason is honest, it does not ask whether the reason is correct—it is enough that the employer believe its own reason in good faith.

Easterbrook cited the example of Mozart's firing by Hieronymus von Colloredo, the Prince-Archbishop of Salzburg, as precedent. Judge Easterbrook actually indulged in the observation that Mozart—and perhaps by implication the plaintiff—was better off for having been fired.

87. *Hosanna-Tabor*, Alito, J., concurring at 200. This is Lawrence Sager's position as well. See Sager, "Why Churches . . . Can Discriminate," 47n69. See also Carol Weissbrod, *The Boundaries of Utopia* (New York: Random House, 1980), for a study of the litigation to enforce contracts among members of four utopian communities formed in nineteenth-century America.

is a relationship rooted in another reading of the history of the church—one that tells a story of the freedom of christians, and eventually of non-christians as well; it is a story founded in a different church history. It is an understanding that sees Perich, not "the church," as the possessor of rights. This other version of church also reflects an American sociology and church history that has naturalized the free church and its ecclesiology. Alito's move to analogize them at once secularizes the church and sacralizes the Boy Scouts and other voluntary associations and corporate bodies.[88]

Church and state

Highlighting the risk that churches and other religious groups take in demanding recognition of their autonomy from the state, a short essay by a Lutheran theologian and former LCMS member written just after the *Hosanna-Tabor* decision shifts the focus back to Perich. George Heider affirms that LCMS teaching has for 150 years distinguished two types of ministry: ordained and commissioned.[89] He further affirms that there was little question that Perich was a minister within the LCMS scheme of things. But he regretted the recourse to the courts and the rights of the church; turning to his pastoral concern for Perich, he addressed what he called "the *supreme* question": "The *real* question to my mind is whether or not Hosanna-Tabor Lutheran Church and School will do right by one who went to considerable effort to become eligible for a call, only to be burned by the consequences of the ministerial status that her additional training and certification enabled."[90] "Burned?" Like Joan of Arc? The analogy is not wholly fanciful given the powers arrayed against her. Other

88. Andrew Koppelman, another First Amendment scholar who has commented on *Hosanna-Tabor*, simply says, like Horwitz, that this is not the Middle Ages, and that the state is now firmly in charge. Koppelman, "The Freedom of the Church in the Modern Era: 'Freedom of the Church' and the Authority of the State," 145–164. The argument of this book is that the state is not firmly in charge.

89. George C. Heider, *The Immanent Frame*, "What's the *Supreme* Question in *Hosanna-Tabor v. EEOC*?" https://tif.ssrc.org/2011/10/27/the-supreme-question-in-hosanna-tabor-v-eeoc/ (accessed November 7, 2017).

90. Heider, "What's the *Supreme* Question?" Hannah Garvey drew my attention to this passage in Françoise Meltzer's book on Joan: "If the mimetic gesture of burning Joan is meant to emphasize the tragedy of her death and the brutality of the Church Militant in her era, there is also a way in which the mimetic gesture mirrors the *desire* to obliterate alterity and to silence all minority discourse." Meltzer, *For Fear of the Fire*, 19. Always.

religious voices commenting at the time of the decision agreed that there was something shameful about the applause that the *Hosanna-Tabor* decision received in some quarters.

In June 2017, the Supreme Court decided another Lutheran case,[91] a case originating in Missouri. The Missouri Department of Natural Resources had, in what they described as an effort to recycle proliferating numbers of used car tires, protect children, and save the environment, created a program to supply shredded tires to cover playground surfaces. Schools and daycare centers were invited to apply to the department, which, unable to fund all applicants, prioritized them based on various criteria, including the economic need of the children they served. Trinity Lutheran Church in Columbia, Missouri, had a daycare center with a cement playground. They applied to the state playground program. Although Trinity ranked high among the applicants because of the financial need of the children they served, their application was denied because the department believed that under the Missouri Constitution it was not able to provide funds to churches for any purpose. (The Missouri Constitution provides that "no money shall ever be taken from the public treasury, directly or indirectly, in aid of any church, sect or denomination of religion.")[92]

Trinity sued the department, claiming that the department had discriminated against it just because it was a religious organization, violating the federal constitutional guarantee to the "free exercise of religion." The US district court for the Eastern District of Missouri and the Eighth Circuit Court of Appeals ruled in favor of the department. In a closely watched decision, the US Supreme Court reversed, in a 7–2 decision, finding that the department had violated the free exercise clause of the First Amendment to the US Constitution by discriminating against the church in the distribution of a public benefit.

There are various ways to talk about this case, but what I want to notice here is that the majority and the minority on the Court had different ideas about what the church is, how it is related to the state, and where to draw the line between religion and nonreligion. The majority in *Trinity Lutheran* saw the issue as being about equality before the law, arguing that the church should be treated the same as any other applicant by the state. Running a daycare center that admitted anyone regardless of religion, as

91. *Trinity Lutheran Church v. Comer*, 582 U.S. ___ (2017).
92. Missouri Const., art. I, § 7.

Trinity did, was seen by the Court as a nonreligious activity but one that both religious and nonreligious folks could and should participate in and for which they could receive state funds. The two dissenters wrote a long and passionate opinion arguing that the majority's decision threatened the separation of church and state. Pointing to Trinity Church materials that described its daycare center as a part of its christian mission, they argued that the decision "discounts centuries of history and jeopardizes the government's ability to remain secular."[93] For the dissenters, allowing Trinity Church to participate in the playground program amounted to an unconstitutional sponsorship of religion—an establishment of religion, if you will, in US constitutional terms.[94]

Was this case about saving the environment and providing safe playgrounds for poor children, or was it a case about the government funding religious conversion? I think that your answer depends in part on what you think the church is, because only then can you draw the line between legal and illegal religion that is necessary for law. For the majority in the *Trinity Church* case, the religion whose free exercise the Constitution protects includes that of churches. As with *Hosanna-Tabor*, the church as an entity appears here as an artificial person whose rights before the law must be protected. For the dissenters, the religion that the Constitution protects is that of individual conscience. Individual conscience needs to be protected from churches, particularly government-funded churches.

Unconverted antinomianism

An iconic text for those writing today in a field broadly constituted as law, culture, and the humanities is Robert Cover's "*Nomos* and Narrative."[95] Cover has also been widely cited by law and religion scholars. In urgent and entrancing words, "*Nomos* and Narrative" proposes to enrich the study of law through an expansion of the field broadly to include all the normative worlds that we inhabit. Famously, Cover opens with this gambit:

93. *Trinity Church*, Sotomayor, J., dissenting.

94. *Trinity Church*, Sotomayor, J., dissenting.

95. Robert M. Cover, "The Supreme Court, 1982 Term—Foreword: *Nomos* and Narrative," *Harvard Law Review* 97, no. 4 (1983): 4–68. Other founding texts include James Boyd White, *The Legal Imagination: Studies in the Nature of Legal Thought and Expression*, 45th anniversary ed. (New York: Wolters Kluwer, 2018), and *Justice as Translation: An Essay in Cultural and Legal Criticism* (Chicago: University of Chicago Press, 1990).

> We inhabit a *nomos*—a normative universe. We constantly create and maintain a world of right and wrong, of lawful and unlawful, of valid and void. The student of law may come to identify the normative world with the professional paraphernalia of social control. The rules and principles of justice, the formal institutions of the law, and the conventions of a social order are, indeed, important to that world; they are, however, but a small part of the normative universe that ought to claim our attention. No set of legal institutions or prescriptions exists apart from the narratives that locate it and give it meaning. For every constitution there is an epic, for each decalogue a scripture. Once understood in the context of the narratives that give it meaning, law becomes not merely a system of rules to be observed, but a world in which we live.[96]

These words have inspired many to enlarge their understanding of law—to see state law as only one normative world among many—and to see the possibilities for justice beyond the narrow limits of the state's capacity. Cover's article goes on to outline a theory of communal law that distinguishes world-creating (religious) from world-maintaining (civil) narratives; the article has been understood in the law and religion field broadly to valorize the role of religious communities in modern life and to support their protection from state law. If one were to give a Coverian reading of *Hosanna-Tabor*, one might approve of the Court's strong recognition of an alternative nomos in its recognition of the rights of the church.

But what of Cheryl Perich? Marie Ashe, in a lengthy and hard-hitting feminist critique of Cover's work, has made the argument that it is time to displace Cover's work with that of American poet Susan Howe:[97]

> Re-reading N&N ["*Nomos* and Narrative"] through the critical lenses of Susan Howe's work, I have tried to show the limits of the liberal-legal project in application to American law's under-explored intersections with religion and gender. At the same time, I have sought to introduce Susan Howe's work of "unconverted antinomianism" to people thinking and writing about legal theory under the headings of Law and Literature, of feminist legal theory, and of law and religion. I have done this in the belief that her searching—beyond law, beyond language, beyond gender, beyond certainty—illuminates the only path

96. Cover, "*Nomos* and Narrative," 4–5.

97. Interestingly, Susan Howe is the daughter of Mark DeWolfe Howe, author of *The Garden and the Wilderness*, cited above at 5n17.

> of possibility that I can discern: "I . . . go on searching for some trace of love's infolding through all the paper in all the libraries I come to."[98]

Ashe underlines Cover's almost exclusive reliance on male authors and narratives of male lineage. She also makes visible the violent exclusion of dissenting women from the very religious communities Cover valorizes, beginning with puritan Anne Hutchinson. Both Ashe and Howe focus on individual female voices of conscience and their exclusion in any civil law recognition of special privileges for patriarchal religious communities.

The epigraph for this chapter is the verses of Paul's Letter to the Ephesians that are often used to underwrite the use of another bodily metaphor for the church, the bride of Christ. New Testament scholar Carolyn Osiek has analyzed this metaphor and the violence it has done to women. Tracing the historical melding of the body language in Paul's Letter to the Corinthians and the bridal imagery of the Letter to the Ephesians, as well as the church's appropriation of the Song of Solomon as a forecasting of Christ's love for the church, Osiek argues that this assimilation has fostered an ecclesiology in which the church's submission to Christ models feminine submission to male leadership in the family and in the church. The argument concludes:

> Herein lies the great danger posed by this ecclesiological metaphor: it encourages men to identify with Christ and women with the church. As everyone knows who teaches or ministers, for most people the line between Christ and God is very thin. As long as the marriage metaphor is in play gender symbolism is fixed. Men will even unconsciously identify with Christ and women with the church and feminine imagery for God or Christ then has no place. Then God is the ultimate male.[99]

Is it possible to have a nonpatriarchal theory of the church—of the collective, as Nancy Levene names it?[100] Is it possible for law to see women's religion? In an important book theorizing the historic importance of

98. Marie Ashe, "Beyond *Nomos* and Narrative: Unconverted Antinomianism in the Work of Susan Howe," *Yale Journal of Law and Feminism* 18, no. 1 (2006): 59. See also Gillian Rose, *Mourning Becomes the Law: Philosophy and Representation* (Cambridge: Cambridge University Press, 1996), and *Love's Work: A Reckoning with Life* (New York: Schocken Books, 1997).

99. Carolyn Osiek, "The Bride of Christ (Ephesians 5:22–33): A Problematic Wedding," *Biblical Theology* 32, no. 1 (Spring 2002): 38.

100. Levene, *Powers of Distinction.*

sacrifice to human political and religious projects, feminist sociologist of religion Nancy Jay argued that the continuity of the Catholic Church has depended on the tight link between the male priesthood and a sacrificial interpretation of the Eucharist.[101] US law about religion seems to agree—about all religion. This tight link is now under acute strain as a result of the clerical sex abuse crisis, prompting some to turn to alternative ecclesiologies.[102]

101. Nancy Jay, *Throughout Your Generations Forever: Sacrifice, Religion, and Paternity* (Chicago: University of Chicago Press, 1992).

102. See, e.g., Massimo Faggioli, "Abuse Crisis: Shifting Boundaries Between Church and State," in "Sex and the Catholic Church: What Does Law Have to Do with It?" discussion on *The Immanent Frame*, https://tif.ssrc.org/category/exchanges/sex-and-the-catholic-church/, February 5, 2019.

CHAPTER TWO

"The Mother of Religion": The Church Property Cases

. . . the church is the mother of religion; and as faith is perpetual, its patrimony must be preserved in its entirety perpetually.—Chief Justice Fuller, *Ponce v. Roman Catholic Apostolic Church*[1]

Virgin Mary, Mother of God.
Be a feminist, we pray thee,
Be a feminist, we pray thee.—Pussy Riot[2]

Introduction

The rule in *Hosanna-Tabor* is founded in a story about "the church" and her imagined ancient and perduring sovereign right to choose her own ministers. But what the church means in this invocation is highly unstable. In what sense are the thirteenth-century medieval English church of King John and Hosanna-Tabor Evangelical Lutheran Church

1. *Ponce v. Roman Catholic Apostolic Church*, 210 U.S. 296 (1904).

2. Lyrics for the performance at https://genius.com/Pussy-riot-punk-prayer-english-translation-lyrics/ [accessed March 24, 2019]. Pussy Riot's performance of "Punk Prayer" on February 21, 2012, in Moscow's Cathedral of Christ the Savior resulted in two of the group's members being imprisoned. See footage of the performance on YouTube at https://www.youtube.com/watch?v=lPDkJbTQRCY/ [accessed March 24, 2019].

in Redford, Michigan, both *the* church? How can/should law acknowledge the phenomenon of the church today?

After the section of his opinion that moves from Magna Carta to the First Amendment, Chief Justice Roberts opens a new section with supporting precedent from another body of law. This section discusses a group of decisions known in US law as the church property cases; these are legal disputes over ownership and control of real property that arise when a religious community becomes irrevocably divided. American courts have striven to find ways to resolve these cases without being drawn into theological issues that they feel neither competent nor perhaps constitutionally permitted to consider.[3] Deciding who is the rightful spokesperson for the church in these cases is perilously close to the prohibited establishment role for government that Americans want to avoid—having civil courts decide which of two bodies is the authentic church. Yet the free exercise clause—and perhaps an unacknowledged commitment to the reality of *the* church—pulls courts the other way—toward an affirmative legal effort to enable the continuity of religious life in the church. The ministerial exception is one product of this unresolved tension. The church property cases are another.

Hosanna-Tabor Evangelical Church and School, the defendant in *Hosanna-Tabor*, is an ecclesiastical corporation under Michigan state law.[4] In response to the EEOC's 2010 complaint in the Eastern District of Michigan charging it with violating the ADA, the church filed a motion for summary judgment claiming that the district court had no subject matter jurisdiction, that is that under the ministerial exception the court lacked authority to hear the case. This was a remarkable claim, that a federal district court lacked the authority to hear a federal employment discrimination suit with respect to the employment relationship between a corporation created by state law and one of its employees.

Why should a disabled schoolteacher be excluded from protection of the law because her employer is a church? There was no explicit statutory

3. This is not just an American problem. Famously, in 1904 the British House of Lords considered whether the Free Church of Scotland (known colloquially as the Wee Frees) or the newly created United Church of Scotland, created out of the fracturing of the established Church of Scotland, was entitled to ownership and control of a vast amount of historic church property. *Free Church of Scotland v. Overtoun* (1904). For a brief description of the case, see Rivers, *The Law of Organized* Religions, 97–99. But such disputes have occurred wherever there are churches with property.

4. Michigan General Corporation Statute Ch. 450, Act 327, § 450.178 (1931).

exemption for the church in this situation. The ministerial exception has sometimes been taken to rest on sovereignty rights inherent in the religion clauses, as discussed in the previous chapter. But the exemption has also been understood to derive from the assumption expressed in *Watson v. Jones* (discussed below) that the decision to work for the church included a conscious waiver of her rights in civil law; the employee is assumed, in effect, to have agreed to a transfer of jurisdiction over the conditions of her employment to the church.[5] In this chapter, we will consider several leading church property cases and the ways in which the rhetoric of choice masks a different reality, one of increasing deference by US courts to the legal regime of another sovereign.

What exactly is an ecclesiastical corporation and what makes it different when it comes to regulation by the state? Is the church a creature of the law or does the church exist independently of law? How should churches be organized in civil law and what role should the secular government have in their constitution and governance? Under what legal theory does a/the church have legal personality with the capacity to contract and to sue and to be sued? These are remarkably difficult questions to answer.

The radical religious diversity of the Americas combined with a decision in the US not to establish a national church led to a fissiparous frenzy of church creation in the early republic but it also resulted in the need for handy generalizations to help law bypass the voluminous cataloging that would have been necessary to take appropriate legal account of each variation on the collective. "Religious organization" and "religious society" have been such words. "Religion" is the word used in the First Amendment to the Constitution. "Church" is used elsewhere—in the tax code and in countless other laws recognizing the legal personality of religious societies. In Michigan law, the words used are "ecclesiastical cor-

5. The waiver in these cases is implied. The increasingly widespread use of formal waivers limiting employee rights is widely recognized today as a threat to the rights of labor and to the rule of law not just in religious contexts but also more broadly. Another domain in which such a threat is recognized is in the explosion of contractual arbitration clauses, mandating that customers submit disputes with companies to private resolution, removing them from the protection of public law, both substantive and procedural. One issue with these clauses is whether they are truly voluntarily entered into. See, e.g., Paul Carrington and Paul H. Haagen, "Contract and Jurisdiction," *Supreme Court Review* 1996: 331–402. Arbitration has an earlier progressive history. For an account of the triumph of individualistic adversarial notions of due process, see Amalia Kessler, *Inventing American Exceptionalism: The Origins of American Adversarial Legal Culture, 1800–1877* (New Haven: Yale University Press, 2017).

poration." The ambiguity of reference cast by these abstractions persists. And the ambiguity of the relationship of church to state also remains, unresolved as it was by constitutional disestablishment. The opinion for the Court in *Hosanna-Tabor* seems to recognize a robust form of sovereignty in the church. But it stopped short of explicitly recognizing the church as its own naturally occurring sovereign jurisdiction, one entirely independent of state and federal law.[6] The church seems still to be subject to law, having a precarious or subordinate independence.[7]

Americans have long had an ambivalent relationship with organized religion, for both theological and political reasons. The model of religion to be avoided was the Church of England, the establishment par excellence and the butt of political and theological scorn; the other related specter was Popery.[8] But nonreligious forms of private governance were also suspect, including corporations of all kinds, as we shall see in the next chapter. Privileging individual conscience has at times produced a theological, political, and legal rhetoric about free religion that denies the need for, even stigmatizes, collective religious life. The contemporary expression "spiritual but not religious" expresses this sentiment as well.

There is no mandate in US law for religious collectivities legally to formalize their activities and not all do. All the same, primarily for practical reasons, groups of both christians and nonchristians have sought legal recognition in order to come together to purchase property and create ongoing legal entities to conduct their affairs, to limit their liability, and to secure tax benefits. These ubiquitous but varied legal arrangements—as well as the law-producing of religion itself—belie the notion that religion and law can ever be separate, as the Court has periodically acknowledged. Disestablishment in the US has meant instead that church and state are each conceived of as governed by the people. It is the people who are sovereign, not the state. Religion is imagined to be free under this arrange-

6. See 26n13 in chapter one concerning the Court's rejection of the jurisdictional bar asserted by Hosanna-Tabor.

7. The borders of this separate but limited jurisdiction were explored at oral argument, with some justices inquiring about whether the ministerial exception would extend to hypothetical cases of child sex abuse or criminal negligence. See oral argument transcript in *Hosanna-Tabor*, No. 10-553, at 5–6. https://www.supremecourt.gov/oral_arguments/argument_transcripts/2011/10-553.pdf/. But the *Hosanna-Tabor* decision itself avoided these questions, leaving them for another day.

8. For a thorough exploration of anticatholicism in US history, see Evan Haefeli, ed., *Against Popery: Anti-Catholicism and the British-American World* (University of Virginia Press, forthcoming 2020).

ment. Disestablishment results in a different legal phenomenology of religion, a different articulation of the church as free than that of most christian-majority countries.

In the christian west, churches arguably gradually acquired legal personality in national law beginning in the early modern period after the break-up of the monopoly of the Roman church. This is a very complicated story, one that is coincident with the development of the modern state. Within the emerging national legal systems in Europe, "ecclesiastical" law, an expression that can include the law of the internal governance of religious organizations as well as the civil law that governed their relationship to the state, took quite different forms in different countries. Subsequent revolutions and changes of government complicated and continue to complicate the situation further. Simultaneously with these changes at home, migrant members of these churches brought various ideas about church with them to North America, deterritorializing their ecclesiologies and often taking the opportunity to reinvent themselves. Even among late eighteenth-century protestant churches in the US, there were already serious differences in the theology of the church and varying strategies for acquiring the legal personality necessary to hold title to property and maintain continuity of doctrine and governance over time, strategies that changed as the politics of law changed. The diversity has only increased, presenting a serious challenge to US law.

Nineteenth-century church transformations and the resulting denominational differences have not usually been understood well in twentieth-century law, as legal historians are now detailing. Nor have we properly understood the approach of the early state governments to their regulation. In contrast to the current deference to church autonomy in many US courts, in the early republic churches were regarded with suspicion and were closely controlled by state law. Over time, there has been a counter-intuitive but increasing bias toward the legal enabling of the legal independence of what the Court has called "hierarchical churches," although the reason given for such deference has varied.[9] Surprisingly, considering the dominance of low church ecclesiology in the US, legislatures and courts have generally moved from an effort to insist on local democratic

9. Several law review writers have noted the bias toward hierarchical churches in these cases. See, e.g., Michael McConnell and Luke W. Goodrich, "On Resolving Church Property Disputes," *Arizona Law Review* 58, no. 2 (2016): 326; and Calvin Massey, "Church Schisms, Church Property, and Civil Authority," *St. John's Law Review* 84, no. 2 (Winter 2010): 23–62.

control in matters of church governance to a deference to national and transnational religious organizations with nondemocratic, often monarchic, forms of governance.

As mentioned in the introduction, legal historian Mark DeWolfe Howe was one of the first to describe this shift in his classic 1967 book on the First Amendment religion clauses.[10] In an earlier article, Howe had analogized the increasing US deference toward what he called group religious rights as a variant of the political pluralism championed by European political theorists in the first half of the twentieth century.[11] This chapter will suggest that while there is naturally some overlap and resonance among these comparative examples the US church property cases that defer to hierarchical church governance are not recognizing group rights as analogous to those of unions and political parties, as Howe suggested, or to voluntary associations such as the Boy Scouts, as Justice Alito suggested in his concurring opinion in *Hosanna-Tabor*, but are rather recognizing alternative forms of sovereignty residing in mystical variants of the body of Christ.

Law professor Perry Dane argues that the anomaly that is religion in US law is best understood as the result of an existential encounter between religion and the state—one in which institutional autonomy—church sovereignty—might properly be understood to be the third pillar of religious freedom law, in addition to disestablishment and free exercise. In other words, he argues that resolution of the tension between the two religion clauses of the First Amendment has in fact often been silently supplied by an unacknowledged church autonomy doctrine—one that recognizes the existential claims of religion as an alternative sovereign.[12] He argues persuasively that the many failures of religious freedom law in the US are the result of "a failure of imagination." "We live," he says, "in many ways in an age of flattened legal, constitutional, and normative discourse, an age reluctant to appreciate complexity, plurality, multivocality, and multidimensionality. The consequences are in odd ways both statist and libertarian."[13] Dane comments on the *Hosanna-Tabor* decision

10. Howe, *The Garden and the Wilderness.*

11. Mark DeWolfe Howe, "Foreword: Political Theory and the Nature of Liberty," *Harvard Law Review* 67 (1953): 91–179.

12. Perry Dane, "Master Metaphors and Double-Coding in the Encounters of Religion and State," *San Diego Law Review* 53, no. 1 (Winter 2016): 53–104. On this reading, *Hosanna-Tabor* just surfaces what is always already there.

13. Dane, "Master Metaphors," 104.

that "[t]he reaffirmation of religious institutional autonomy—at least in the context of the ministerial employment problem found in *Hosanna-Tabor*—might stand out as a sort of exception. Or perhaps religious institutional autonomy is, in some sense, and uniquely among the three strands of religion and state jurisprudence, just flat enough itself to survive the bulldozer."[14] It is the law's imaginative flatness with which this chapter is concerned.

This chapter will read the church property cases with a view to further specifying the peculiar phenomenology of the church in US law, the legal and theological occlusions that have made possible the law of church property—and the current church autonomy movement. The unexpected judicial recognition and solicitude for what the Supreme Court called "the mother of religion"—that is, the church—since ancient times, including their effort to preserve the transhistorical and transnational sovereignty of the Russian Orthodox and Serbian Orthodox churches as over against orthodox laypersons in the midst of the Cold War, reveals a Court more and more in thrall to *the* church.

But first a return once more to the opinion for the Court in *Hosanna-Tabor*.

Justice Roberts enlists James Madison

The chief justice concluded his history lesson in *Hosanna-Tabor* in support of the right of the church to choose its own ministers with a quotation from President James Madison explaining his 1811 veto of a bill to incorporate a church in the District of Columbia.[15] With the opening of a new legal and political regime, churches were at that time coming before legislative bodies seeking incorporation in order to hold property, govern themselves, and perpetuate their polities beyond the founding generation.

14. Dane, "Master Metaphors," 104. See also John D. Inazu, "The Freedom of the Church (New Revised Standard Version)," *Journal of Contemporary Legal Issues* 21, no. 1 (2013): 335–368.

15. This case arose before the enactment of general incorporation laws. In the early republic, each corporation was created by a special act of the legislature. The leading history of corporation law history is James Willard Hurst, *The Legitimacy of the Business Corporation in the Law of the United States, 1780–1970* (Charlottesville: University Press of Virginia, 1971).

In the particular case before Madison, "Congress had passed a bill incorporating the Protestant Episcopal Church in the town of Alexandria in what was then the District of Columbia."[16] As Roberts explains, "Madison vetoed the bill, on the ground that it 'exceeds the rightful authority to which Governments are limited, by the essential distinction between civil and religious functions, and violates, in particular, the article of the Constitution of the United States, which declares, that "Congress shall make no law respecting a religious establishment."'"[17] Madison had a famously astringent view of disestablishment, viewing even incorporation of a church as an establishment of religion in violation of the First Amendment.

Roberts went on to quote Madison's own explanation for his veto in the Virginia case: "The bill enacts into, and establishes by law, sundry rules and proceedings relative purely to the organization and polity of the church incorporated, *and comprehending even the election and removal of the Minister of the same*; so that no change could be made therein by the particular society, or by the general church of which it is a member, and whose authority it recognises" [italics supplied by Roberts].[18] Roberts italicizes Madison's words here to underline what he takes to be the rule that in the US the church has in law the right of appointment with respect to her own ministers. But Madison himself was making that statement in the context of his expressed opposition to church incorporation. Insisting on "the essential distinction between civil and religious functions," Madison emphasized the ways in which incorporation could be understood to be a form of religious establishment, fixing church law as state law, and limiting the capacity of churches to change over time both as to property ownership and as to church governance. Madison saw church governance as existing wholly apart from civil law. Roberts quotes him in support of a church very much incorporated in state law, one seeking state legitimation by way of the ministerial exception.

History has granted James Madison, as principal author of the Constitution and the Bill of Rights, as well as of the preconstitutional "Memorial and Remonstrance against Religious Assessments" in support of the Virginia Statute on Religious Freedom, which he wrote together with Thomas Jefferson, an iconic role in defining the meaning of the First Amendment religion clauses. Indeed, his views are often cited as prescriptive in the

16. 565 U.S. at 184.
17. 565 U.S. at 184–85.
18. 565 U.S. at 185.

jurisprudence of the First Amendment.[19] Here, however, we see him in his presidential role as interpreter in chief insisting on the independence of religious life from civil oversight—even to the extent of denying churches the right to incorporate. Madison understood the risk to churches of playing footsie with the state.[20] Today's churches seem to want to have their Madisonian cake and eat it too. They want the benefits of incorporation under law without the regulation that incorporation necessarily brings.

The Court has long had recourse to a carefully selective history of the disestablishment in Virginia as a model for interpreting the federal constitutional arrangement.[21] There are various ways in which this habit has cramped the Court's interpretive resources, as Justice William Rehnquist argued in his dissent in *Wallace v. Jaffree*.[22] However, while courts often go to the legislative history of the Virginia statute to interpret the First Amendment, in this area in particular the Commonwealth has always been an outlier among the states, scrupulously banning all forms of church incorporation from the beginning.[23] Following Madison, until 2002 churches

19. This is a form of originalist fundamentalism shared by left and right. Legal historian Farah Peterson writes of the foreshortening of history caused by over-attention to the founding. "Monuments and Memory: How the Law Writes American History."

20. See "Memorial and Remonstrance against Religious Assessments, [ca. 20 June] 1785," *Founders Online*, National Archives, accessed April 11, 2019, https://founders.archives.gov/documents/Madison/01-08-02-0163. [Original source: *The Papers of James Madison*, vol. 8, *10 March 1784–28 March 1786*, ed. Robert A. Rutland and William M. E. Rachal (Chicago: University of Chicago Press, 1973), 295–306.]

21. For an exploration of the Virginia statute on the occasion of its bicentennial, see Merrill D. Peterson and Robert C. Vaughn, eds., *The Virginia Statute for Religious Freedom: Its Evolution and Consequences in American History* (New York: Cambridge University Press, 1988).

22. *Wallace* concerned an Alabama law prescribing a moment of silence at the beginning of the school day. Justice Rehnquist, dissenting from the majority's finding that the law was unconstitutional, took the occasion to review the history of the court's interpretation of the religion clauses, concluding that:

> The Framers intended the Establishment Clause to prohibit the designation of any church as a "national" one. The Clause was also designed to stop the Federal Government from asserting a preference for one religious denomination or sect over others. Given the "incorporation" of the Establishment Clause as against the States via the Fourteenth Amendment in *Everson*, States are prohibited as well from establishing a religion or discriminating between sects. As its history abundantly shows, however, nothing in the Establishment Clause requires government to be strictly neutral between religion and irreligion, nor does that Clause prohibit Congress or the States from pursuing legitimate secular ends through nondiscriminatory sectarian means.

472 U.S. 38, 113 (1985) (Rehnquist, J., dissenting).

23. Virginia Constitution art. IV, § 16.

in Virginia were not legally permitted to incorporate. A church could be legally constituted only as an unincorporated association—with a consequently more limited set of legal capacities and rights. While Virginia took this restrictive position on church incorporation, all other states over time passed laws permitting the incorporation of churches,[24] suggesting that continuing to privilege the Virginia experience constitutes a kind of originalist fundamentalism. Unlike Madison's churches, the churches that seek recognition of a ministerial exemption today, including Hosanna-Tabor, are all creatures of state law. It is for that reason that they are subject to it. An entirely voluntary Madisonian church with a voluntary unpaid clergy would not run afoul of civil law regulating employment because their clergy would not be employees.

Reluctantly conceding that the matter of ministerial appointment had not been conclusively laid to rest by Madison's letter, Roberts' opinion in *Hosanna-Tabor* seeks further authority for its reading of the preconstitutional rights of the church to self-government in the church property cases. Madison, acting from the conviction that there was an essential distinction between civil and religious functions, apparently envisioned churches governing themselves entirely through private law. Indeed, many American churchmen then and now might agree with the desirability of such an arrangement.[25] But many more have chosen to come before the courts to settle their internal disputes and gain the government's imprimatur on their arrangements, even enlisting the government in their enforcement. It is to those cases that Roberts next turns. He moves straight from Madison's 1811 letter to the Supreme Court's 1872 decision in *Watson v. Jones* in order to bolster what he takes to have been Madison's view, that is, that US courts are prohibited from deciding matters that are deemed "strictly ecclesiastical."[26]

One effect of this historical leap across the nineteenth century is to omit the important early legal history of church incorporation in the US, a history that is only now being fully understood.[27] The occlusion assists

24. For a summary of current law on church incorporation, see James Serritella, ed., *Religious Organizations in the United States: A Study of Identity, Liberty, and the Law* (Durham, NC: Carolina Academic Press, 2006).

25. See Kellen Funk, "Shall These Bones Live? Property, Pluralism, and the Constitution of Evangelical Reform," *Law and Social Inquiry* 41, no. 3 (Summer 2016): 742–774.

26. *Watson v. Jones*, 80 U.S. 679 (1872). On the significance of the phrase "strictly ecclesiastical" for the *Hosanna-Tabor* court, see Lupu and Tuttle, "The Mystery of Unanimity."

27. This historical foreshortening allows the Court to ignore the strong preference that the antebellum courts had for local democratic congregational governance of churches. See

the Court and legal commentators to make slippery transhistorical claims about the US constitutional order, about the legal personality of churches, and about religion more generally. It flattens out theological change and difference, a flattening necessary to the consolidation of religion in First Amendment religion clause jurisprudence.

Yet more avatars of the church appear in this section of the *Hosanna-Tabor* opinion, but one difficulty with using the church property cases to establish the right of "the church" to choose its ministers is that, by definition in such cases, there are at least two churches at issue and two groups of people who lay claim to a right to define who is a minister. In each case, after the courts have decided the issue, one version of the church did not get to select its own minister or had to abandon the church property in question and found its own new congregation in order to do so. The problem presented to the court is how to resolve two churches into one. US courts have mostly solved that problem by attempting to discern and side with what it took to be the established order—that is, with what it took to be *the* church, *the* church having an ancient and exclusive jurisdiction over matters "strictly and purely ecclesiastical."[28] It is such an affirmation of *the* church's rights that Roberts seeks.

In attempting to give some shape to the variety of churches before them, and in order to form a typology of church governance, US courts have typically divided American churches into free-standing local congregations, on the one hand, and what they have called hierarchical churches, on the other, the latter a set that awkwardly encompasses such very different entities as the Presbyterian Church USA and the Serbian Orthodox Church. This typology originates in federal law with the Court's decision in *Watson v. Jones*.[29]

Howe, *The Garden and the Wilderness*. It also permits the court to ignore early state statutory limits on church wealth and governance. See Sarah Barringer Gordon, "The First Disestablishment: Limits on Church Power and Property Before the Civil War," *University of Pennsylvania Law Review* 162, no. 2 (January 2014): 307–372; Kellen Funk, "Church Corporations and the Conflict of Laws in Antebellum America," *Journal of Law and Religion* 32, no. 2 (July 2017): 263–284, https://doi.org/10.1017/jlr.2017.31/, and McConnell and Goodrich, "On Resolving Church Property Disputes," 311.

28. This position is the one English legal historian Julian Rivers, in his discussion of the English church property cases, terms the strong version of the departure from doctrine position, the one that, in cases of schism, always "prefers the party which maintains the historic position of the church." Rivers, *The Law of Organized Religions*, 96.

29. *Watson v. Jones*, 80 U.S. 679 (1872). The *Watson* decision precedes incorporation of the First Amendment into the Fourteenth Amendment (see explanation at pp. 2–3). The doc-

Watson v. Jones

The case most commonly cited with respect to judicial guidance in church property cases, *Watson v. Jones*, was an 1872 Kentucky dispute concerning a schism that had developed in a local Presbyterian church between those who supported slavery and those who were antislavery. Such splits developed in many US protestant congregations, particularly along the border between north and south. The question for the Kentucky courts was which faction should retain control of the church building and lead the congregation going forward. In other words, "[i]t [wa]s a question as to which of two bodies shall be recognized as the Third or Walnut Street Presbyterian Church."[30] Actual possession of the property was held by church trustees but disposition of the property was under control of the church elders. The question for the court was who of two different sets of claimants had authority to act as elders in the local congregation.

The Kentucky Supreme Court having decided for the abolitionists, the defendant proslavery claimants appealed to the US Supreme Court. *Watson* famously characterized such cases to fall into three types:

1. The first of these [known in US law as the English Rule] is when the property which is the subject of controversy has been, by the deed or will of the donor, or other instrument by which the property is held, by the express terms of the instrument devoted to the teaching support, or spread of some specific form of religious doctrine or belief.
2. The second is when the property is held by a religious congregation which,

trine of civil court incompetence in matters "strictly ecclesiastical," attributed by Roberts to the decision in *Watson*, formally originates then not in the Court's role as interpreter of the First Amendment, but in what is called federal common law—the extraconstitutional law developed by the federal courts as an adjunct to its authority over textual interpretation of the Constitution. Because the religion clauses were not understood to have been incorporated into the Fourteenth Amendment until 1940, leaving religion mostly to state law, federal church property cases before that date should be understood to be elaborations of federal common law, not of constitutional law. Nevertheless, this distinction is blurred in practice by the fact that these earlier cases are often cited by federal courts and can be understood as being constitutionalized by reference.

In 1938, in *Erie R.R. v. Tompkins*, 304 U.S. 64 (1938), the Court held that it had no power to create federal common law, formally nullifying the *Watson* doctrine. Yet while often cited as marking the end of federal common law, the *Erie* doctrine remains contested and *Watson* continues to be cited in constitutional cases.

30. 80 U.S. at 717.

by the nature of its organization, is strictly independent of other ecclesiastical associations, and so far as church government is concerned, owes no fealty or obligation to any higher authority.

3. The third is where the religious congregation or ecclesiastical body holding the property is but a subordinate member of some general church organization in which there are superior ecclesiastical tribunals with a general and ultimate power of control more or less complete, in some supreme judicatory over the whole membership of that general organization.[31]

The first two types, according to the *Watson* court, are understood to admit of solution through secular legal reasoning, the law applicable to the enforcement of trusts generally in the first case, and those pertaining to all private associations in the second. "But," the *Watson* court said, "the third of these classes of cases is the one which is oftenest found in the courts, and which, with reference to the number and difficulty of the questions involved, and to other considerations, is every way the most important."[32] Finding its current case to fall into the third class—"a religious congregation which is itself part of a large and general organization of some religious denomination, with which it is more or less intimately connected by religious views and ecclesiastical government"[33]—the *Watson* Court held that the abolitionist faction, because they were backed by the national General Assembly of the Presbyterian Church, were the rightful elders and should win.

The *Watson* Court gave extended consideration to the reasons for this ruling, repeatedly asserting the importance of allowing ecclesiastical bodies independently to decide "matters of faith, discipline, and doctrine."[34] As Mark DeWolfe Howe argued, however, the Court's deference to the national Presbyterian Church in this case could be more plausibly explained ideologically or politically by Union victory in the Civil War. Indeed, Howe regarded the *Watson* decision as a case of gross overreach by the Court given a lack of colorable federal jurisdiction. It was for him, as a dispute between and among Kentuckians alone, a case clearly sounding in state law.[35] While antebellum church property disputes had been biased in favor of the desires of the local congregation, Howe argues that a new

31. 80 U.S. at 722.
32. 80 U.S. at 726.
33. 80 U.S. at 726.
34. 80 U.S. at 732.
35. Howe, *The Garden and the Wilderness*, 80–81.

nationalism seized the Court after the War, giving license to move these cases from state to federal jurisdiction, and from congregational to hierarchical decision-making authorities.

Summarizing its theory of church property law, the *Watson* Court contrasted it to that of the United Kingdom. Under the first option, the trust doctrine, predominant in English law, the court is required to make a finding as to which faction in the church in question continued to be faithful to its doctrine. In contrast, in the US, the *Watson* Court announced: "[t]he law knows no heresy, and is committed to the support of no dogma, the establishment of no sect." Freedom of religion in the US, they said, meant that

> [t]he right to organize voluntary religious associations to assist in the expression and dissemination of any religious doctrine, and to create tribunals for the decision of controverted questions of faith within the association, and for the ecclesiastical government of all the individual members, congregations, and officers within the general association, is unquestioned. All who unite themselves to such a body do so with an implied consent to this government, and are bound to submit to it.[36]

Voluntary religious associations were understood, under this theory, to give the congregants what they wanted—that is, their right to establish a form of church polity and governance of their own choosing. Once having chosen, they were bound by it. They were understood to have consented to the church's jurisdiction.

The *Watson* language is often proudly quoted as evidence of America's commitment to religious freedom. It was quoted in *Hosanna-Tabor*. It has acquired a strong normative valence in First Amendment cases. It is important to note, however, that the language of "implied consent" in this new doctrine is understood to derive from a voluntariness understood to be characteristic of voluntary associations more broadly. Justice Samuel Miller insists at the beginning of his decision for the Court in *Watson* that

> [r]eligious organizations come before us in the same attitude as other voluntary associations for benevolent or charitable purposes, and their rights of property, or of contract, are equally under the protection of the law, and the actions of their members subject to its restraints. Conscious as we may be of the excited feeling engendered by this controversy, and of the extent to which it has agi-

36. 80 U.S. at 728–29.

> tated the intelligent and pious body of Christians in whose bosom it originated, we enter upon its consideration with the satisfaction of knowing that the principles on which we are to decide so much of it as is proper for our decision, are those applicable alike to all of its class, and that our duty is the simple one of applying those principles to the facts before us.[37]

In deferring to the national presbytery of the Presbyterian Church, the Court in 1872 suggested that it was simply deferring to that form of church government its members preferred, notwithstanding the schism before them.

In contrast to the *Hosanna-Tabor* decision, there is little whiff of incense that wafts through the opinion. The church in *Watson* appears in the Court's language entirely a creature of this world. Or, one could say that the lack of mystification reflects the thoroughly protestant ecclesiology that informs the Court's opinion.[38] It affirms an ecclesiology founded in the political theological fiction of a voluntary christian community governed by secular democratic law, rather than in the fictions of governance by the holy spirit more typical of the liturgical traditions.

Current Supreme Court jurisprudence tends to a theory of the church and its sovereignty that focuses less on the presumed consent of the member, and more on the corporate rights of the church. Sometimes the two are combined in mutual support, the fiction of individual choice blurring into and enabling the givenness of the religious organization's own self-understanding. The Court in *Hosanna-Tabor* insists that "our opinion in *Watson* 'radiates . . . a spirit of freedom for religious organizations, an independence from secular control or manipulation—in short, power to decide for themselves, free from state interference, matters of church government as well as those of faith and doctrine.'"[39] Who exactly is exercising this "power to decide for themselves" is carefully elided.

The church in its mystical incarnation has only further gained in importance since its appearance as an avatar of Union victory in 1872, leaving behind its imagined status as just another voluntary democratic organization whose members consent to its leadership and decision-making structures. The entrenched nature of this shift was headlined with the improbable appearance of the Russian patriarch in a US court.

37. 80 U.S. at 713.
38. Inazu, "The Freedom of the Church (New Revised Standard Version)," 337.
39. 565 U.S. at 186.

The orthodox cases

By the middle of the twentieth century, to which Roberts, in his review of church property doctrine, now quickly passes, things have changed in the US, in terms of religious, legal, and political culture, and in terms of constitutional doctrine. Dominant concerns are now international, not domestic, and the incorporation of the religion clauses through the due process clause of the Fourteenth Amendment has constitutionalized law with respect to religion.[40] In a pair of church property cases, *Kedroff v. St. Nicholas Cathedral of Russian Orthodox Church*[41] and *Serbian Eastern Orthodox Church v. Milivojevich*,[42] the Court in the second half of the twentieth century, as a matter of constitutional free exercise doctrine, oddly affirmed in US law the authority of patriarchal church governance in the eastern churches, giving them a constitutional trump card in their disputes with North American orthodox litigants.[43] The religious freedom recognized by *Watson*, that is, "[t]he right to organize voluntary religious associations to assist in the expression and dissemination of any religious doctrine, and to create tribunals for the decision of controverted questions of faith within the association, and for the ecclesiastical government of all the individual members, congregations, and officers within the general association,"[44] through the operation of these two decisions, became the freedom of the corporeal church, not of its members. (Justice Roberts does not cite the Court's 1904 decision in *Ponce v. Roman Catholic Apostolic Church*,[45] a rarely cited church property case which also asserts a robust view of church sovereignty, although the opinions in the two orthodox cases do cite *Ponce*. The next section will discuss briefly this remarkable missing decision.)

Both judges and legal commentators often simply pass from a discus-

40. See discussion in Howe, *The Garden and the Wilderness*, 88–90.

41. *Kedroff v. St. Nicholas Cathedral of Russian Orthodox Church*, 344 U.S. 94 (1952).

42. *Serbian Eastern Orthodox Diocese v. Milivojevich*, 426 U.S. 696 (1976).

43. I particularly want to thank my Indiana colleague Patrick Michelson and Aram Sarkisian, Ph.D. student at Northwestern University, for help in understanding the orthodox context of these cases. That these church polity disputes in the orthodox churches continue to be live can be seen in the recent declaration of independence by the Ukrainian Orthodox Church. Bohdan Hladio, "Schismophrenia: A Reflection on Ukrainian Autocephaly," *Public Orthodoxy*, https://publicorthodoxy.org/2019/04/12/schismophrenia-a-reflection-on-ukrainian-autocephaly/.

44. 80 U.S. at 728–29.

45. *Ponce v. Roman Catholic Apostolic Church*, 210 U.S. 296 (1904). The significance of this case was drawn to my attention by David Maldonado Rivera, who has written about this case at greater length in Hurd and Sullivan, *At Home and Abroad*.

sion of the nineteenth-century Presbyterian Reconstruction-era cases to the eastern orthodox cases as if they are essentially addressing the same problem and the same object—the problem of church organization and church property—or even of something they call religious societies or organizations more broadly. It seems worth asking again whether and how the First Presbyterian Church in Louisville, Kentucky, and the Russian Orthodox Church in New York City or the Serbian Eastern Orthodox Church are the same kind of thing. As Mark DeWolfe Howe says in the conclusion to his discussion of these twentieth-century church property cases, "The recognition of that special institutional freedom [the church's liberty to govern herself]—a freedom, I believe, enjoyed by no other collegiate body—suggests that the justices either do not quite mean what they say or do not say quite what they mean when they assert that aid to religion is outlawed by our Constitution."[46]

What were the orthodox cases actually about? The 1952 case, *Kedroff*, was a suit in ejectment, an old common law action brought to remove from the property a person alleged to be in illegal possession. Two different Russian Orthodox bishops lay claim to leadership of St. Nicholas Cathedral in New York City, one appointed by the Russian patriarch in Moscow and one elected by a group of Russian Orthodox churches in North America that had declared themselves independent of Moscow. The lawsuit was only the latest in a very long dispute among Russian Orthodox communities in North America, including litigation across decades.[47] The Moscow appointee, Benjamin Fedchenkoff, was the target of the ejectment action. The legal issue was the constitutionality of a 1945 New York statute by operation of which leadership of the North American Orthodox churches had formally been transferred away from the Moscow patriarchate to a then recently created North American metropolitan, Archbishop Leonty.[48] Appealing from the court of appeals' affirmation of the opera-

46. Howe, *The Garden and the Wilderness*, 90.

47. See Aram Sarkisian, "The Cross Between Hammer and Sickle: Russian Orthodox Christians in the United States, 1908–1928" (Northwestern University dissertation, 2019).

48. New York State, then and now, provides for the incorporation of churches through a statute that individuates incorporation denomination by denomination. In this case, as the Court explained:

> Article 5-C was added to the Religious Corporations Law of New York in 1945 and provided both for the incorporation and administration of Russian Orthodox churches. Clarifying amendments were added in 1948. The purpose of the article was to bring all of the New York Russian Orthodox churches, formerly subject to the administrative jurisdiction of the Most Sacred Governing Synod in Moscow or the Patriarch of Moscow, into an administratively autonomous metropolitan district. That district was North American in area,

tion of the statute, Fedchenkoff, citing the fourth-century Edict of Milan, argued that the New York statute had, in effect, converted the Russian Orthodox church from a hierarchical to a congregational church in violation of Orthodox canon law. The Orthodox Church, like the Roman Catholic Church, claims its authority by way of apostolic succession.[49]

The majority opinion in the US Supreme Court in *Kedroff*, in an 8–1 decision, was written by Justice Stanley Reed. Rejecting the judgment of both the New York State Legislature and the New York Court of Appeals that the atheism of the Soviet regime justified their actions, and citing its decision in *Watson*, the Court found that authority remained in Moscow and that for hierarchical churches, free exercise of religion as guaranteed by the First Amendment to the US Constitution meant deferring to the traditional authority structure of the church in question.

We see in the *Kedroff* decision an unexpected solicitude on the part of an American court, in the middle of the Cold War, for the rights of a Russian church deeply entangled with the Soviet government.[50] We also see the church-in-law here epitomized by a church largely unfamiliar to most Americans, certainly in 1952. How to explain Justice Reed's romantic and idealized, even fantastical, depiction of a unified transhistorical Russian church and of apostolic succession as the foundation of his strong assertion of the rights of collective Christianity under the US Constitution?[51]

> created pursuant to resolutions adopted at a *sobor* held in Detroit in 1924. This declared autonomy was made effective by a further legislative requirement that all the churches formerly administratively subject to the Moscow synod and patriarchate should for the future be governed by the ecclesiastical body and hierarchy of the American metropolitan district. 344 U.S. at 97–98.

For an explanation of the meaning of *sobor* in Russian Orthodox theology, see Vera Shevzov, *Russian Orthodoxy on the Eve of the Revolution* (Oxford: Oxford University Press, 2004), 33–35.

49. See Brief for Appellants at 9: "The official name of the Eastern Church is 'The Holy Orthodox Catholic Apostolic Eastern Church.' The Russian Orthodox Church is an integral, though autocephalous, part of this Catholic and Apostolic Church. The traditional position of the Russian Orthodox Church is that it is apostolic in origin and descent, that this apostolic succession is preserved through the institution of its Ecclesiastical Hierarchy in an unbroken succession from Christ and His disciples, that its bishops have been consecrated by those duly qualified and duly authorized by Higher Authority to perform this sacrament, and that there must be no defect anywhere in the line of descent for the transmission of grace."

50. It would be incorrect to describe the Russian church as entirely captive to Soviet politics. See Sarkisian, "The Cross Between Hammer and Sickle," for an extensive analysis of the complex politics of Russian Orthodoxy in North America.

51. See F. William O'Brien, *Justice Reed and the First Amendment: The Religion Clauses* (Washington, DC: Georgetown University Press, 1958) in which O'Brien explores the reasons

As in *Hosanna-Tabor*, the Court told a long and somewhat arcane story of the history of church and state. Justice Reed began:

> The Russian Orthodox Church is an autocephalous member of the Eastern Orthodox Greek Catholic Church. It sprang from the Church of Constantinople in the Tenth Century. The schism of 1054 A. D. split the Universal Church into those of the East and the West. Gradually self-government was assumed by the Russian Church until in the Sixteenth Century its autonomy was recognized and a Patriarch of Moscow appeared.[52]

In Reed's telling, it is a story of springing and of appearances! Pushing back before Magna Carta to the Great Schism of the first millennium, Reed traced the Russian church forward through the reign of Peter the Great, its missions to the Aleutian Islands, and the formation of North American orthodox churches, then through the church/state transformations of the Bolshevik Revolution.

Reed carefully explained how the North American churches came to separate themselves from Moscow. On the one hand, he said, Russian Orthodoxy in America looked with horror at the transformation back home: "The Russian upheaval caused repercussions in the North American Diocese. That Diocese at the time of the Soviet Revolution recognized the spiritual and administrative control of Moscow. White Russians, both lay and clerical, found asylum in America from the revolutionary conflicts, strengthening the feeling of abhorrence of the secular attitude of the new Russian Government."[53] At the same time, he said, these émigrés were also becoming Americans, accustomed to "our" ways: "The church members already here, immigrants and native-born, while habituated to look to Moscow for religious direction, were accustomed to our theory of separation between church and state."[54] The 1945 New York statute, Justice Reed said, had given effect to this newfound commitment to separation.

Surprisingly then, notwithstanding this apparently very American story of religious freedom and New World church re-founding, the Supreme Court characterized the New York legislation as an effort to interfere

---

for Reed's position in *Kedroff*, placing the decision alongside his other religion clause decisions. He observes, among other things, that this was the first case in which the Constitution was applied extraterritorially. O'Brien, *Justice Reed*, 189.

52. 344 U.S. at 100.

53. 344 U.S. at 102–03.

54. 344 U.S. at 103.

in the administration of the Russian Orthodox Church and found that the statute violated the First and Fourteenth Amendments. Reed cited *Watson* in support. While noting that *Watson* predated the incorporation doctrine extending the reach of the free exercise clause to the states, he announced that "[t]he [*Watson*] opinion radiates . . . a spirit of freedom for religious organizations, an independence from secular control or manipulation—in short, power to decide for themselves, free from state interference, matters of church government as well as those of faith and doctrine."[55] (These words would later be appropriated by Chief Justice Roberts in *Hosanna-Tabor*.)[56]

How does this radiating "spirit of freedom for religious organizations" to which Justice Reed refers actually work? How does the court locate the proper organization when who speaks for the organization is precisely what is at issue? Does the court look to the members who have voluntarily associated themselves or does it look to the corporate entity that association has become? The history of the North American orthodox churches might have suggested that many, perhaps most, Russian orthodox in North America had decided that they preferred their own leadership to that of Moscow. Indeed, the New York state legislature had found—and the New York courts had taken judicial notice of—the Russian church's captivity to a hostile political regime.

According to Reed's own historical account, there were arguably two churches before the Court and one was just the kind of voluntary lay organization extolled in *Watson*. Yet Reed found a unified church with a millennia-old unbroken right to freedom of governance in Moscow. His conclusion was that the New York statute had improperly inserted itself into "matters strictly ecclesiastical":

> The record before us shows no schism over faith or doctrine between the Russian Church in America and the Russian Orthodox Church. It shows administrative control of the North American Diocese by the Supreme Church Authority of the Russian Orthodox Church, including the appointment of the ruling hierarch in North America from the foundation of the diocese until the Russian Revolution. We find nothing that indicates a relinquishment of this power by the Russian Orthodox Church.[57]

55. 344 U.S. at 115.

56. 565 U.S. at 186.

57. 344 U.S. at 120. Reed also distinguished the case from an earlier decision approving the US federal government's seizure of the assets of the Mormon Church. 344 U.S. at 119. The *Kedroff* plaintiffs had claimed that the Court's earlier decision approving the dismantling

Notwithstanding decades of upheaval and division in Russia and in the US, Justice Reed found Moscow to have been in firm control of "matters strictly ecclesiastical" all along. Given both his own description of the ragged history of the orthodox churches in North America and the even more disjointed description in the briefs, Reed's certainty about where the Russian church and its authority were located is wildly belied by the history of the Russian church from the time of the 1861 emancipation of the serfs to the Bolshevik Revolution. As Vera Shevzov details in her book on this period in Russian Orthodox history, ecclesiology was a highly fraught topic in the Russian church after emancipation of the serfs.[58]

Precisely where the church is located and who is in charge is always radically indeterminate, but it was particularly so in the Orthodox Church at this moment in Russian history. Shevzov traces Russian Orthodox Christian preoccupation with the proper nature of christian community back to the Reformation and to Luther's proclamation of a priesthood of all believers. She argues that the rise of democratic politics had led to a stronger sense of lay belonging to the body of Christ in the Russian church. Emancipation and improvement in education had also changed lay understanding of their relationship to the church and its governance. Shevzov explains that "[t]he very meaning of church, the conceptualization of its character and life, and the internal principles by which it should be ordered—these fundamental issues were being radically questioned and reexamined."[59] With Russians roughly divided between those who took a congregationally centered and those who took a hierarchical view of the church, Shevzov further explains that there "were two powerful yet often diverging understandings of religious authority. One was focused on the bishop; the other was focused on the perceived workings of the Holy Spirit and the responsibility of all believers to bear witness to the Spirit.

---

of the Mormon Church in *Late Corporation* was controlling in *Kedroff*. Justice Reed distinguished that case, saying that "[t]he seizure of the [LDS] property was bottomed on the general rule that where a charitable corporation is dissolved for unlawful practices, the sovereign takes and distributes the property according to the *cy-pres* doctrine to objects of charity and usefulness, e.g., schools. . . . None of these elements exist to support the validity of the New York statute." 344 U.S. at 120, referencing *Late Corporation of Latter-Day Saints v. United States*, 136 U.S. 1 (1890). In other words, the Mormon Church, unlike the Russian church, was a criminal enterprise and therefore subject to dissolution by the government. See Sarah Barringer Gordon, *The Mormon Question: Polygamy and Constitutional Conflict in 19th Century America* (Chapel Hill: University of North Carolina Press, 2002), for a thorough discussion of the federal government's persecution and disciplining of the Mormon Church.

58. Shevzov, *Russian Orthodoxy*. See also Nicholas Ferencz, *American Orthodoxy and Parish Congregationalism* (Piscataway, NJ: Gorgias Press, 2006).

59. Shevzov, *Russian Orthodoxy*, 13.

Tensions were also aggravated by the manifestation of two different tendencies in ecclesial ordering: a centralizing one and a decentralizing, localizing one."[60] Shevzov sees the same tension in the Russian church today.

Yet notwithstanding this history and the fractured religious politics described by Reed in his own opinion, the Supreme Court affirmed a high hierarchical and static view of church governance, strangely negating what might have been understood to be a historically more American form of local lay-led church governance. On what constitutional basis could the US Supreme Court decide that American Russian Orthodox people who understood the church to be located in North America were wrong? It is hard to avoid the conclusion that the Court bought the argument of the appellants that the church—the hierarchical church—is a sacramental as well as a sovereign entity entitled to extraconstitutional legal deference.

If one looks to the briefs in *Kedroff*, one finds the two versions of the church to have been clearly laid out. Lawyers for Moscow carefully explained that "[t]here is and can be only one Russian Orthodox Church." Indeed, it is *the* church:

> An Orthodox Church is not an aggregate or collection of separate or discrete parts, of parishes and dioceses, which are free to federate or separate at pleasure. An Orthodox Church is an indivisible whole. Indeed, it has no parts. It is a unity and, by hypothesis, no diocese or parish may of its own will, leave the Church—or consider itself a part of the Church and live "autonomously", without breaking the unity, the indivisibility, of the whole.[61]

Their brief further explains that "[t]he traditional position of the Russian Orthodox Church is that it is apostolic in origin and descent, that this apostolic succession is preserved through the institution of its Ecclesiastical Hierarchy in an unbroken succession from Christ and His disciples . . . and that there must be no defect anywhere in the line of descent for the transmission of grace."[62] The church in a mystical theological sense is clearly evident here.

The Americans answer with their own ecclesiology. The Russian church, they say, is not hierarchical. It is sobornal—governed collectively by the

60. Shevzov, *Russian Orthodoxy*, 262.
61. *Kedroff* Brief of Appellants at 6–7.
62. *Kedroff* Brief of Appellants at 24.

community of clerical and lay members.[63] Furthermore, they say, their theology of the church was in concert with US foreign policy toward the USSR:

> An American Church of the Eastern Confession, safe from Soviet interference and secure in its temporalities, would not only contribute a great heritage to the religious culture of America—in spirituality, faith, dogma, worship, liturgy and general ethos—but would be a beacon to the multitudes of Eastern Christians now under the Soviet yoke. The Voice of America and Radio Free Europe could proudly inform the oppressed populations that in America there exists an autocephalous branch of their own confession free from all governmental control, at home or from abroad, and at liberty to criticize any government including its own. Such a bond of sympathy between the Christian populations behind the Iron Curtain and their fellow believers here would, it is submitted, be the equivalent of many billions of dollars in military preparedness.[64]

An American Orthodox Church was worth its weight in missiles.

Not only did the Court's majority in *Kedroff* take sides in an ecclesiological dispute within the Russian church, it did so in apparent violation of Cold War politics. It also stood against a tide of reform in the Russian church. Why? Because, I would argue, the Court had come to believe in the church.[65] In his brief concurring opinion in *Kedroff*, Justice Felix Frankfurter felt called upon to underline this last point. "St. Nicholas Cathedral is not just a piece of real estate," he said.

> It is no more that than is St. Patrick's Cathedral or the Cathedral of St. John the Divine. A cathedral is the seat and center of ecclesiastical authority. St. Nicholas Cathedral is an archiepiscopal see of one of the great religious organizations. What is at stake here is the power to exercise religious authority. That is the essence of this controversy. It is that even though the religious authority becomes manifest and is exerted through authority over the Cathedral as the outward symbol of a religious faith.[66]

63. For an explanation of the sobornal in orthodox theology, see Shevzov, *Russian Orthodoxy*, 33–35.

64. *Kedroff* Appelle's Brief at 4.

65. Justice Reed wrote a lengthy and passionate dissent in *McCollum*, the released time case, protesting the invalidating of an Illinois statute requiring schools to accommodate students for voluntary religious education during the school day. *Illinois Ex Rel. McCollum v. Board of Education*, 333 U.S. 203 (1948), Reed, J., dissenting.

66. 344 U.S. at 121.

"What is at stake here," Frankfurter says, "is the power to exercise religious authority." The power of what he calls "one of the great religious organizations." Such authority, it seems, is natural, is pre- or extra-constitutional, and is top-down.

And yet, the sad irony is that, as historian Aram Sarkisian makes clear, ultimately religious authority was exercised by the courts, not by the patriarch: "The cathedral cases [*Kedroff* and other related ones] made civil courts an arbiter of doctrine and dogma, the spiritual authority and legitimacy of ecclesiastical leadership, the holder of the church's purse, and even the nature of religious life in Soviet Russia. In these ways, non-Orthodox judges became critical mediators of what it meant to be a Russian Orthodox Christian in the United States after 1917."[67] Just as in *Hosanna-Tabor*.

For an entirely different view of the *Kedroff* case, it is helpful to turn to Justice Robert Jackson, in dissent, who saw the case as presenting no constitutional issue at all. All he saw was a simple property dispute, one properly left to state law. The Russian orthodox of New York had no obligation to incorporate their church, Jackson pointed out; they had chosen to do so. Having decided to incorporate, he said, the church was subject to New York law.

For Jackson, there was no issue of religious freedom. The New York statute had not inhibited anyone's exercise of religion. Indeed, it was not about religion, but politics, he wrote:

67. Sarkisian, "The Cross Between Hammer and Sickle," 351. Interestingly, each faction looked to a different US protestant church for support:

> [T]hese cases highlight the extent to which Orthodoxy remained in tension with American life, struggling for legibility and recognition in a country that still perceived Christianity almost exclusively in its Western forms. To compensate, John Kedrovsky and Platon would instead rely on surrogates, mostly mainline Protestants, who traded on their prominence and respectability to champion one Orthodox faction or another, often to further their own ecumenical or denominational interests. Kedrovsky would be supported by Methodists who acted out of progressive Christian altruism, seeing an opportunity to breathe new life into a church rife with over nine centuries of what they saw as backward superstitions, arcane ritual, and a reluctance to engage with the modern world. What was more, they viewed cooperation with a renovated Russian Orthodox Church—and a benevolent Soviet government—as a means to preserve a small, yet active Methodist community clinging to survival under Bolshevik rule. Platon drew on the Episcopal Church, whose longstanding links to the "Eastern Churches" stemmed from nineteenth-century Branch Theory, and which had long been a critical ally to American Orthodox Rus'.

Sarkisian, "The Cross Between Hammer and Sickle," 351–352.

> It is important to observe what New York has not done in this case. It has not held that Benjamin may not act as Archbishop or be revered as such by all who will follow him. It has not held that he may not have a Cathedral. Indeed, I think New York would agree that no one is more in need of spiritual guidance than the Soviet faction. It has only held that this cleric may not have a particular Cathedral which, under New York law, belongs to others. It has not interfered with his or anyone's exercise of his religion. New York has not outlawed the Soviet-controlled sect nor forbidden it to exercise its authority or teach its dogma in any place whatsoever except on this piece of property owned and rightfully possessed by the Cathedral Corporation.[68]

Jackson also revealed his jaundiced view of the church-state politics of the situation:

> This Cathedral was incorporated and built in the era of the Czar, under the regime of a state-ridden church in a church-ridden state. The Bolshevik Revolution may have freed the state from the grip of the church, but it did not free the church from the grip of the state. It only brought to the top a new master for a captive and submissive ecclesiastical establishment . . .
>
> I shall not undertake to wallow through the complex, obscure and fragmentary details of secular and ecclesiastical history, theology, and canon law in which this case is smothered. To me, whatever the canon law is found to be and whoever is the rightful head of the Moscow patriarchate, I do not think New York law must yield to the authority of a foreign and unfriendly state masquerading as a spiritual institution.[69]

Jackson's bracing lawyerly secularism, and hostility to what he takes to be ecclesiastical obfuscation and state dissembling, as well as his insistence that the Court is after all there to enforce the laws of the United States, reveals the eight-justice majority to be apparently under the spell of the church—or perhaps of corporeal sovereignty more generally.

It could be said that what is revealed in *Kedroff* is a new and broader constitutional solicitude for the rights of private groups to self-governance, even to sovereignty, with christian theology here providing the theory of the case. Legal historian Mark DeWolfe Howe, writing in the 1953 *Harvard Law Review*'s annual volume on the Court's prior term, saw in the

68. 344 U.S. at 129–30.
69. 344 U.S. at 127, 131.

Kedroff decision an affirmation of political pluralism. As he explained, "The heart of the pluralistic thesis is the conviction that government must recognize that it is not the sole possessor of sovereignty, and that private groups within the community are entitled to lead their own free lives and exercise within the area of their competence an authority so effective as to justify labeling it a sovereign authority."[70] Comparing the Court's decision to the work of the British pluralists John Figgis and Harold Laski,[71] Howe admiringly commented that "[n]ot only has the Court recognized the liberty of the group as something different from the individual liberties of its members but it has extended this recognition to an international body with its home office for spiritual government in a foreign country."[72] The rights of the church and the rights of other corporate entities seem to gain strength from one another, passing back and forth the charisma of the collective.

American Jesuit John Courtney Murray, celebrated for his role in the drafting of the Declaration on Religious Freedom promulgated by the Second Vatican Council, also argued that the church in the US enjoyed a sovereignty in law shared with other groups.[73] He asserted that the US lacked the unitary sovereignty of European governments. Citing *Kedroff*, he concluded that "[t]he juridical result of the American limitation of governmental powers is the guarantee to the Church of a stable condition of freedom as a matter of law and right." "[T]his guarantee," he said, "is made not only to the individual Catholic but to the Church as an organized society with its own law and jurisdiction . . . Nowhere in the American structure is there accumulated the plenitude of legal sovereignty possessed in England by the Queen in Parliament." "The American state has no sovereignty in the classic Continental sense," he insisted.

70. Howe, "Foreword," 91.

71. John Neville Figgis, *Churches in the Modern State* (London: Longmans Green, 1914), was responding to the plight of the free church of Scotland; see 60n3 above. Harold Laski, "The Pluralistic State," *Philosophical Review* 28, no. 6 (November 1919): 562–575. See also David Nicholls, *The Pluralist State: The Political Ideas of J. N. Figgis and His Contemporaries* (Oxford: St Anthony's Press, 1975).

72. Howe, "Foreword," 93. Legal scholar Richard Garnett goes further: "[n]ot only does [*Kedroff*] imply that the Church as a spiritual body has liberties which will be given protection directly rather than derivatively, but it gives that protection to liberties which, in their essence, differ from those possessed by the members of the Church." Richard W. Garnett, "The Story of *Kedroff v. St Nicholas Cathedral*," *Journal of Supreme Court History* 38, no. 1 (2013): 80–93.

73. John Courtney Murray, *We Hold These Truths: Catholic Reflections on the American Proposition* (New York: Sheed and Ward, 1960).

"Within society, as distinct from the state, there is room for the independent exercise of an authority which is not that of the state."[74] Lacking the encompassing sovereignty of the modern European state epitomized for Murray by English Parliamentary supremacy, a US government of limited constitutional power leaves room for other sovereigns.

As will be discussed in the next chapter, what Howe called "pluralism" and what Murray understood to be "the independent exercise of . . . authority" in the US has, in fact, always been controversial—and often understood as antidemocratic. While both Howe and Murray entertain the possibility that the *Kedroff* court might have been affirming a willingness to recognize the positive political value of pluralism more generally, not just that of the church, current First Amendment scholars Lupu and Tuttle see *Kedroff* to be about what is strictly ecclesiastical, that is, a specific exclusion from the Court's remit of those matters not subject to rational decision-making.[75] They do not see these cases as affirming the sovereignty of these bodies.

Roberts concluded his discussion of the church property cases in *Hosanna-Tabor*, including *Watson* and *Kedroff*, with the announcement of the rule that "'the First Amendment commits [church governance] exclusively to the highest ecclesiastical tribunals' of the Church."[76] Citing its 1976 decision in *Serbian Eastern Orthodox Diocese for United States and Canada v. Milivojevich*,[77] another Cold War dispute, this one over who should control the American-Canadian Diocese of the Serbian Orthodox Church, Roberts explained that the First Amendment "permit[s] hierarchical religious organizations to establish their own rules and regulations for internal discipline and government, and to create tribunals for adjudicating disputes over these matters."[78]

In the Serbian Orthodox case, the Court had again insisted on the incompetence of courts to inquire into the justice of ecclesiastical decisions. Reversing the decision of the Illinois Supreme Court finding that the Serbian Church had not followed its own internal process in removing and replacing a bishop, Justice William Brennan explained that "it is the

74. Murray, *We Hold These Truths*, 71–72.

75. Lupu and Tuttle, "The Mystery of Unanimity," 1278.

76. 565 U.S. at 187.

77. *Serbian Eastern Orthodox Diocese for United States and Canada v. Milivojevich*, 426 U.S. 696 (1976).

78. 565 U.S. at 187.

essence of religious faith that ecclesiastical decisions are reached and are to be accepted as matters of faith whether or not rational or measurable by objective criteria. Constitutional concepts of due process, involving secular notions of 'fundamental fairness' or impermissible objectives, are therefore hardly relevant to such matters of ecclesiastical cognizance."[79] Ecclesiastical decisions are "matters of faith," not subject to due process.

Justices Rehnquist and John Paul Stevens dissented in the Serbian case, refusing to accede to the majority's anxiety about the special incompetence of the courts in such matters and insisting that secular courts could indeed answer the question of who "the real bishop" was using ordinary secular legal principles. Like Justice Jackson in his dissent in *Kedroff*, they refused to be moved by the charisma of the church. "A casual reader of some of the passages in the Court's opinion," the dissenters said,

> could easily gain the impression that the State of Illinois had commenced a proceeding designed to brand Bishop Dionisije [the Serbian Orthodox bishop in the case] as a heretic, with appropriate pains and penalties. But the state trial judge in the Circuit Court of Lake County was not the Bishop of Beauvais, trying Joan of Arc for heresy; the jurisdiction of his court was invoked by petitioners themselves, who sought an injunction establishing their control over property of the American-Canadian Diocese of the church located in Lake County.[80]

Having been petitioned for help, the court, they said, was entirely capable of deciding the question, "just as they would have attempted to decide a similar dispute among the members of any other voluntary association."[81] In other words, application of the canon law of the Serbian Eastern Orthodox Church by the Illinois courts was the appropriate and inescapable secular route to such a question.

Whether church property cases should be considered special and different from other disputes within voluntary organizations continues to be an issue in the US. Indeed, since the 1990s, when an openly gay man was consecrated as Episcopal bishop of New Hampshire, efforts by local Episcopal churches to disaffiliate from the national church in the US have led to hundreds of such disputes.[82]

79. 426 U.S. at 714–15.

80. 426 U.S. at 725.

81. 426 U.S. at 726.

82. See Jeremy Bonner, "What Is Truth? Ecclesiology, Law, and the Historian Expert Witness in Twenty-First Century America," Ecclesiastical History Society, Summer Conference,

The Church of Rome

Oddly missing among the church property cases to which Roberts referred in *Hosanna-Tabor* is any consideration of *Ponce v. Roman Catholic Apostolic Church*,[83] a 1908 church property case cited in *Kedroff*.[84] This remarkable case arose as a result of the accession of Puerto Rico as a territory of the United States after the Spanish-American War. The city of Ponce in the newly acquired possession, taking advantage of the change of administration, argued that the Roman Catholic Church in Puerto Rico lacked legal personality and therefore was incapable of owning two church properties in the city. After a careful discussion of the formal transition from Spanish to American law, as provided for in the Treaty of Paris and the Foraker Act, Chief Justice Melville Fuller considered the genealogy of the church's ancient rights—as reflected in the exceptions to the mandates of property registration in colonial era Puerto Rican law. Taking a very long view indeed, Fuller endeavored to explain why church property has been a special class of property since ancient times.

Fuller began with the Emperor Constantine: "[T]he Roman Catholic Church has been recognized as possessing a legal personality and the capacity to take and acquire property since the time of the Emperor Constantine."[85] Referring to the sixth-century Code of Justinian, Fuller insisted that "[t]he strictest prohibition against alienating the property of the church exists in that code, and it provides that the alienation of church property shall not take place, even with the assent of all the representatives of the church, since these rights 'belong to the church,' and the church is the mother of religion; and as faith is perpetual, its patrimony must be preserved in its entirety perpetually."[86] Then, reaching even further back, the chief justice quoted a church historian on the prechristian legal rights of temples:

> In his History of Latin Christianity (vol. 1, p. 507), Dean Milman says: The Christian Churches succeeded to that sanctity which the ancient law had at-

Cambridge, July 24, 2018, for an entertaining account of the thorny ecclesiological disputes among Episcopalians being presented to US courts for resolution.

83. *Ponce v. Roman Catholic Apostolic Church*, 210 U.S. 296 (1908).

84. 344 U.S. at 120.

85. 210 U.S. at 302.

86. 210 U.S. at 311–12.

> tributed to the temples; as soon as they were consecrated they became public property, and could not be alienated to any other use. The ground itself was hallowed, and remained so even after the temple had been destroyed. This was an axiom of the heathen Papinian. Gifts to temples were alike inalienable, nor could they be pledged; the exception in the Justinian code betrays at once the decline of the Roman power, and the silent progress of Christian humanity. They could be sold or pledged for the redemption of captives, a purpose which the old Roman law would have disdained to contemplate.[87]

Fuller then extended the story of christian progress forward to the law of the barbarians: "[I]n the barbarian codes most sweeping provisions are found, recognizing the right of the church to acquire property and its inalienability when acquired. Church property everywhere remained untouched by the rude hands of invading barbarians. Trespass upon or interference with such property was severely punished, and gradually it became exempted from taxation."[88] For the chief justice the history of the rights of the church was a story of heathens, barbarians, and christian humanity. It was also a story told in the time of US imperialism.[89]

The story Justice Fuller renders in *Ponce* reveals a deep misunderstanding of the nature of the church's legal personality across time. As Julian Rivers explains in his important book, *The Law of Organized Religions*, legal establishment of the christian churches is something that happened as a result of the conjunction of the early modern reformations with the rise of the modern state. Recounting the now slow disestablishment of the church in England, he explains that

> establishment was an unrepeatable historical moment in the development of the Christian church and the modern State, the legal incidents of which can be identified with precision in any one legal system, and with broad comparability across Latin Christendom. The impact of that historical moment can be seen not only in the legal residue of establishment as it still affects the Church of England, but also in the legal position of other organized religions as they were partially included in the incidents of establishment, and even in our

87. 210 U.S. at 312.

88. 210 U.S. at 312.

89. See Christina Duffy Burnett and Burke Marshall, eds., *Foreign in a Domestic Sense: Puerto Rico, American Expansion, and the Constitution* (Durham, NC: Duke University Press, 2001).

> understanding of the modern concept and function of the State. In this sense, the established Church of England is an ever-receding memory.[90]

As Rivers goes on to explain, the partial autonomy of organized religious institutions differently acknowledged by different governments reflects the ongoing ambiguities of what it might mean "for one system of law (State law) fully to respect the autonomy of another system (religious law) within its boundaries."[91] More provocatively, he asserts that

> [i]f religious communities are to have a role in the preservation of civil liberty, they must to some extent compete with the institutions of the State. They cannot be purely spiritual communities, in the ethereal sense of the word, but must be expressed in the material goods common to all humankind. They must lay claim to the proper ordering of those goods which presents itself as superior to the claims of the State. They can only do this by being somewhat threatening to the authority of the State.[92]

Conclusion

While today the concept of the church may seem to some to be bound to an exclusive and even unitary christian narrative, profoundly compromised by its history and only one among many religious others, variation within the conceptual category church is and has been extensive. Over the course of the two thousand plus years of christian history, many ecclesia have appeared, and an ongoing disagreement about where the church is located has been omnipresent. Many of these forms have been present over the course of US history. What unity is there within and among churches and what unity should law acknowledge?

First Amendment scholars Ira Lupu and Robert Tuttle argue that the unanimity in *Hosanna-Tabor* can be explained by an agreement among the justices that courts have no competence when it comes to deciding church matters, that is, with respect to "matters ecclesiastical."[93] Such matters are understood by the justices, they say, to be singularly difficult of resolution,

90. Rivers, *The Law of Organized Religions*, 324.
91. Rivers, *The Law of Organized Religions*, 335.
92. Rivers, *The Law of Organized Religions*, 336.
93. Lupu and Tuttle, "The Mystery of Unanimity."

requiring skills that the judges lack; such matters display a singular level of nonrationality, perhaps. Questions of church governance are understood by them to be radically irresolvable questions. Courts, of course, make very difficult decisions all the time. Is religion different? Lupu and Tuttle—and the Court, when it acts on this theory—reproduce the enlightenment critique of religion and perform once again the separation necessary to support the modern state and its particular appropriation/suppression of religion.

It is now a commonplace among comparative religio-legal scholars to see secularism and secular law in particular as essentially about constantly drawing and redrawing the line between religion and nonreligion on behalf of the state's own projects.[94] There is an anxious effort on the part of secular legal thinkers and courts to narrow the scope of what might be considered purely religious matters in which the state has no competence or maybe no interest—matters so irrational as to not admit of legal cognizance. In the church property cases in the US, that line-drawing is made by way of the word "ecclesiastical."

There is little pretense in the Supreme Court's decisions that other religious communities are protected by this rule of deference. It is a rule about "the church."[95] The ministerial role described by the Court is one explicitly and historically defined by and confined to Christianity.[96] Indeed, the rationality of the ministerial exemption is enhanced when the particular history of the right of the church to choose her own ministers is emphasized.[97] The further one gets from this particular version of English

94. See, e.g., Hussein Ali Agrama, *Questioning Secularism: Islam, Sovereignty, and the Rule of Law in Egypt* (Chicago: University of Chicago Press, 2012). See also Benjamin L. Berger, *Law's Religion: Religious Difference and the Claims of Constitutionalism* (Toronto: University of Toronto Press, 2015), and Laborde, *Liberalism's Religion*.

95. See Lupu and Tuttle on why the Court all agreed on the history of the "perfect convergence of establishment and free exercise." "The Mystery of Unanimity," 1284. See also *Pfeil v. St. Matthews Evangelical Lutheran Church of the Unaltered Augsburg Confession*, 877 N.W.2d 528 (Minn. 2016), cert. denied, in which the Supreme Court of Minnesota, citing *Kedroff, Serbian Orthodox*, and *Hosanna-Tabor*, denied civil jurisdiction on the ground of the "ecclesiastical exemption" doctrine in a suit for defamation based on alleged falsehoods uttered during a church adjudicatory.

96. The role they insist is "functional" not ecclesiastical is about "teaching, leading others in worship, and otherwise communicating the faith through words." Lupu and Tuttle, "The Mystery of Unanimity," 1278. With Justice Alito, they assume that this role is universal among religious traditions.

97. According to Lupu and Tuttle, the constitutional settlement is essentially about "transmission of the faith." "The Mystery of Unanimity," 1314.

church history, the less the exemption can be explained or managed. Lupu and Tuttle insist that "*Hosanna-Tabor* reaffirmed the limited competence of a secular state."[98] But that affirmation has come in service of a particular view of the church-in-law.

Turning to this chapter's epigraph from the performance of Pussy Riot in the Cathedral of Christ the Savior in Moscow, how might their intervention be understood to challenge the consolidation of the church-in-law? Melissa Caldwell, in a recent article about religious pluralism and sacred spaces in Moscow, explains that Pussy Riot's performance should not be understood as a sacrilegious transgression of the ur-sacred space of Russian Orthodoxy, but rather as a religious violation of a civic space of a certain Russian nationalism, one that in many ways is quite secular.[99] Christ the Savior, she explains, is not a diocesan church but a nationalist monument built with private funds and maintained by the state, not by the church. In the memorable words of Bruce Grant, quoted by Caldwell, Christ the Savior can be described as a "strategem of innocence" in which public monuments and other forms of monumental architecture "tranquilize or freeze time."[100] Echoing the story told by Vera Shevzov about the late-nineteenth-century Russian lay movements, it is not there, according to Caldwell, but in the other distinctively post-Soviet improvised spaces, former office buildings and factories, that religious and political work is actually being done today by any number of appealing characters ministering to those caught in the gaps: "Robust cooperative partnerships have emerged between otherwise competing religious communities and between religious and governmental organizations and even security agencies."[101]

Turning to Pussy Riot's complex performance in Christ the Savior, cited in an epigraph to this chapter, both their words and gestures have been read by some as laying claim to being prophetic calls from within the tradition rather than as sacrilegious.[102] On this reading, it is Pussy Riot who

98. Lupu and Tuttle, "The Mystery of Unanimity," 1315.

99. Melissa Caldwell, "Sacred Spaces and Civic Action: Topographies of Pluralism in Russia," *Religion and Society* (forthcoming).

100. Bruce Grant, "New Moscow Monuments, or, States of Innocence," *American Ethnologist* 28, no. 2 (2001): 332–362.

101. Caldwell, "Sacred Spaces and Civic Action."

102. Vera Shevzov, "Women on the Fault Lines of Faith: Pussy Riot and the Insider/Outsider Challenge to Post-Soviet Orthodoxy," *Religion & Gender* 4 (2014): 121–144.

is arguably *the* church, not Christ the Savior. As we will see in the next chapter, the church-in-law can be seen to present a convergence between the capacity of both religion and law to traffic in imagined beings while at the same time limiting and excluding the possibility of such collective reform.

CHAPTER THREE

Hobby Lobby: The Church, the State, and the Corporation

The corporation entered the twentieth century as an immortal super-citizen.—Bethany Moreton, *To Serve God and Wal-Mart*[1]

Introduction

In the church property cases, it is what US courts call the hierarchical church that is increasingly deferred to in US law. One might offer various explanations for this apparent anomaly, but partly it seems it is because it is only in the church that an ever more ambitious federal legal power sees an alternative legal regime that it can recognize and respect as a partner in governance and trust as a regulator of religious freedom. We can see in that deference recognition of the church-state mimesis described by Kantorowicz, Rivers, and others.[2] The Court apparently believes that it can divide what is truly religious from what is not through jurisdictional thinking. Local congregational churches can be seen over the same period to have been secularized by their closeness to other associational forms and are therefore more porous, being available for secular

1. Bethany Moreton, *To Serve God and Wal-Mart: The Making of Christian Free Enterprise* (Cambridge: Harvard University Press, 2010), 13.

2. See above at 43–44, 88.

forms of regulation and demands for democratic and contractual accountability. Hierarchical churches, coevolutionary with the state, even while in some fundamental sense un-American, retain a separate and sacred distinctiveness.

Churches, whether congregational or hierarchical, are not the only form of religious organization in the US, of course. Nonchristian forms of religious collectivity also organize themselves in American law, although when they do so, they do so primarily by analogy with the church, as for example with the Native American Church and the Buddhist Churches of America.[3] But arguably more pertinent—and certainly more prevalent—is the corporation, both for-profit and not-for-profit corporations; businesses also turn out to be bodies demanding sovereign recognition and deference. Indeed, the corporation turns out to be more church-like, more "strictly ecclesiastical" even than the congregation in some ways, because it also shares sovereignty with the state. Further development of the doctrine of *Hosanna-Tabor*, that is, the doctrine that the religious collective has constitutional rights that are prior to the individual, was next taken up by the Court in the case of the business corporation. There is a sense in which there is a profound interchangeability among the church, the state, and the corporation—the state and the corporation borrowing from the church the sign of the sovereign as sacred.[4]

In its 2014 decision in *Burwell v. Hobby Lobby*,[5] a suit to prevent enforcement of the contraceptive mandate in the Affordable Care Act, the Supreme Court found Hobby Lobby, Inc., a nationwide company selling crafts materials through retail outlets, and two other corporate plaintiffs each to have a right of exemption from operation of the act, exemptions founded in the 1993 Religious Freedom Restoration Act (RFRA).[6] As with *Hosanna-Tabor*, the Court in *Hobby Lobby* again appeared to honor

3. These formations were deliberate efforts to mimic the christian church. Other less obvious christianizing of imported religious traditions can be seen in the conforming of nonchristians to protestant Sunday worship, fundraising, religious education, and forms of pastoral care, thereby making themselves legible to an overwhelmingly Christian American religious imaginary.

4. See Yelle, *Sovereignty and the Sacred* and Cavanaugh, *Migrations of the Holy*.

5. *Burwell v. Hobby Lobby Stores*, 573 U.S. 682 (2014).

6. 42 U.S.C.S. § 2000bb et seq. The companies had no claim based in the free exercise clause of the First Amendment under the holding in *Employment Division v. Smith*. The Religious Freedom Restoration Act was passed by Congress to remedy the Court's decision in *Smith*. See Winnifred Fallers Sullivan, "The World Smith Made" in Winnifred Fallers Sullivan, Elizabeth Shakman Hurd, Saba Mahmood, and Peter Danchin, eds., *Politics of Religious Freedom* (Chicago: University of Chicago Press, 2015).

the religious rights of the corporate over the individual, giving the corporate religious entity a power to resist the law—a kind of sovereignty—that was denied to individuals within it.[7]

That Hobby Lobby was a natural successor in law to Hosanna-Tabor and should be recognized as a religious organization was immediately assumed by lawyers before the high Court. In the oral argument in the *Hobby Lobby* case, Don Verilli, then solicitor general of the United States, commenting on the status of religious exemptions for religious organizations, referred to "that special solicitude, which the Court recognized in *HosannaTabor*."[8] Michael McConnell, a senior religion clause scholar and author of an amicus brief filed in *Hobby Lobby* on behalf of religious publishers, said of the Court's decision in *Hosanna-Tabor*: "It is not too much to say that the decision augurs a 'new birth of freedom' for the religious communities of America."[9] Both lawyers assumed that *Hobby Lobby* was such a religious community.

Is Hobby Lobby a religious organization deserving of special solicitude? Is it a church? Both McConnell and Verilli speak generally of religious communities or religious organizations, but what they are both talking about is *the* church. Phenomenologically speaking, it is *the* church that the Court recognizes in *Hobby Lobby*, just as it did in *Hosanna-Tabor*. It is the corporation as church that grounds the religious status of conscientious opposition to abortifacients for the Court.

Three separate cases were consolidated in *Hobby Lobby*. In each case, a for-profit commercial corporation (Hobby Lobby, Conestoga Wood Specialties, and Mardel) claimed that compliance with the contraceptive mandate in the Affordable Care Act would burden that company's exercise of religion as protected by the Religious Freedom Restoration Act because each company would be required to purchase health insurance for its employees that covered four kinds of contraception that each company sincerely believed to be an abortifacient. The Secretary of the Department of Health and Human Services argued in response that for-profit

7. Radical citizens groups have long demonstrated against corporate power of various kinds. On the sovereign citizen movement, see Spencer Dew, *The Aliites: Race and Law in the Religions of Noble Drew Ali* (Chicago: University of Chicago Press, 2019).

8. Oral argument transcript, *Hobby Lobby*, No. 13-354 at 57. https://www.supremecourt.gov/oral_arguments/argument_transcripts/2013/13-354_3ebh.pdf/.

9. McConnell, "Reflections on *Hosanna-Tabor*," 837. The brief he wrote in *Hobby Lobby* was on behalf of the Christian Booksellers Association, Deseret Book Company, Feldheim Publishers, and Tyndale House Publishers, Inc., as Amici Curiae in support of Hobby Lobby and Conestoga. See Brief of the Christian Booksellers Association et al.

corporations are not persons within the meaning of RFRA and therefore do not enjoy the protection of the act. The secretary also argued that even if the companies were protected by RFRA, the burden on them of compliance with the law was too insubstantial and attenuated to require exemption. In the secretary's view, it is only the decisions of individual employees that triggers coverage, not the decisions of the companies.[10] Some of the amicus briefs supporting the government in *Hobby Lobby* argued that corporations—especially perhaps for-profit corporations—are incapable of exercising religion. Only natural persons can do that, they said.[11]

Many observers were shocked at the *Hobby Lobby* decision's seeming endorsement of the view that religion and profit might be mixed. Their secularist creed teaches them that religion is not of this world. Yet the religious story told by the Greens, the owners of Hobby Lobby, and by the other plaintiffs in the case, is one with a long pedigree in religious history. Explicitly realizing your religious commitments through your working life can be traced back to Martin Luther, at least, and Max Weber explored these developments in *The Protestant Ethic and the Spirit of Capitalism*.[12] In the US the history of the corporate form is itself deeply entwined with the history of the church. The same people undertook to organize both religion and business in the early republic.[13] Such an admixture is also a feature more generally of the evangelical movement and of evangelical ecclesial consciousness, broadly understood.

In recognizing the three corporations as persons within the meaning of the act, the *Hobby Lobby* Court was able to privilege the corporation over the employees, giving preference to the corporation's views on contraception over that of the employees. Consistent with the political theology expounded by Douglas Laycock at oral argument in *Hosanna-Tabor*, discussed in chapter one, the corporation in *Hobby Lobby* was understood, like the church, to be responsible for forming the consciences of those employees—and perhaps also of its customers. To enforce the Affordable Care mandate against Hobby Lobby was, in this theology, akin to enforcing the ADA against Hosanna-Tabor. It would have constituted interference with "the faith and mission of the church itself."[14]

10. Oral argument transcript Hobby Lobby, No. 13-354 at 80. https://www.supremecourt.gov/oral_arguments/argument_transcripts/2013/13-354_3ebh.pdf/.

11. See, e.g., Amicus Curiae Brief of Corporate and Criminal Law Professors in Support of Petitioners.

12. Max Weber, *The Protestant Ethic and the Spirit of Capitalism*, trans. Talcott Parsons (London: G. Allen & Unwin, Ltd., 1930).

13. See, e.g., Funk, "Church Corporations."

14. 565 U.S. at 173.

The *Hobby Lobby* decision is one more chapter in the long and complex story of the intertwining of religion, business, gender, and sexuality in the US. The exercise of religion for which RFRA protection was claimed in *Hobby Lobby* was the refusal to provide insurance coverage for contraception. That this refusal was an exercise of religion was simply accepted by the Court—by both the majority and the dissent. Opposition to legal contraception and abortion was assumed to be religiously motivated. No evidence was required. The eliding of the possibility that evidence might be needed on such an assertion disregards scholarship showing that while the regulation of women's bodies and of sexuality more generally has long been a preoccupation of both church and state, the particular recent thematizing of reproductive rights and other political issues around sex and gender in the US, has a very specific history that can in many ways be understood as primarily, maybe even quintessentially, secular and economic.[15]

This chapter will look closely at the *Hobby Lobby* decision, placing it within both the history of the business corporation in US law and the history of the regulation of sex and reproduction. Counterintuitively perhaps, it is the former that is the better religion story. One can make a more persuasive case that Hobby Lobby is an instantiation of the church than that its decision not to cover certain forms of contraception is the product of a specifically religious conscience.

Burwell v. Hobby Lobby

The Affordable Care Act (ACA)[16] requires employers with fifty or more full-time employees to offer "a group health plan or group health insurance coverage" that provides "minimum essential coverage."[17] The guidelines promulgated by the US Department of Health and Human Services

15. See Elizabeth Bernstein and Janet R. Jakobsen, "Sex, Secularism, and Religious Influence in US Politics," *Third World Quarterly* 31, no. 6 (September 2010): 1023–1039; R. Marie Griffith, *Moral Combat: How Sex Divided American Christians and Fractured American Politics* (New York: Basic Books, 2017); Scott, *Sex and Secularism*; Saba Mahmood, *Religious Difference in a Secular Age: A Minority Report* (Princeton: Princeton University Press, 2015); and Melinda Cooper, *Family Values: Between Neoliberalism and New Social Conservatism* (Cambridge, MA: MIT Press, 2017).

16. 26 U.S.C. §5000A(f)(2); §§4980H(a), (c)(2).

17. It is important to note that this case arises because health insurance in the US is generally provided through employers. Universal health care through a single payer would significantly reduce these kinds of cases.

(HHS) define "minimum essential coverage" to mean that nonexempt employers are, among other things, generally required to provide "coverage, without cost sharing" for "[a]ll Food and Drug Administration [(FDA)] approved contraceptive methods, sterilization procedures, and patient education and counseling for all women with reproductive capacity."[18] The guidelines also authorized the establishment of specific exemptions from the contraceptive mandate for "religious employers."[19] Exhibiting a clear privileging of christian corporate bodies and their lobbying power, "[r]eligious employers" are defined by the guidelines, to include only "churches, their integrated auxiliaries, and conventions or associations of churches," as well as "the exclusively religious activities of any religious order."[20] "Religious order" here denotes Roman Catholic orders of monks and nuns. HHS has also exempted certain religious nonprofit organizations, described under HHS regulations as "eligible organizations," from the contraceptive mandate.[21] Other employers are exempted or grandfathered for other reasons.[22]

The three plaintiffs joined in *Hobby Lobby* all claimed that they enjoyed a RFRA exemption from the ACA mandate. RFRA provides that

> (a) In general
>
> Government shall not substantially burden a person's exercise of religion even if the burden results from a rule of general applicability, except as provided in subsection (b) of this section.
>
> (b) Exception
>
> Government may substantially burden a person's exercise of religion only if it demonstrates that application of the burden to the person—

18. 77 Fed. Reg. 8725.

19. 45 CFR §147.131(a). These exemptions were the result of powerful lobbying of Congress and direct negotiations with the White House.

20. 78 Fed. Reg. 39874 (2013).

21. See 45 CFR §147.131(b). An "eligible organization" is tautologically described as a nonprofit organization that "holds itself out as a religious organization" and "opposes providing coverage for some or all of any contraceptive services required to be covered . . . on account of religious objections."

22. The many exemptions in the ACA, politically necessary to passage of the bill, set the government up for the successful argument by the companies in this case that the government's interest in universal coverage was not sufficiently "compelling" under RFRA to justify the substantial burden on the companies. If the government had regarded the mandate as really compelling, so the argument goes, it would not have granted exemptions so readily.

(1) is in furtherance of a compelling governmental interest; and

(2) is the least restrictive means of furthering that compelling governmental interest.[23]

Each argued that enforcement of the contraceptive mandate against them would, in the language of the statute, "substantially burden" their exercise of religion because it would require them to do something in contravention of their religious beliefs, effectively prohibiting them from exercising their religion. They further argued that the government failed to meet the statutory override provision in section (b) by making a convincing showing that the mandate was "in furtherance of a compelling governmental interest" and was "the least restrictive means of furthering that interest."

A majority of the justices in *Hobby Lobby* held that the plaintiffs' exercise of religion had indeed been burdened by the requirements of the ACA, and that, while the government had shown a compelling interest in women's health care, it had not shown that the contraceptive mandate was the least restrictive means of furthering that interest. As evidence that other means of insuring quality women's healthcare were available to the government, the Court cited accommodations the government had made to other kinds of employers, as well as the available remedy of simply providing government-funded coverage for those employees disadvantaged by the exemptions.[24] The four dissenting justices argued that corporations are not persons for purposes of RFRA, but that even if they were found to be persons under that statute, the three corporate plaintiffs had not shown that they were substantially burdened by the law because the relationship between an employer and the decision of an individual employee to avail herself of the coverage is too distant and attenuated to constitute a burden on the company's exercise of religion. The dissent effectively challenged the plaintiffs' position on theological grounds, refusing the plaintiffs' claim that complying would involve them in what is called in theology "complicity with evil."[25]

Proof that an exercise of religion is involved is foundational to a RFRA claim. An "exercise of religion" is defined tautologically by the statute to include "any exercise of religion, whether or not compelled by, or central to, a system of religious belief."[26] The language of this broad and gener-

23. Religious Freedom Reformation Act, 42 U.S. Code §2000bb et seq.
24. 573 U.S. at 72.
25. M. Cathleen Kaveny, "Complicity with Evil," *Criterion* (2003): 20–29.
26. 42 U.S. Code § 2000cc-5, (7) (a).

ous legislative gesture beyond what courts have sometimes termed "core beliefs" emerged in the congressional hearings leading up to passage of RFRA. Congress evinced a clear and very American intention to throw a wide protective net around religion of all kinds. Most courts, too, given both a broadly shared sense of judicial incompetence in such matters and the inherent difficulty of distinguishing religious from nonreligious exercise have tended to simply accept plaintiffs' assertions of its presence. It is rare for the religiousness or not of a particular practice to be in dispute. In the absence of red flags, religion is mostly just silently assumed. In its briefs, Hobby Lobby simply asserted that its beliefs were religious without reference to religious authorities or texts.

This chapter will separately consider the argument for regarding plaintiff corporations as churches, and the religiousness of the plaintiffs' objections to the mandate but it is important to recognize that the two are an inseparable pair. There is a sense in which the recent cultural naturalization of the necessary link between religion and conservative views on sex and reproduction gives added weight in *Hobby Lobby* to its corporate claim to churchness. In other words, the Court's logic seems to be that Hobby Lobby Inc., as a person protected by RFRA, opposes reproductive choice and therefore it must be doing so on religious grounds. The corporateness of religiousness and the religiousness of corporateness is finessed in this elision, turning on the assumed essentialism of religion's distinctive concern for women's bodies.

As religious corporations, Hobby Lobby and Conestoga and Mardel connect to a longer history of overlapping and interchangeable fictive personalities, church, state, and corporation.[27]

Corporate religion

Scholars of the corporation today do not agree about the legal nature of the corporation.[28] Some argue that the corporation is merely a contractual

27. The university also belongs in the roster of historical sovereigns, sharing a history with church, state and corporation. The Court recognized the First Amendment's protection of academic freedom in *Sweezy v. New Hampshire*, 354 U.S. 234 (1957), recognizing also that the right belongs to the institution, not to the individual. See Tomoko Masuzawa, "The University and the Advent of the Academic Secular: the State's Management of Public Instruction," in Winnifred Fallers Sullivan, Mateo Taussig-Rubbo, and Robert Yelle, eds., *After Secular Law* (Palo Alto: Stanford University Press, 2011).

28. For a general introduction to the history of the corporation in the US, see Naomi R. Lamoreaux and William J. Novak, eds., *Corporations and American Democracy* (Cambridge: Harvard University Press, 2017).

arrangement reducible to the economic interests and activities of those who own and control it. Others argue that it is something more, an entity of its own—more, in other words, than the sum of its parts.[29] These two legal theories are understood to correspond to theories of the appropriate spheres of public and private authority. While the long history of the corporate form might be traced back to medieval guilds and towns (or further into Roman law antecedents), during most of its early modern history each corporation was created by special legislation only after proof was made of its benefit to the public. It was that benefit that justified the limited liability enjoyed by its owners. That practice changed in the US over the course of the nineteenth century. The corporation took on a distinctively new legal life, one that enabled its private contractual power.

This new life is often traced to the opinion of Chief Justice John Marshall in the famed and much argued about 1819 *Dartmouth College* case.[30] The case concerned the constitutionality of New Hampshire legislation designed to provide public oversight over Dartmouth College, then a small christian college. Marshall, interpreting the 1769 charter granted to Dartmouth College by George III in light of the subsequent US Constitution, found that what had been, prior to the Revolution, a public institution subject to regulation by Parliament had been converted by the US Constitution's clause forbidding impairment of contract into a private entity.[31] On this theory, New Hampshire's effort to regulate it in the public interest was found to be "repugnant to the Constitution."[32] In affirming the sanctity of contract under the US Constitution, Marshall underlined the privileged space of private economic activity in the US.

Dartmouth College is also understood to have marked a change in the relationship of the church to the state, as historian Mark McGarvie explains:

> In protecting Dartmouth College's authority as an incorporated Christian school, the Court recognized religion as belonging in the private sector . . . The separation of church and state, completed everywhere except in New England

29. Margaret M. Blair summarizes the history of this scholarship in the US in "Corporate Personhood and the Corporate Persona," *University of Illinois Law Review* 3 (2013): 785–820. See also her coauthored chapter, "The Supreme Court's View of Corporate Rights: Two Centuries of Evolution and Controversy," in Lamoreaux and Novak, *Corporations and American Democracy* (with Elizabeth Pollman).

30. *Trustees of Dartmouth College v. Woodward*, 17 U.S. 518 (1819).

31. U.S. Const. art. I, §10.

32. 17 US at 654.

> by 1819, ultimately reached the northeastern states through the court's clarification of the contract clause as a delineation of private and public sectors.[33]

Together with the corporation, the church was arguably now an entirely private matter; as such it had an ambiguous relationship to the state with no formal right of participation. McGarvie has argued that "[*Dartmouth College*] was a pyrrhic victory for the church," depriving it of a public role.

The case did not have these effects instantly. Historian Margaret Blair argues that this notion of the corporation as simply private and transactional did not actually take firm hold until after the creation of general incorporation acts in the mid-nineteenth century under which proof of a public benefit was no longer required. With the passage of those acts, private individuals could form corporations, and benefit from the limited liability they provided, for virtually any noncriminal purpose. These statutes hugely diffused the focus on the public benefit that corporations were formerly understood to bring and the justification for their myriad privileges in law.

The earlier public entity theory did not entirely recede. By the end of the nineteenth century, as the number of corporations had increased and private corporate power had become a source of anxiety, the idea that corporations were real entities began to take the place of private contract theories, under the influence of such European legal theorists as Otto Gierke and William Maitland.[34] Blair argues that American scholars too "began exploring the idea that groups of people organized into associations, and especially those organized into corporations, might take on a group personality that was different from the personality of each member of the group."[35] They "came to perceive the corporation as something more than either a creation of the state or just an aggregate of the

33. Mark McGarvie, "The Dartmouth College Case, the Contract Clause, and the Creation of the Private Sector." HistPhil forum, https://histphil.org/2019/07/23/the-dartmouth-college-case-the-contract-clause-and-the-creation-of-the-private-sector/.

34. Blair, "Corporate Personhood," 806. See also Antony Black, ed., *Community in Historical Perspective*, a translation of selections from Otto von Gierke, *Das Deutsche Genossenschaftrecht* (The German Law of Fellowship), trans. Mary Fisher (Cambridge: Cambridge University Press, 1990); and Frederic William Maitland, *State, Trust, and Corporation*, ed. David Runciman and Magnus Ryan (Cambridge: Cambridge University Press, 2003).

35. This was partly in an effort to explain and justify the holding of the Supreme Court in *Santa Clara County v. Southern Pacific Railroad Company*, 118 U.S. 394 (1886). *Santa Clara*, a case concerning corporate taxation, is often taken to be the first case in which corporate personhood was recognized as having constitutional status, although the actual holding in the case is a great deal more ambiguous.

shareholders—rather, it was 'an organic social reality' with an existence independent of, and constituting something more than, its changing shareholders."[36] Thus a phenomenological, as well as a contractual argument, was made as to the source of corporate power.

Blair concludes her history with the rise of the law and economics movement at the end of the twentieth century and a subsequent scholarly return to a contractual theory of the corporation. "The dominant theory of corporations in the last few decades," she says, "in finance and in law has been a reductionist, finance inspired approach that regards corporations as mere contractual devices, with no truly separate existence, for which it is misleading and even foolish to speak of such things as the goal, reputation, will, or moral duties of the corporation apart from its contracting agents."[37] However, she continues, "The effort by financial market players in recent years to create value by simply repackaging the assets and liabilities of corporations without regard to the impact of such maneuvers on reputation and trust in the entity as a whole, let alone on the financial markets as a whole, it seems to me, is one expression of this mentality."[38] Blair argues then that the recent return to a contractual theory of the corporation has led to serious moral lapses because such a theory makes it more difficult to locate and punish corporate misdeeds. The entity theory, she believes, makes visible the corporation as a person who can act for or against the public interest.

Scholars have disagreed about whether corporations are in fact distinct entities in a phenomenological sense, they have also disagreed about which legal theory of the corporation promotes better corporate behavior. Blair concludes that it is "time for financial and legal economics to rethink the contractarian theories and models that have been guiding much corporate law scholarship in recent years . . . The idea that corporations can have a separate persona would be a useful part of that inquiry."[39] For her, recognition of corporate personhood—and its necessary public responsibilities—would curtail overreaching by corporations and foster corporate responsibility, even while they remain constitutionally protected by *Dartmouth College*.

36. Blair, "Corporate Personhood," 806, quoting Phillip I. Blumberg, "The Corporate Personality in American Law: A Summary Review," *American Journal of Comparative Law* 38:49 (1990).

37. Blair, "Corporate Personhood," 819.

38. Blair, "Corporate Personhood," 819.

39. Blair, "Corporate Personhood," 820.

There is an interesting parallel here to the legal theory of the nature of the church discussed in the previous chapter. The risk involved in treating corporations or churches as simply private contractual vehicles for individual persons, as *Watson* suggests that churches are, is interestingly illustrated in the recent coming home to roost of the *Dartmouth College* decision for the college itself, celebrating its bicentennial this year. A group of students staged a rearguing of the case for the occasion.[40] While Justice Marshall's opinion affirming Daniel Webster's argument on behalf of the independence of the college was celebrated by some as having helped to unleash capitalist growth in the US, other students argued that American law had lost sight of the public purpose argued for at the time by the losing party, the state of New Hampshire, that is, its charter obligations to Native students: "the education and instruction of youth of the Indian tribes in this land in reading, writing, and all parts of learning which shall appear necessary and expedient for civilizing and christianizing children of pagans."

The nature of the corporation has also recently enjoyed the attention of political and cultural historians telling longer histories of extra-state corporate activities.[41] Histories of one of the early modern precursors to the modern business corporation, the English East India Company, for example, arguably one of the most successful corporations in history, have become resources to those critical of the power of the current multinational corporation. Historian Philip Stern comments of the new fascination with the East India Company by contemporary legal theorists of the corporation that it is "perhaps unsurprising given the great legal, political, and economic conundrums surrounding the modern multinational corporation, from questions about global management to controversial issues such as tax inversions, monopoly, state-owned corporations, as well as the corporate person's rights to free speech, religion, and so on."[42] But this new work, Stern says, often misunderstands the nature of the Company.

40. Robert Bonner, "How Dartmouth College Commemorated the Bicentennial of the Dartmouth College Case," HistPhil forum, https://histphil.org/2019/07/16/how-dartmouth-college-commemorated-the-bicentennial-of-the-dartmouth-college-case/.

41. See, e.g., John O'Brien, *Literature Incorporated: The Cultural Unconscious of the Business Corporation, 1650–1850* (Chicago: University of Chicago Press, 2016).

42. Philip Stern, "The English East India Company and the Modern Corporation: Legacies, Lessons, and Limitations," *Seattle University Law Review* 39, no. 2 (Winter 2016): 424.

Stern divides interest in the English East India Company into two main threads. Those telling the history of capitalism see it as a form of proto-capitalism in embryo. Others, more interested in the company's state-like qualities, focus on the extraordinary sovereignty enjoyed by the company. Because the company was in many ways quite unlike the modern business corporation as an economic and legal matter, what is most potent in the comparison, Stern urges, is to see the ways in which the company exercised sovereignty; seeing those aspects of the company's exercise of its power can help us, in Stern's view, to see how contemporary transnational corporations do so as well–religious ones as well as secular ones.

At various points in its almost four-century existence, the East India Company drafted its own laws, held its own courts, printed its own currency, engaged in treaty-making, and exercised military authority over populations. What this history shows us, Stern suggests, is an entity more state-like than business-like—one that exercised both private and public functions in a field more characterized by divisible and overlapping sovereignty than by exclusively territorial sovereignty. Indeed, Stern concludes that "what the East India Company's history shows us is how state and corporation are mutually constituted, and in fact, derive from similar and shared ideological and historical contexts."[43] "The unique power of the corporation as an institution," he says, "created by the state and constantly standing in opposition to and outside of it can be seen as an extension of the early modern corporate sovereignty exhibited by bodies like the East India Company which are only amplified in an age of modern globalization."[44] The East India Company was not the only such company. Others enjoying plenary powers over land and peoples included the Hudson's Bay Company.[45]

One might extend Stern's observations about the nature of the sovereignty of the East India Company to the church. Churches, like corporations and states, operate transnationally, create law, exercise authority over populations, negotiate with governments, and control territory. They too have been transformed by the same early modern history, exchanging properties with their sovereign siblings, the corporation and the state. Indeed, the English East India Company itself

43. Stern, "The English East India Company," 441.

44. Stern, "The English East India Company," 441.

45. Edward Cavanagh, "A Company with Sovereignty and Subjects of Its Own? The Case of the Hudson's Bay Company, 1670–1763," *Canadian Journal of Law and Society* 26 (2011): 25–50.

had its own church-like aspects: for example, ministerial employees of various kinds, including hundreds of chaplains, offered pastoral care to its own employees and missionized the population within the territory it governed. The hiring process included delivering sample sermons to the directors.[46]

Geographer Joshua Barkan has also studied the history and personality of the modern corporation. He describes its sovereign powers and its frequent legally sanctioned immunity from law, adding policing and the right to decide who lives and who dies to the list of its extralegal powers, powers seen by Barkan to constitute an exercise of biopolitical control in the logic of the ban, in the Schmittian and Agambenian sense.[47] Corporations, Barkan argues, increasingly do all the work of the state—education, punishment, war-making, arbitration—and, of course, the provision of health care. According to Barkan, the key to understanding corporate power is understanding the tragedy of its doubleness. In its collectivity, the corporation both empowers and oppresses the individual. Also like the church and the state, the corporation is embedded in a web of bourgeois capitalist commitments that determine its emancipatory potential.[48]

While Justice Alito in his opinion for the majority in *Hobby Lobby* paid lip service to the idea that any rights enjoyed by Hobby Lobby were simply traceable to the rights of the owners, in a kind of pass-through contractual theory of the corporation (one recognizable as the private law and economics model mentioned by Blair and Barkan), he also continually recognized and spoke of the corporate plaintiffs in *Hobby Lobby* as having personalities and capacities independent of those of their owners. Indeed, notwithstanding Justice Alito's occasional efforts to describe the views and affects of the corporate plaintiffs as simply a shorthand for

46. "The East India Company . . . employed hundreds of chaplains. Many of those were promised shares in the company as a part of their pay for preaching sermons and tending to the moral character of the employees. Chaplains were understood to be critical to ensuring the company's success, together with that of the empire, as a political, commercial, and spiritual enterprise." Sullivan, *A Ministry of Presence*, citing Daniel O'Connor, *The Chaplains of the East India Company 1601–1858* (New York: Continuum, 2012), 61.

47. Joshua Barkan, *Corporate Sovereignty: Law and Government under Capitalism* (Minneapolis: University of Minnesota Press, 2013).

48. Literature scholar Henry Turner focuses on sixteenth- and seventeenth-century England to further specify the nature of the emerging modern corporation and the character of the corporate person. Henry S. Turner, *The Corporate Commonwealth: Pluralism and Political Fictions in England, 1516–1651* (Chicago: University of Chicago Press, 2016). Interestingly, both Barkan and Turner turn in the end to the university to illustrate what they each see to be the necessary emancipatory potential of the corporate as a location for reinvigorating the commons.

those of their owners, there is recurrent slippage between the two locutions in the opinion.

That Hobby Lobby and the other corporate plaintiffs in the *Hobby Lobby* case are recognized as churches in the *Hosanna-Tabor* sense can be shown by a close reading of the majority opinion in *Hobby Lobby* against the background of this longer history of corporate personhood—even sovereignty—as well as the Court's decision in *Citizens United* recognizing the political free speech rights of corporations.[49] Justice Alito repeatedly characterizes the plaintiff companies themselves as having missions, ethical obligations, and religious commitments. The dissenters engage in the same semantic blurring.

In introducing plaintiff Conestoga, Alito writes that "[t]he Hahns believe that they are required to run their business 'in accordance with their religious beliefs and moral principles' . . . the company's mission, as they see it, is to 'operate in a professional environment founded upon the highest ethical, moral, and Christian principles.'"[50] Further, he says: "The company's 'Vision and Values Statements' affirms that Conestoga endeavors to 'ensur[e] a reasonable profit in [a] manner that reflects [the Hahns'] Christian heritage.'"[51] As for Hobby Lobby, Alito explains that Hobby Lobby's statement of purpose commits the Greens to "[h]onoring the Lord in all [they] do by operating the company in a manner consistent with Biblical principles." He writes that

> [e]ach family member has signed a pledge to run the businesses in accordance with the family's religious beliefs and to use the family assets to support Christian ministries. In accordance with those commitments, Hobby Lobby and Mardel stores close on Sundays, even though the Greens calculate that they lose millions in sales annually by doing so. The businesses refuse to engage in profitable transactions that facilitate or promote alcohol use; they contribute profits to Christian missionaries and ministries; and they buy hundreds of full-page newspaper ads inviting people to "know Jesus as Lord and Savior."[52]

One can find further testimonials to Hobby Lobby's corporate mission in the many, many laudatory articles about the Greens in trade journals and

49. *Citizens United v. FEC*, 558 U.S. 310 (2010).
50. 573 U.S. at 701.
51. 573 U.S. at 701.
52. 573 U.S. at 703.

in christian media—about their intimately conjoined financial success and religious commitments.

In the first four paragraphs of his *Hobby Lobby* opinion Justice Alito is scrupulous in attributing religious views only to the individual owners, asserting that any legal rights with respect to religion are the rights of the owners who are natural human persons.[53] As he explains somewhat later, when he is defending the inclusion of the companies in the RFRA category of person, a corporation is a legal fiction: "Congress provided protection for people like the Hahns and Greens by employing a familiar legal fiction: It included corporations within RFRA's definition of 'persons.'" But, he continues, "it is important to keep in mind that the purpose of this fiction is to provide protection for human beings. A corporation is simply a form of organization used by human beings to achieve desired ends . . . protecting the free-exercise rights of corporations like Hobby Lobby, Conestoga, and Mardel protects the religious liberty of the humans who own and control those companies."[54] Alito here underlines the private contractual reading of the *Dartmouth College* legacy. But Alito's care to make this distinction lessens as the opinion proceeds, especially in the section in which he reads RFRA as protecting corporations as persons; the artificial person, the legal fiction, gains weight and independence and personality.[55] It also gains sovereignty. The slippage is revealing.

Alito makes the transition this way. While, on the one hand, he says that "[c]orporations, 'separate and apart from' the human beings who own, run, and are employed by them, cannot do anything at all,"[56] he also shows us the plaintiff corporations doing things. He describes them as having rights and as exercising them. He refers to "the religious liberty of religious nonprofit corporations" and he announces that "religious nonprofits . . . have religious objections."[57] He also underlines the government's concern to protect corporate as well as individual bodies: "HHS [United States Department of Health and Human Services] also authorized the HRSA [Health Resources and Services Administration] to establish exemptions

53. 573 U.S. 688–92.

54. 573 U.S. at 707.

55. Natural persons, or individuals, do not, of course, all enjoy the same legally enforceable rights. Prisoners, those deemed mentally disabled, children, and others (historically including slaves, indentured workers, and women) have fewer rights in the US today than the freely contracting white male imagined in *Dartmouth College*. All rights-bearing persons, individual and corporate, are in that sense artificial, enjoying such rights in law, not in nature.

56. 573 U.S. at 707.

57. 573 U.S. at 692.

from the contraceptive mandate for 'religious employers.' That category encompasses 'churches, their integrated auxiliaries, and conventions or associations of churches,' as well as 'the exclusively religious activities of any religious order.'"[58] And he adds that "HHS has effectively exempted certain religious nonprofit organizations, described under HHS regulations as 'eligible organizations,' from the contraceptive mandate."[59] An "eligible organization" means a nonprofit organization that "holds itself out as a religious organization" and "opposes providing coverage for some or all of any contraceptive services required to be covered . . . on account of religious objections."[60] And he describes the corporate parties as "refus[ing] to engage in profitable transactions that facilitate or promote alcohol use . . . contribut[ing] profits to Christian missionaries and ministries . . . buy[ing] hundreds of full-page newspaper ads inviting people to 'know Jesus as Lord and Savior.'"[61] The companies "have religious reasons for providing health-insurance coverage for their employees . . ." and "sincerely believe that providing the insurance coverage demanded by the HHS regulations lies on the forbidden side of the line."[62]

The plaintiff companies are repeatedly described by Alito and also by the dissenters as "having religious reasons" and as "believing." We are encouraged to understand these entities as having religious consciences, religious consciences that deserve our respect. The Court is at pains to explain that the corporate form and profit-making objectives do not in any way of themselves formally disqualify the three companies from being persons whose exercise of religion is protected by RFRA. Arguably that is what Chief Justice Marshall promised in his *Dartmouth College* decision.

One line of critique against the *Hobby Lobby* decision has been founded in a raw emotional reaction against the mixing of religion and profit. And yet corporateness and profit making have always been a part of US religion.[63] That is not new. A great many American businesspersons would describe themselves the way the Greens of Hobby Lobby and the Hahns

58. 573 U.S. at 698.
59. 573 U.S. at 698.
60. 573 U.S. at 698.
61. 573 U.S. at 703.
62. 573 U.S. at 685, 725.
63. For history of Wanamaker's department store in Philadelphia (1861–1986) that tells of Mr. Wanamaker's thoroughgoing evangelical piety and the way it infused the whole operation, see Nicole C. Kirk, *Wanamaker's Temple: The Business of Religion in an Iconic Department Store* (New York: New York University Press, 2018).

of Conestoga do. A friend who grew up in a small town in Tennessee describes her own father's mixing of church and business in the running of his store as follows: "the code for the invoice price of items—as opposed to retail—in my grandfather's and father's store (1900–1980) was the numerical values of the letters in the phrase 'By God's help.' There was also a sign on the door that read 'Closed Sundays. See you in church.'" "Holy Cow!," she added, "That seemed so natural when I was a kid!"[64]

In his amicus brief for the Christian Booksellers Association in the *Hobby Lobby* case, Michael McConnell forcefully argues this point:

> The government's cramped view of the purposes of for-profit corporations also flies in the face of the ordinary practice of the Christian and Jewish religions, the faiths most familiar to the framers of the First Amendment. Contrary to the government's anachronistic assumptions, these religions do not concern themselves only with worship on specified occasions, but encourage or require their members to adhere to the commands of God in their daily lives, including in the conduct of their businesses. Within those traditions, business is ideally a vocation to be conducted to the glory of God and in conformity to His commandments . . . Revealingly, the Puritans in New England often headed their business ledgers with the phrase "In the name of God and profit"—and did not see those purposes as a contradiction.[65]

That is not to say that there were/are not in all of these communities people with anxieties about the mixing, a concern, that is, that one cannot in good conscience serve both God and mammon without risking your soul. But profit making alone need not prevent these businesses from being considered a part of church life, just as the worldly work of Catholic religious orders and charities, work that is explicitly recognized by HHS and by the Court's dissenters as exempt and deserving of special protection, does not defeat their special status as a part of the church-in-law.

It is not just that the corporate plaintiffs in HobbyLobby should be understood to be entities capable of religious affect—as, in effect, avatars of *the* church. It is that churches are heir to the same modern history of

64. Personal email communication from Alexandra Brown, November 24, 2015. See Peter van der Veer, *The Modern Spirit of Asia* (Princeton: Princeton University Press, 2014), for a discussion of the religious power of modern money and financial transactions.

65. Brief of the Christian Booksellers Association at 16–17.

the sovereign corporate entity as the commercial company. The church of *Hosanna-Tabor* and the corporation of *Hobby Lobby* are both exercising sovereignty, a sovereignty they share with the state, a sovereignty that emerges from a common history.

Justice Ruth Bader Ginsburg's dissent in *Hobby Lobby*, in its effort to deny RFRA personhood to Hobby Lobby, ironically further enhances the corporate sovereignty of churches, particularly of the Roman Catholic Church. While she insists that "the exercise of religion is characteristic of natural persons, not of artificial legal entities,"[66] she also says, in making the further distinction between for-profit and not-for-profit corporations,[67] that she "would confine religious exemptions under that Act to organizations formed 'for a religious purpose,' 'engage[d] primarily in carrying out that religious purpose,' and not 'engaged . . . substantially in the exchange of goods or services for money beyond nominal amounts.'"[68] The exempt entities she is describing here are named in the regulations as "churches, their integrated auxiliaries, and conventions or associations of churches," as well as "the exclusively religious activities of any religious order."[69] In other words, she would limit exemption to the churchier church of the *Hosanna-Tabor* decision, arguably discriminating against the evangelical/pentecostal free church tradition of the *Hobby Lobby* plaintiffs, originating in the reformation era, as well as against non-christians.

Reproductive religion

Evidence that there had been the requisite *religious* exercise by the corporate plaintiffs in this case, one that might be substantially burdened and therefore entitled to protection under RFRA, was established in the majority opinion with simple declarations as to the convictions of the Hahns and the Greens, owners of the three companies joined as plaintiffs in *Hobby Lobby*: Conestoga Wood Specialties, Hobby Lobby, Inc., and Mardel, a chain of christian bookstores. No supporting evidence was of-

66. 573 U.S. at 752.

67. The distinction between profit and not-for-profit corporations is often blurred, legally speaking. See Jonathan Levy, "From Fiscal Triangle to Passing Through: Rise of the Nonprofit Corporation," in Lamoreaux and Novak, *Corporations and American Democracy*.

68. 573 U.S. at 772.

69. 573 U.S. at 697.

fered as to the religiousness of the plaintiffs' objection to the mandate of the Affordable Care Act.

Beginning with Conestoga, Alito tells us that "Norman and Elizabeth Hahn and their three sons are devout members of the Mennonite Church, a Christian denomination. The Mennonite Church opposes abortion and believes that '[t]he fetus in its earliest stages . . . shares humanity with those who conceived it.'"[70] With respect to Hobby Lobby, which is owned by David and Barbara Green, and Mardel, which is owned by their son, Alito states that "David and Barbara Green and their three children are Christians who own and operate two family businesses . . . Like the Hahns, the Greens believe that life begins at conception and that it would violate their religion to facilitate access to contraceptive drugs or devices that operate after that point."[71] In other words, the owners of these companies are represented by the Court to be devout christians who have objections to certain forms of contraception. Alito introduces the assertion with respect to the Hahns with the words "[l]ike the Greens," as if the elision were natural. Yet the Hahns and the Greens belong to very different church traditions, neither of which have always or consistently opposed abortion as a matter of religious conviction. How does the Court know that these convictions are religious ones? What if we called them moral? Or political? Or aesthetic? Or secular?

What makes an objection to abortion religious?[72] Why would a nonreligious objection to abortion not deserve the same exemption? In contrast to the Court's opinion in *Hosanna-Tabor*, there is no learned reference to church history. The Court seemingly expects that we somehow all know that devout christians oppose abortion. That is how you recognize a religious person these days. And yet that is not in fact the case, empirically speaking. Neither christians in general nor these christian churches in particular have always or unanimously opposed abortion. Furthermore, prohibition of abortion and restricted access to reproductive care has often been a policy of supposedly secular authorities.

The Court acknowledges no history of diversity within or change over

70. 573 U.S. at 700.

71. 573 U.S. at 702–03.

72. This question could be posed in a number of current contexts in which opposition to legislative mandates is premised on ostensibly religious grounds. What counts as religion for the exemptions being offered is deeply arbitrary and subject to shifting political discourses. See, e.g., with respect to opposition to vaccination, Gina Bellafonte, "Why Should Religion Be a Bar to Vaccines?" *New York Times* (April 14, 2019); J. D. Grabenstein, "What the World's Religions Teach, Applied to Vaccines and Immune Globulins," *Vaccine* 31 (2013): 2011–2023.

time in theological reflection on contraception in any of these religious communities, although there is now—and always has been—considerable difference of opinion. It is apparently obvious to the Court that beliefs about controlling reproduction are specifically religious and worthy of constitutional protection. The implication by contrast is that pro-choice positions are secular. How did that branding come about? (It is not just the Court that makes these assumptions, of course. These assumptions are widespread in the US today.)

With respect to the particular religious communities before the Court in *Hobby Lobby*—pentecostals and mennonites—there is in fact a complex history of concern with and attention to contraception and abortion.[73] Opinion is uniform neither over time nor across the various church communities that consider themselves mennonite or pentecostal. Indeed, that varied history can be seen in the variety of views expressed by the very mennonite and pentecostal churches whose members were before the Court in *Hobby Lobby*.

Mennonite churches in the US are descendants of churches formed in Germany and in Dutch-speaking central Europe in the sixteenth century. They take their name from Menno Simons, a former Catholic priest who was a leader of sixteenth-century anabaptist groups persecuted both by catholics and by other protestants. The first mennonite communities in North America were formed in the 1680s. Many more immigrated during the eighteenth century. With other anabaptist christians, including the amish, mennonites are conventionally distinguished from other protestant christians by their rejection of infant baptism, their refusal of certain aspects of modern industrial society, and also by their pacifism. Most were separatists—they opposed state patronage of churches[74]—and most also

73. Thank you to Courtney Bender for calling my attention to the mennonite story.

74. See from a website maintained to define mennonite theology, an article denominated "Church, Doctrine of":

> One of the most characteristic features of Anabaptism is its church concept. The church (*Gemeinde*), according to the Anabaptists, is a voluntary and exclusive fellowship of truly converted believers in Christ, committed to follow Him in full obedience as Lord; it is a brotherhood, not an institution. It is completely separated from the state, which is to have no power over the church; and the members of the church in turn do not hold office in the magistracy. There is to be complete freedom of conscience, no use of force or compulsion by state or church; faith must be free. In these principles the Anabaptists were pioneers and forerunners of modern religious liberty and the free church. This church concept was held in sharp distinction from the prevailing inclusive concept of both Catholic and Protestant state-churchism, namely, that of the mass church (*Volkskirche*) coterminous with the

opposed slavery. In the last several hundred years, mennonites have split over various issues, mostly with respect to the degree to which mennonites should accommodate to modern ways of life, some more insistent on retaining the plain way of life of the old order amish, others modernizing in various ways.

The Hahns belong to the Lichty Mennonite Church in East Earl, Pennsylvania, a church that is affiliated with a group of nineteen congregations that broke with the Lancaster Conference of the Mennonite Church in 1999 because of differences over sanctity of life politics, among other issues. Together they formed the Keystone Mennonite Fellowship.[75] Opposition to contraception or to legalized abortion has not historically been a distinguishing feature of mennonite theology. It is opposition to military service that has historically distinguished mennonites in the public square. The Keystone Fellowship, with which the Hahns' church is affiliated, opened a new chapter in mennonite politics when it pledged itself to a sanctity of life politics in 1999. Historians would trace the shift in the sexual politics of some mennonite groups as being better understood as in dialogue with US politics rather than as an expression of theological positions inherent historically to mennonite identity.[76] It is therefore not the case, as Justice Alito averred in his opinion, that "[t]he Mennonite Church opposes abortion and believes that '[t]he fetus in its earliest stages . . . shares humanity with those who conceived it.'"[77] Some mennonites do.

A similarly shifting politics might be said to characterize the pentecostal churches to which the Greens belong. David Green, the owner of Hobby Lobby, is the son of an Assembly of God preacher. His five siblings entered pentecostal ministry. In many interviews David Green has said that he could not be a preacher because he was not a good student, but that he and his wife regard their business as a religious venture. He and

---

> population of a state, into which all citizens are in effect born and are to be formally incorporated by universal and compulsory infant baptism and in which they remain until death.

http://gameo.org/index.php?title=Ecclesiology/.

75. http://gameo.org/index.php?title=Keystone_Mennonite_Fellowship (accessed January 22, 2018)

76. Mennonites have also had a shifting relationship to market capitalism. Courtney Bender explained to me in a personal communication that "Mennonites have long been anti-governmental or anti-state in some way, at least theologically. And, not consistently anti-capitalist." March 11, 2019. The ending of the military draft in the US might be understood to mark a moment in which some mennonites chose other means to display their opposition to the state.

77. 573 U.S. at 700.

his wife are billionaire philanthropists on a very large scale, having, among other projects, successfully established a Museum of the Bible in Washington, DC, to house their vast collection of ancient manuscripts.[78]

Pentecostal christianity is a global phenomenon. And a very diverse one. With scattered origins in the late nineteenth and early twentieth centuries, pentecostals—and other charismatic christians—center their religious practice in the works of the spirit. They anchor their witness in the events of Pentecost as described in the biblical book of Acts. They celebrate the work of the spirit in such experiences as glossolalia, ecstatic movements of the spirit, and what is called spirit baptism. They are not alone in this focus on the spirit. Periodic charismatic revivals have been experienced across christian denominations. Like mennonites, many pentecostals today are typically socially quite conservative. As with some mennonites, since the 1970s there has also been a political convergence in the US between some pentecostals and some evangelicals making common cause over political issues, including opposition to abortion.

As American religious historian Marie Griffith details in her new book, abortion has not always been an identifiably and exclusively religious issue in the US.[79] Griffith traces a mostly twentieth-century story of religion, sex, and politics in the US, beginning with the story of how, under the prodding of the newly organized and assertive medical profession, abortion came to be criminalized at the end of the nineteenth century. Until then abortion before "quickening" was not only not criminalized but was largely unregulated. After criminalization, and the subsequent creation of a black market in abortions, churches got involved. Many clergy joined a coalition expressing growing concern for the harm inflicted on women by back alley abortions. Indeed, up until the decision in *Roe v. Wade* in 1973,[80] many protestants across the theological spectrum, as well as many lay catholics, favored legalization as an alternative to the butchery of illegal abortions. On the eve of that decision, "the Southern Baptist Convention had passed a resolution calling on members to work for abortion's legalization . . . Ninety percent of Texas Baptists surveyed in 1969 had felt their state's abortion law should be loosened."[81] These groups were motivated largely by the widespread suffering endured by women.

78. https://www.museumofthebible.org/ (accessed March 26, 2018).
79. Griffith, *Moral Combat.*
80. *Roe v. Wade*, 410 U.S. 113 (1973).
81. Griffith, *Moral Combat*, 202.

Opposition to abortion legalization before *Roe* was led largely by Catholic clergy. But as Griffith tells it, a constellation of events, including the growth of the women's movement, led to a realignment after *Roe* was decided, with some conservative lay Catholics making common cause with evangelicals. This alliance intensified during the 1980s as a result of expressed opposition to what was perceived by conservatives to be a rise in secular humanism, feminism, and sexual libertinism. According to Griffith, it was only then that opposition to abortion was specifically identified as religiously based and it proved a convenient political position on which to stake a new cultural politics.

Policies entrenching gender and sexual inequality are both religious and secular, as Elizabeth Bernstein and Janet Jakobsen argue in an article on the politics of anti-sex-trafficking efforts. Bernstein and Jakobsen see a peculiar conjunction of religious and secular politics that have combined in the US to produce assumptions about sex and gender that result in "imperial subordination and heterosexual familialism, particularly in the form of the nuclear family."[82] "[I]t is easy to think that the removal of religion from the American political process," they say, "would also directly further gender equality . . . however, American secular politics includes a gender and sexual conservatism which . . . has often combined a Christian secularism with neoliberal imperatives in support of policies that are punitive towards women and that undercut possibilities for gender equality."[83]

Historian Joan Scott makes a similar argument on a somewhat broader geographic canvas. "Euro-Atlantic modernity," she says, "entailed a *new order of women's subordination*, assigning them to a feminized familial sphere meant to complement the rational masculine realms of politics and economics."[84] She insists that "the notion that equality between the sexes is inherent to the logic of secularism is false . . . Gender inequality is not simply the by-product of the emergence of modern Western nations, characterized by the separation between the public and the private, the political and the religious." "Inequality," she says, "is at its heart."[85]

In other words, the current sexual politics that subordinates women is modern, not medieval. And it is secular as much as it is religious. But the Court in *Hobby Lobby* reproduces a common contemporary US discourse

82. Bernstein and Jakobsen, "Sex, Secularism, and Religious Influence in US Politics," 1026.

83. Bernstein and Jakobsen, "Sex, Secularism, and Religious Influence in US Politics," 1023–1024.

84. Scott, *Sex and Secularism*, 3.

85. Scott, *Sex and Secularism*, 3–4.

in which control of women is assigned to the religious, at once winning them special constitutional consideration and letting secularists off the hook. The double effect apparently wins votes on the Court and in the legislature.

This new cultural alignment is reflected in the dissenting opinions as well as in those of Justice Alito and those who separately concurred. It is a narrative that serves the interests of secular progressives, obscuring their complicity in maintaining and regulating capitalist forms of family life. In her chapter on sexual emancipation, Scott, following Foucault, traces how sexual liberation and secularism, partly by way of the othering of Islam, became equated through "the logic of concupiscence and desire" even though there is "no necessary connection between emancipation and equality."[86] Religious freedom came to be about the maintenance of female subordination through the association of women with religion.

The adjective "religious" appears 296 times in the opinions in the *Hobby Lobby* decision. It is as if constant adjectival repetition will make it real and stable. Yet, as many have explained, "religious" as a universal modifier in this sense is both a comparatively recent phenomenon and a deeply fluid one. It cannot be understood to mark an essential difference. As Talal Asad and others have shown, the practice of identifying objects and ideas and practices as either religious or secular today has its roots in the history of modernity and in the history of the ways modernity has been and continues to be narrated.[87] Hussein Agrama sees the particular effort to make the distinction as a characteristic move of the modern state.[88] In the US, this distinction in law took on new salience with the nationalization of the religion clauses of the First Amendment to the US Constitution in the mid-twentieth century and again with the post-9/11 politics of the twenty-first, placing new pressure on the distinction, but also raising the stakes for maintaining ambiguity about its meaning, allowing the government to police good religion and bad religion.[89] Increasing polarization and an intractable politics contribute to perpetuating this unresolvable problem.

When both the majority and the dissent in *Hobby Lobby* defer to the plaintiffs' assertions that opposition to certain forms of birth control are

86. Scott, *Sex and Secularism*, 161–162.

87. See, e.g., Asad, *Formations of the Secular*.

88. Agrama, *Questioning Secularism*.

89. See Elizabeth Shakman Hurd, *Beyond Religious Freedom: The New Global Politics of Religion* (Princeton: Princeton University Press, 2015).

both naturally religious and naturally the position of devout christians, they are performing roles in a historically constituted discourse, not a timeless and necessary connection. The discourse is useful in bolstering the recognition of the plaintiff corporations as religious. Indeed, it is also helpful in bolstering both the personhood and the churchness of the plaintiff corporations. The bolstering works both ways. In other words, Hobby Lobby, Conestoga, and Marden are churches because they oppose the contraception mandate and they oppose the contraceptive mandate because they are conservative christians. They are *the* church-in-law.

Low church ecclesiology

The churches present in the *Hobby Lobby* litigation reflect a distinctive evangelical low church ecclesiology, one that finds origin points in the establishment of various alternative christian communities in the medieval and early modern periods, but which develops into full-blown ecclesiologies with the establishment of new churches in the reformations—and then with their reinvention in the New World, where religious societies needed to find new legal forms. Low church ecclesiology is deeply committed to the priesthood of all believers and to the works of the Spirit; it is skeptical of "organized religion"—and of the institutional implications of the "body of Christ" language implicit in the *Hosanna-Tabor* decision. It is also often anticlerical. Organized religion for these christians includes Roman Catholics and the high liturgical churches of lutheranism and episcopalianism. For many low church christians, all of their enterprises, including their retail enterprises, are ministries.

The Court groups the Hahns in with the Greens. The Hahns, however, have a different religious pedigree, as we have seen. While in practice these particular mennonites share some religious terrain today with other conservative christians whose political theology is in some ways centered into opposition to contraception and abortion, they are latecomers to this politics. Mennonite theology of business—and its ecclesiology—is distinctive. They would not be considered evangelicals by most church historians. Anabaptists are protestant but not evangelical. But the Court sees them as religiously related because of their opposition to certain forms of contraception. It is that which is seen to confirm their status as protected religious persons under RFRA.

A useful compendium of essays on evangelical protestant theologies of the church edited by John Stackhouse explores the complexity of this ecclesial terrain.[90] Protestant theorizing of the church, following on the reformers' critiques of the medieval church, is anchored in biblical models. While all protestants who understand the Nicene Creed to be an essential statement of christian doctrine see the church as necessary, the forms that protestant church communities have taken are enormously varied, as are their modes of governance. There is a sense in which for the evangelical movement, taken as a whole, perhaps particularly in the US, elective affinity might be a better description of their unity; church order and polity have often been subordinated to piety and work in the world, in part because of the collective trauma of the religious wars and the persecutions of the sixteenth and seventeenth centuries, understood to be brought on by christian division and confessionalization, among other things.

In the recitation of the Nicene Creed, christians affirm a belief in "one holy catholic and apostolic church." (Others do this through affirmation of the Apostles' Creed or other confessions or statements of faith.) In a very real way, all of these christians, not just catholics, thereby affirm that *extra ecclesiam nulla salus* (there is no salvation outside the church), as christians have since the fourth century; but salvation, after Augsburg, is no longer tied to the imagined institutional unity of western Christendom. As Stackhouse and the other contributors to his volume note, each of the words "one," "holy," "catholic," and "apostolic" remains unsettled for protestants. In what precisely the unity, holiness, catholicity, and apostolicity of the church now consist, and how to understand the relationship between the visible church and the invisible church, given the shattering of the medieval consensus, protestants do not agree. From the magisterial churches of the Reformation to the myriad new churches of the dissenters and of the new foundations in the New World after various awakenings, how the injunction to love each other should be lived out in everyday lives, how to recognize who is a christian, and where the authority of church community, whether local or otherwise, fits in, is tremendously fraught. In this connection, because of these origins, the relationship to the state is not external to protestant self-understandings of the church; it is constitutive. Separatism is in their DNA, even while they are deeply dependent on the state. As is their symbiotic relationship to the economy.

90. John G. Stackhouse, ed., *Evangelical Ecclesiology: Reality or Illusion?* (Grand Rapids, MI: Baker Academic, 2002).

Bruce Hindmarsh, in "Is Evangelical Ecclesiology an Oxymoron?," describes the puzzling organizational challenges that the awakenings of the eighteenth century posed for pietist christians, who were then spread among different protestant denominations. He sees them as modern individuals who had inherited a corporate consciousness in their theology: "[A]lthough evangelicals gathered together as an act of free association, they also understood this to be because of a prior 'calling out' and 'calling together' of the Holy Spirit through the means God ordained. If these early evangelicals acquired a new sense of individual agency under the modern conditions of life that emerged in this period, they could still be described as deeply communitarian in their common life."[91] They understood themselves to face new challenges. What was to be the new work of God in this new world? And how was it to be organized?

Ernst Kantorowicz teaches the power of the migration of religious metaphors across the various domains, religious and secular, of late medieval and early modern life.[92] One might similarly trace a Kantorowiczian exchange among religious, political, and economic domains in the US, following, for example, such religious metaphors as "servant leader," "covenant," etc. Seeing the *Hobby Lobby* decision as reducible simply to conservative religious views on sex in such a pliable and fissiparous context is founded in a division of the religious from the secular—and the private and the public—that cannot be defended, except on a political basis—as many current critics of the secularization thesis have argued. They are always profoundly entangled.

Conclusion

As was mentioned at the beginning of the chapter, law professor Michael McConnell and former solicitor general Don Verilli seem to have assumed that *Hosanna-Tabor*'s affirmation of the rights of churches had implications for *Hobby Lobby*. Is Hobby Lobby then a church as well as a corporation? What is a church?[93] What is the difference between a church and a corporation?

91. Bruce Hindmarsh, "Is Evangelical Ecclesiology an Oxymoron? A Historical Perspective," *International Journal for the Study of the Christian Church* 7 (2007): 302–322.

92. See above at 43–44.

93. The entry on ecclesiology in a leading encyclopedia of religion tries to describe the opaque complex theological reality that is the church:

Most historical theologians today believe that it was not Jesus who created the church. The church was formed after Jesus' death. The biblical warrants for the church are found in Paul's letters and the Acts of the Apostles—finding further consolidation in the church councils of the next few centuries and the political and discursive establishment of the church as the religion of the empire with Constantine's reign.[94] While there continued to be other theologies of the church in the churches of the east, the theologies of the Roman church dominated in Western Europe until the reformation, when first Martin Luther, then John Calvin and others, introduced distinctive new reforms to the Roman model, emphasizing the primacy of faith over works, scripture over sacrament, the priesthood of all believers, the abolishing of apostolic succession, and the removing of the ontological distinction between clergy and laity. The establishment of national churches as well as the appearance of dissenting congregationally based polities followed. This is a highly complex and dense story. All types of church polity have been imported into North America, where they have been indigenized and where both old and new religious groups invented new forms. A wide spectrum of ecclesiologies resulted. A web of biblical and theological ideas is understood to support the various forms that the church takes today. All US religious groups also engage in a complex negotiation and translation among particularist ecclesiological traditions and public versions of the church both in legal formulations and in political discourse.

The church, legally speaking, can be understood to be but one example of the legal fictions that have been created in order to enable the creation and maintenance of collective human projects over time. Others include

---

> The word *church* refers to the visible community in which Christians come together for worship, prayer, communal sharing, instruction, reflection, and mission. Most Christian bodies, but not all, see this visible community as imperfectly representing on earth an invisible communion of saints called together by God in Jesus Christ. The church can thus be viewed as one social institution among many, but also as a shared form of life shaped by profound theological self-understandings. Seen institutionally, the church has subsisted in a variety of communal forms and structures of governance throughout a long and very complex history. Understood theologically, the church has been the object of many varying images, descriptions, terminologies, and conceptualities interwoven with the circumstances of that history.

Lewis S. Mudge, "Church: Ecclesiology," in *Encyclopedia of Religion*, 2nd ed., ed. Lindsay Jones.

94. A key text in the invention of the church is *The History of the Church* by Eusebius of Caesarea, written in the fourth century of the common era. Eusebius, *The History of the Church*, tr. Jeremy M. Schott (Oakland: University of California Press, 2019).

trusts, charitable foundations, universities, unions, corporations—and states. Such collective legal persons have always been controversial from a republican political point of view in the US, as their establishment has been seen as risking the enabling of inequality and control by a dead hand, resulting in the fostering of private governance. Revolutionaries such as Thomas Jefferson and Thomas Paine believed that life belongs to the living and that political decisions should be made by living individuals. That revolutionary creed competed with political ideologies founded in the protection of private property. There is an important parallel here as well to debates about divided sovereignty more generally, including debates about federalism and states' rights—that is, of what is called the *imperium* in the *imperio*.

The history of the corporation in the US begins immediately after the Revolution. As the story usually goes, it was the passage of general incorporation statutes, no longer requiring individualized approval of a public purpose by the legislature, that enabled the growth of capitalism. But Pauline Maier argues that the story is more interesting, that the undeniable proliferation of corporations in the early US actually served a number of purposes. "Americans," she says, "substituted for the old bonds between superiors and dependents new social ligaments voluntarily contracted by equal citizens through constitutions of their own design and within voluntary associations that frequently received official sanction through the process of incorporation."[95] For these early capitalists, then, "the proliferation of corporations could signal, in effect, an extension of American federalism down into day-to-day, local associational relationships, so that 'the whole political system' was 'made up of a concatenation of various corporations, political, civil, religions, social and economical,' in which the nation itself was a 'great corporation, comprehending all others.'"[96] She traces how this impulse to collectivization began in New England with the creation of towns and churches by the first settlers.

For many today, the liberal right to religious freedom is understood properly to pertain only to the individual—to honor what is taken to be the inviolability of private conscience—but US law has long recognized collectivities under various names and rubrics as religious and as protected,

95. Pauline Maier, "The Revolutionary Origins of the American Corporation," *William and Mary Quarterly* 50 (1993): 82.

96. Maier, "The Revolutionary Origins of the American Corporation," 82, citing "Corporations," in Lieber, *Encyclopedia Americana*, vol. 3.

as McConnell noted in his brief.[97] Indeed, all modern law about religion is arguably indebted to the church-in-law and its history of cooperative governance arrangements with modern states. It is also haunted by the heritage of Westphalia, by the minority concessions of the late Ottoman period, as well as by the gradual accommodation—or not—of religious minorities in European and other countries, an accommodation often managed by ceding a level of self-governance to such communities. It has never been just about the individual. Or just about conscience. Or just about christians.

The question perdures. Is the proper object of protection in the case of religious freedom the conscience of the individual or is it the protection of the continuity of communities, whether newly or historically discriminated against, communities that may espouse unfamiliar or unpopular ideas and practices and wish to discipline their members in those practices? Can the law do both? Can the individual be protected without protecting a community? Can a community be protected without sacrificing the rights of the individual? Finally, is this just about religion? Are religious collectivities phenomenologically, and legally, like (or unlike) secular assemblies, associations, and corporations—and emerging virtual electronic communities? In what ways? Are churches simply entitled to the same rights as the Boy Scouts or Citizens United? What is the relationship of all of these collectivities, quasi-sovereignties, to the modern state?

Over the course of their own constitutional history, American states moved unevenly and incompletely after disestablishment from initial efforts in the early republic to limit and tightly control organized religious groups and their wealth to an enabling of hierarchical religion in the late nineteenth and early twentieth centuries, with an increasingly ascendant federal constitutional affirmation of individual conscience, whether religious or not, in the mid-twentieth century. This history is now actively being revised with older and previously submerged "corporate" threads of the debate reemerging.

As Sarah Barringer Gordon explains in her article on the legal implementation of disestablishment in the new states, the initial impulse was to keep churches small and local and poor:

> The decision to disestablish represented an end in some ways but a beginning in many others. It was the prelude to a gradual yet broad-ranging, nationwide attempt to limit the ability of religious organizations to acquire and hold

97. See above at 110.

> wealth. Equally important, states imposed strict controls on church governance, mandating the election of lay trustees to hold and manage church property. The desire to keep religious organizations both limited in size and firmly under lay control was key to the ongoing administration of disestablishment in the states. The rules were by no means identical, but they resembled each other enough to create a rough system. This first system of disestablishment imposed discipline on religious institutions, especially in terms of property and internal governance, based on concerns for individual conscience and lay control.[98]

Deference to hierarchical religious authority was far from the minds of these early reformers, as Gordon explains:

> The most startling aspect of this history is the direct control states exercised over religious organizations' property and power through statutes allowing "religious societies" (as they were commonly called) to incorporate. Consider, for example, the limitations on wealth imposed by most states, which capped real property acreage: two acres in Virginia, Maryland, and the congressionally governed District of Columbia; four acres in Kentucky; and five acres in Pennsylvania, Georgia, and Tennessee. Limits were also imposed on total annual income: $1000 in New Hampshire; $2000 in Maryland; and $3000 in Maine, Wisconsin, and Minnesota. Similar restrictions were enacted around the country.[99]

Gordon's article tells the fascinating early nineteenth-century story of church incorporation and the efforts of the states to limit church wealth and insist on local governance.

Church politics shifted after the Civil War, when church and state joined hands in a new imperial enterprise. State control of church wealth and governance gave way to a new deference to the power of religious institutions in regulating the population. It is interesting that today, thanks in part to the *Smith* decision, we have the religious and political heirs to both of these strands of church history linked in a new assertion of corporate religious freedom.

Robert Cover, in his well-known article commenting on the Court's *Bob Jones University* decision,[100] which affirmed the IRS decision to re-

98. Gordon, "The First Disestablishment," 311.

99. Gordon, "The First Disestablishment," 311–312.

100. See discussion above at 55–58; *Bob Jones University v. United States*, 461 U.S. 574 (1983).

voke the university's charitable status because of the university's racially discriminatory rules about student behavior, discussed the capacity of the state to tolerate alternative nomic communities in its midst. "We ought not lightly to assume a statist perspective here," he said, "for the nomos of officialdom is also 'particular'—as particular as that of the Amish. And it, too, reaches out for validation and seeks to extend its legitimacy by gaining acceptance from the normative world that lies outside its core."[101] He warned too of the attendant violence used to maintain the state's position in any matter.

Cover's article advocating for legal recognition of normative pluralism concludes that:

> [i]t is not the romance of rebellion that should lead us to look to the law evolved by social movements and communities. Quite the opposite. Just as it is our distrust for and recognition of the state as reality that leads us to be constitutionalists with regard to the state, so it ought to be our recognition of and distrust for the reality of the power of social movements that leads us to examine the nomian worlds they create. And just as constitutionalism is part of what may legitimize the state, so constitutionalism may legitimize, within a different framework, communities and movements. Legal meaning is a challenging enrichment of social life, a potential restraint on arbitrary power and violence. We ought to stop circumscribing the nomos; we ought to invite new worlds.[102]

Cover believed that only by acknowledging the promise and danger of a plural set of nomoi would a robust engagement with the zero-sum sovereignty claimed by the modern state be possible. He urged us not to be too quick to dismiss those alternative worlds, as both majority and dissenting justices do in *Hobby Lobby*, particularly if we are unable to articulate our own.

101. Cover, "*Nomos* and Narrative," 33.
102. Cover, "*Nomos* and Narrative," 68.

CHAPTER FOUR

The Body of Christ in Blackface

Signifying is worse than lying.—Charles H. Long, *Significations*[1]

Introduction

Hosanna-Tabor and the church property cases display the startling legal deference toward hierarchical state-like churches over the course of the last century and a half of US history. *Hobby Lobby* reveals mimetic forms of the church and the corporation as well as the shifting politics of the gendered church-in-law. The story of the black church-*in-law* reveals another claustrophobic legal consolidation of religion in the US, one that, like the others, both enables and controls.

The black church has been the explicit object of regulation through slave law and Jim Crow, an aspirational vehicle of social uplift, as a result of the work of W. E. B. Du Bois and other early twentieth-century sociologists, a heroic figure in narrative retellings of the civil rights movement, an object of derision by Elijah Muhammad and others seeing in it the stamp of backwardness and white supremacy, and, through its deployment by law enforcement today, once more a means of social control.[2] These figures

1. Charles H. Long, *Significations: Signs, Symbols, and Images in the Interpretation of Religion* (Minneapolis: Fortress Press, 1986), 1.

2. Writing about African-American religious life is today, for a white author, difficult terrain—and appropriately so, in my view. Understanding the way in which black life has

of the black church-in-law—the body of Christ in blackface, perhaps—dominate the public legal consciousness even while other assemblies of the black sacrality flourish in the inbetween spaces of law's dominion. The realities of black churches-in-law are always being subverted by outlaw black religious sovereignties, by those who refuse religion, and by religions of blackness.

The first thing to say, to quote Barbara Dianne Savage, is that "there is no such thing as the black church."[3] As Curtis Evans too insists, the black church, or the Negro Church, in Du Bois' words, as a US phenomenon, was not, as it is often described, an organically occurring and unified phenomenon originating in the African religious experience and culminating naturally in the work of Martin Luther King, Jr.[4] What created that narrative was, to a large extent, the invention of the new fields of the social sciences that emerged at the end of the nineteenth century. And it continues to be useful to them. The linguistic gesture of naming "the black church" obscures a vastly more varied and dispersed history of institution building by African Americans and by those who would tell their stories.[5] The fact is that the apostrophized black church corresponds only at times to the religious lives of actual African Americans, lives that have always been religiously diverse and changing. African Americans, like other Americans, have not all been christian nor have they all been religious.[6] But that is not the same thing as saying there are no black collective christian imaginaries or that they do not have political power.[7]

---

been, and continues to be, represented in American law is a complex and unfinished project. Nevertheless, there is an exceptionally rich and growing literature. This chapter engages a piece of that story.

3. Barbara Dianne Savage, *Your Spirits Walk Beside Us: The Politics of Black Religion* (Cambridge: Harvard University Press, 2008).

4. Evans, *The Burden of Black Religion*, 10–11.

5. For a summary of this history, see Kathryn Lin Gum and Lerone Martin, "American Religion and the Rise of Internal Security: A Prologue," in *The FBI and Religion: Faith and National Security before and after 9/11*, ed. Sylvester A. Johnson and Steven Weitzman (Berkeley: University of California Press, 2017).

6. See, among others, Judith Weisenfeld, *New World A-Coming: Black Religion and Racial Identity During the Great Migration* (New York: New York University Press, 2016), and Anthony Pinn, *The End of God-Talk: An African American Humanist Theology* (Oxford: Oxford University Press, 2012), each focusing on a different set of nonchristian African Americans, Weisenfeld on the new religious groups formed during the Great Migration and Pinn on contemporary humanists.

7. For a comparative discussion of black churches and city politics in New York and Detroit, see Ronald Brown, "The Black Church in a Post–Church Federation Era," preface to Henry Pratt, *Churches and Urban Government in Detroit and New York* (Detroit: Wayne State University Press, 2004). See also Joseph Winters, *Hope Draped in Black: Race, Melancholy,*

What I name in this chapter as the black church-in-law is a through thread of the consolidation of the legal recognition of the disestablished church as a form of racial enslavement in the Americas stretching from the seventeenth-century Caribbean to the present-day Louisiana State Penitentiary at Angola. The genealogies of this particular body, like the other bodies in this volume, reveal an elusive and shifting legal fiction, one, like her siblings, arguably indispensable in myriad ways to the legal life of religion in the US. This chapter will focus on the very particular way in which signifying consolidations of black religion have been and continue to be put to use in law enforcement and corrections today in the US,[8] "signifying" in the sense elaborated by Charles Long in *Significations*. This black church-in-law, like the churches-in-law of *Hosanna-Tabor*, *Hobby Lobby*, and the church property cases, inhabits and constrains the US legal imagination of the sacred.

The Angola Church

In an essay for *Commonweal* magazine describing his research study of the Baptist Seminary in the Louisiana State Penitentiary at Angola, criminologist Michael Hallett admiringly asserts that "Angola is the only prison in America that allows inmates to run their own churches—a practice with roots in the prison's history as a plantation, where slaves organized their own churches."[9] He explains:

> These inmates' religious communities were expanded in the aftermath of a 1974 federal consent decree, which found that conditions at the prison "shocked the conscience of any right-thinking person." From then on, prisoners were encour-

---

and the Agony of Progress (Durham, NC: Duke University Press, 2016). For a subtle account of the complexities of black catholicism and its relationship to the black church, see Cressler, *Authentically Black and Truly Catholic*. For a discussion of black religion "after" the black church, see Josef Sorett, "A Fantastic Church?: Literature, Politics, and the Afterlives of Afro-Protestantism," *Public Culture* 29, no. 1 (January 2017): 17–26.

8. In addition to the example of the black church-in-law in prison discussed in this chapter, see also, for example, on police/clergy urban partnerships, Rod K. Brunson, Anthony A. Braga, David M. Hureau, and Kashea Pegram, "We Trust You, But Not *That* Much: Examining Police–Black Clergy Partnerships to Reduce Youth Violence," *Justice Quarterly* 32, no. 6 (2015): 1006–1036.

9. Michael Hallett, "Faith at Angola Prison," https://www.commonwealmagazine.org/print/39240 (accessed March 12, 2019).

> aged to turn what had been described as "inmate-led religious clubs" into active "churches." And so they did, forming Baptist, Pentecostal, Catholic, Methodist, and other Christian worship communities—collectively referred to as the "Angola Church." The size of these communities at Angola mirrors almost exactly the percentages of Baptists, Pentecostals, and Catholics in surrounding Louisiana. Adherents of other faiths, including a small contingent of Muslim inmates, also openly practice at the prison.[10]

Hallett presents today's churches at Angola, which he and others name in the collective personality of *the* Angola Church, as the heirs to slave religion, collapsing hundreds of years of African-American religious and penal history into an unbroken story of the black church-in-law, naturalizing the religiousness of African Americans in service of what will become a narrative of personal redemption and rehabilitation. The prisoners' rights revolution of the 1960s and 1970s is seen in this story to make visible and free what, he says, had been latent since slave times; the result is the religious diversity of Louisiana being happily accommodated by the penal church at Angola.

The Louisiana State Penitentiary at Angola occupies 18,000 acres of a former plantation and has a prison population of approximately 6,300, of whom at least two-thirds are serving life sentences and three-quarters are black. Historically, it is one of the most notorious and violent prison camps in the US. Angola has, in the last several decades, undergone a reformation of sorts, most recently under the guidance of Superintendent Burl Cain. There is an extensive literature on Angola; it is the subject of a great deal of academic, journalistic, and artistic analysis, some of it disturbingly voyeuristic, of which only a selection will be referred to here.[11]

Hallett's jejune celebration of what he takes to be the long history of

10. Hallett, "Faith at Angola Prison." The last sentence of this quoted excerpt serves to forestall claims of Christian exclusivism even while the church defines prison religion at Angola and many other US prisons. The finished study has been published as Michael Hallett, Joshua Hays, Byron Johnson, Sung Joon Jang, and Grant Duwe, *The Angola Prison Seminary: Effects of Faith-Based Ministry on Identity Transformation, Desistance, and Rehabilitation* (New York: Routledge, 2018).

11. For a review of the litigation that challenged conditions at Angola, see Wilbert Rideau and Billy Sinclair, "Prisoner Litigation: How It Began in Louisiana," *Louisiana Law Review* 45 (1985): 1061–1076. (Note in article concerning authors: "Wilbert Rideau and Billy Sinclair are prisoners at the Louisiana State Penitentiary where they are serving life terms. They are editors of *The Angolite*, the prison's newsmagazine, which under their direction has reaped some of the nation's most prestigious journalism awards.")

the Angola Church, bolstered in his subsequent book with references to the black church in the work of W. E. B. Du Bois and Cornel West,[12] can usefully be paired with another recent study of the US penal imaginary by literary scholar Dennis Childs: *Slaves of the State: Black Incarceration from the Chain Gang to the Penitentiary*.[13] Childs has also visited Angola. He also tells a long story of what might be called the black church-in-law.

Seeking to explain the continuation of slave auctions after emancipation, Childs finds in the "exception clause" of the Thirteenth Amendment the pivot/link between the incarceration of slavery and the post-emancipation black neoslavery practices of convict leasing, lynching, and prison farms such as Angola. Section one of the Thirteenth Amendment reads, in its entirety: "Neither slavery nor involuntary servitude, except as a punishment for crime whereof the party shall have been duly convicted, shall exist within the United States, or any place subject to their jurisdiction."[14] Usually understood simply to abolish the chattel slavery accommodated by the Constitution, the implications of the amendment's exception clause remains little understood or explored.[15]

That the exception clause was in fact specifically and immediately understood by some as permitting the continuation of slavery by other means is illustrated by Childs with a passage from congressional testimony in an 1866 hearing. The committee report quotes a northern clergyman recounting a conversation with a southern preacher: "Alluding to the amendment to the constitution that slavery should not prevail, except as

12. W. E. B. Du Bois, *The Negro Church* (New York: AltaMira Press, 2003), as cited in Hallet et al., *The Angola Prison Seminary*, 41; Cornel West, *Prophetic Fragments: Illuminations of the Crisis in American and Religious Culture* (Grand Rapids, MI: Eerdmans, 1988), as listed in bibliography in Hallet et al., *Angola*, 58.

13. Dennis Childs, *Slaves of the State: Black Incarceration from the Chain Gang to the Penitentiary* (Minneapolis: University of Minnesota Press, 2015).

14. The second section reads: "Congress shall have power to enforce this article by appropriate legislation." The language of the Thirteenth Amendment was based on the language about slavery in the Northwest Ordinance of 1787. Article 6 of the Northwest Ordinance provided: "There shall be neither slavery nor involuntary servitude in the said territory, otherwise than in the punishment of crimes whereof the party shall have been duly convicted: Provided, always, That any person escaping into the same, from whom labor or service is lawfully claimed in any one of the original States, such fugitive may be lawfully reclaimed and conveyed to the person claiming his or her labor or service as aforesaid."

15. See Childs, *Slaves of the State*, 200 n17. See also Jack M. Balkin and Sanford Levinson, "The Dangerous Thirteenth Amendment," *Columbia Law Review* 112, no. 7 (November 2012): 1459–1499. Incarceration was not the only legal means by which emancipation was delayed. See Hendrik Hartog, *The Trouble with Minna: A Case of Slavery and Emancipation in the Antebellum North* (Chapel Hill: University of North Carolina Press, 2016).

punishment for a crime, [the southern preacher said] 'we must make a code that will subject many crimes to the penalty of involuntary servitude, and so reduce the Negroes under such penalty again to practical slavery.'"[16] Childs' book goes on to set what he, and others, have described as the attempted nullification of the Thirteenth Amendment's abolition of slavery through implementation of the exception clause, in the context of both the legal and literary history of black punishment.[17] He describes how the plan to perpetuate what he terms the euphemistic violence of "involuntary servitude" then played, and plays out still today, in US prisons, including a harrowing account of his own visit to Angola prison.

Hallett's study of the Angola Church was prompted most immediately by the recent establishment of a free-standing Baptist seminary on the grounds of the prison. It was also motivated by a recent and ongoing academic and political effort to show that "faith works" in personal rehabilitation of many kinds. Regarding secularist academics as unreasonably skeptical of the work religion does, and responding to a changing political climate and the apparent openings provided by shifts in interpretations of the First Amendment, Hallett and others have sought to lend social scientific support to advocates of the faith-based initiative. They see in the work of the Angola Church evidence of the unrecognized beneficial effects of the right kind of religion.

Among the many changes attributed to the charismatic and controversial prison reformer Burl Cain, who was superintendent at Angola from 1995 to 2016, was the introduction into the prison of a degree-granting college program administered by the New Orleans Baptist Theological Seminary. Cain is an outsized personality, both reviled and revered, who has been the subject of numerous media profiles, in video and in print. He is credited by some with transforming Angola into a place of nonviolence through christian conversion. He was also forced to step down as a result of charges of massive corruption.[18] He apparently did, however, make some necessary reforms at the prison.

16. Childs, *Slaves of the State*, 64.

17. US Constitution, Amendment 13 (1865). His reading of the Thirteenth Amendment narratively links the exception clause to a reading of Toni Morrison's *Beloved* (New York: Vintage Books, 1987) and Chester Himes' *Yesterday Will Make You Cry* (New York: W. W. Norton and Company, 1998).

18. See, e.g., an admiring film, *The Farm: Angola USA*, directed by Liz Garbus, Wilbert Rideau, and Jonathan Stack, featuring Burl Cain as himself, produced by A&E (1998), and a muckraking biography, James Ridgeway, "The Overseer," *Mother Jones* 36, no. 4 (July/August 2011): 44–51.

With the precipitous defunding of prisons in the 1990s on the grounds, popular across the political spectrum, that prisons should be places of punishment and not rehabilitation, and after the ending in 1994 of national Pell Grants subsidizing college educations for prisoners, Cain, like many prison administrators all over the country, looked for a way to create other kinds of programming. Religious institutions of various kinds stepped up in many states. Beginning with a few extension courses, the New Orleans Baptist Theological Seminary eventually established a full degree program at Angola. That innovation raised some eyebrows among constitutional separationists but there has been no successful legal challenge to its presence there.[19]

Hallett and his colleagues understand what they call the "Angola model" to be the future of prison reform. They argue that "[r]eligiously motivated identity transformation at Angola carries a host of benefits for both inmates as individuals and for the prison at-large."[20] They believe these many benefits to be the result of a symbiotic relationship between church and state:

> Transformed inmates now look for ways to deliver, support, and encourage prosocial behavior, or what others have referred to as "acts of kindness" through "Relationship Theology." The many positive changes in Angola over the last several decades are in part the result of the Bible College supporting the Angola churches and the Angola churches supporting the Bible College. Working in tandem, these two faith-infused entities have unleashed hundreds of inmates who are involved in a host of prosocial activities that build social and spiritual capital. Many prisoners have told us the next great religious awakening will come from the prisons.[21]

19. After the decision in *Americans United v. Prison Fellowship*, 555 F. Supp. 2d 988 (S.D. Iowa 2008), advocates of faith-based prison programming believe they have found the key to insulating such programs from constitutional challenge in a combination of ensuring prisoner "choice" and building a wall between public and private funding. See Brad Stoddard, "The New Prison Reformers: Florida's Faith-Based Prisons and the Politics of Religious Pluralism," Ph.D. dissertation, Florida State University, 2015. See also Sullivan, *Prison Religion*, and Edward S. Herman and Noam Chomsky, *Manufacturing Consent: The Political Economy of the Mass Media* (New York: Pantheon, 1988).

20. Hallett et al., *The Angola Prison Seminary*, 233.

21. Hallett et al., *The Angola Prison Seminary*, 233. Depressingly, nineteenth-century christian social reformers also saw prisons as the potential source of social reform more broadly, providing a model for godly and socially productive behavior. See Sullivan, *Prison Religion*, 4–5.

Rich with quotations from prisoners testifying to their conversions, and bolstered by surveys and charts that translate religious language into the language of correctional statistics and criminology, the authors claim to show that a "New Prosocial Gospel is a model that is efficacious and can be a part of the kind of smart justice response that so many practitioners, scholars, and decision-makers agree we so desperately need in corrections."[22] Hallett and his colleagues stake this claim on the hard data of quantitative social science, purporting to show that religion is the cause of positive change among prisoners at Angola.

Criticism of the Hallett study can be made on a number of methodological grounds, including the obvious problems of selection bias, given the voluntary nature of these programs, as Hallett and his coauthors acknowledge.[23] But they underestimate the reach of this challenge. Identifying specifically religious motivations and effects is arguably impossible, making the use of religion as an independent variable in statistical analysis without value. Furthermore, from a theological perspective, the idea that a reading of the New Testament characterized as pro-social is an innovation in christian history is a startling idea, the plausibility of such a claim is arguably more a product of the presentism of neoliberal projects of self-improvement than an effect of christian teaching. The claim that a pro-social gospel can change lives ignores the history of theology

22. Hallett et al., *The Angola Prison Seminary*, 234. *The Angola Prison Seminary* is positioned in part as a response to my own book on legal challenges to prison ministries; Hallett and his coauthors frequently invoke and, in my view, mischaracterize my work. Of course, as an author, one cannot and should not attempt to control interpretation of one's published work. Readers will make their own judgments about that. But my own view is that my book, *Prison Religion*, does not, as Hallett and his coauthors suggest, make a case for or against the effectiveness of faith-based prison rehabilitation projects. I do not believe that such a case can be made either way because of the instability of the distinction between secular and faith-based programming and the unavailability of adequate ways of measuring and testing such a proposition. The argument of *Prison Religion* concerns rather the ways in which the jurisprudence of the First Amendment religion clauses abets a confusion between secular and religious languages of individual transformation, one that leads to a collusion between state and church.

23. For a critique of the methods of the quantitative social scientific study of religion more generally, see Leonardo Ambasciano and Thomas J. Coleman, "History as a Canceled Problem? Hilbert Lists, du Bois-Reymond's Enigmas, and the Scientific Study of Religion," *Journal of the American Academy of Religion* 87 (2019): 366–400. The nonrandomized nature of the Angola study, as well as the lack of a control group, is characteristic of a broad range of studies in the behavioral social sciences, not limited to those inquiring into the effects of religion. For a general critique of survey knowledge of religion, see Robert Wuthnow, *Inventing American Religion: Polls, Surveys, and the Tenuous Quest for a Nation's Faith* (Oxford: Oxford University Press, 2015).

and church history and forgets the always tragic histories of projects of christian civilization. That what these authors take to be a feature of the black church should be interpellated by corrections professionals in this way into the US criminal justice system without the scathing critique of the betrayals that such an interpellation conceals, eloquently outlined by James Cone, is also startling.[24]

The Angola Prison Seminary makes a strong claim that what they have seen in Angola—what they call a newly pro-social gospel—is also an instantiation of what they call "the black church," a church present, they say, since slave times. It is both new and old. Citing a century-old tradition of church activity at Angola, the authors conclude that "religious practice as it actually worked on plantations, during slavery—and, as we argue here, today at Angola—works not simply to legitimize oppressive social relations for outsiders but also to provide subaltern populations means to mediate and confront them."[25] The legitimation of oppression is excused, even affirmed by, the opportunities for mediation, even confrontation, the church-in-law being seen to neatly create its own necessity.

"[W]e found religion at Angola playing basically the role it has arguably always played: that of healing the wounded, of caretaking for the poor, and of uplifting the broken hearted."[26] How can one argue against the value of such work? Surely "healing the wounded, caretaking for the poor, and uplifting the broken hearted" are desirable? Particularly in US prisons. But this passage, and others in the book, attribute such work to a "religious practice" that works "as it actually worked on plantations, during slavery." How is it imagined that such a religious practice "actually worked?" What does "work" mean? And why would something that worked "during slavery" work now in the twenty-first century under the supervision of the Louisiana correctional system? Why would anyone want to replicate slavery in any of its parts? Somehow a reference to the "subaltern" legitimates such a reference, healing being dependent on reproducing the plantation. There is a disturbing admission in these words that because conditions at Angola are akin to the condition of slavery, they demand the reproduction of the same slave church. Angola prison today is presented as a kind of theme park historical reproduction of the plantation, the ideal laboratory for the codependent working of the new pro-social gospel.

24. James Cone, *The Cross and the Lynching Tree* (Maryknoll, NY: Orbis Books, 2011).
25. Hallett et al., *The Angola Prison Seminary*, 42.
26. Hallett et al., *The Angola Prison Seminary*, 42.

There are a growing number of ethnographic studies of the relatively new faith-based programming and prisons in the US.[27] Some of these studies make valuable and important contributions to our understanding of the precise nature of the theological anthropology fostered by the penal church, revealing the indebtedness of these programs to an atomized view of each individual as responsible for becoming a productive member of society. But for the most part, neither advocates for faith-based programming nor their many critics take on the prison itself.

In the larger world of the sociology of crime and the literature of mass incarceration, the abolition of prisons is increasingly advocated by a range of academic researchers and policy analysts today across the political spectrum.[28] This is not an entirely new position. In 1974, the great Australian criminologist Norval Morris optimistically predicted that by the end of the twentieth century, "prison in [its current] form will become extinct."[29] He and other researchers of the time concluded that prisons do not work and that their proliferation in the US had increasingly been shown to result from a highly racialized understanding of crime. Now, fifty years later, their views are being confirmed. And the end of prisons is being called for once more.

The motivations that caused mass incarceration then and now can be seen to be rooted in a politics of racial fear, among other things.[30] There

27. See, e.g., the work of Stephanie Gaskill, Joshua Dubler, and Brad Stoddard, cited in the bibliography. See also the work of Jason Sexton, self-described as a formerly incarcerated person, who has done ethnographic studies of what he calls the "prison church." Sexton makes the argument that a prison church organized by inmates is doing valuable work in the prisons in California: "There is, I would like to argue, an altogether different order operating within the prison that both resists and subverts carceral structures, which considers the prison as a formal structure foreign to the essence of the church's life and also notes the church's real existence operating among both formal and informal governance structures within the prison context." Jason Sexton, "Redeemed on the Inside: Radical Accounts of *Ecclesia* Incarcerate," *Ecclesial Practices* 5/2 (2018): 174. See also Sexton, "Greystone Chapel: Finding Freedom in Folsom Prison's Walls," *Boom: A Journal of California* 6/2 (Summer 2016): 104–111; and "Toward a Theology of California's *Ecclesia* Incarcerate," *Theology* 118 (2015): 83–91.

28. See, e.g., Heather Schoenfeld, *Building the Prison State: Race and the Politics of Mass Incarceration* (Chicago: University of Chicago Press, 2018). The online forum of the *Harvard Law Review* has published a Developments in the Law collection on abolition. https://harvardlawreview.org/issues/volume-132-issue-6/.

29. Norval Morris, *The Future of Imprisonment* (Chicago: University of Chicago Press, 1974), 268.

30. Schoenfeld, *Building the Prison State*. See also David Garland, *The Culture of Control: Crime and Social Order in Contemporary Society* (Chicago: University of Chicago Press, 2001). See Sullivan, *Prison Religion*, for a summary of this history.

is a sense in which focusing on faith-based prison programs in particular, as both advocates and critics of the new faith-based social service initiatives do, always draws attention away from these well-established facts. Understanding the religiousness of mass incarceration arguably lies not in a focus on the presence of christian ministers in prisons, whether they are liberal or conservative, but properly begins with the horror of black suffering across centuries.

Abolitionists argue that all prison reform projects, whether they are the progressive projects promoted by liberal arts colleges or the conservative ones promoted by evangelical christian para-church organizations,[31] enable the continuation of incarceration because all focus primarily on the prisoner and his opportunities for self-improvement, not with the social-legal machinery that produces mass incarceration. Prisons are a seductive environment for well-meaning do-gooders of all stripes. The gap between left and right in the personalist relational theology promoted in these projects is slimmer than either side imagines.[32]

The Angola Prison Seminary valorizes the black church insofar as it is successful in converting black prisoners into well-behaved inmates—for life. Once more, law is being urged to make room for the right kind of religion, this time at the heart of the carceral state. If American law needs "the church" to think religion, as this book argues, it seems to need the black church in particular to think crime and punishment. Insertion of the figure of the black church into the narrative of the criminalization of blackness and the hope for reform also fixes an account of the black American as essentially religious.

It is not just at Angola. The black church-in-law is a fixture in urban sociology as well, as its role in preventing delinquency is endlessly studied and promoted. Many cities have formal partnerships between the police and black pastors. Beyond the religious/secular debate, it is important to note that identifying the black church as the source of social control, as these sociologists and criminologists do, associates that identification with criminological theories of risk that carry with them unmarked racial

31. Para-church organizations are a distinctively American religious formation: interdenominational protestant organizations that have been created throughout US history to accomplish various tasks. Examples include the American Bible Society and the American Tract Society from the early nineteenth century, and more recently, such international aid associations as World Vision.

32. See Melani McAlister, *The Kingdom of God Has No Borders: A Global History of Evangelicals* (New York: Oxford University Press, 2018).

biases. Bernard Harcourt and others argue that the only way to reduce racial disparity in the criminal justice system is by criminalizing fewer activities, reducing sentences, and decarcerating because criminal risk assessments, now often performed through the use of algorithms, are largely proxies for race.[33]

But it is also important to realize that the take-up by prisoners of these various initiatives is also more complex than is acknowledged in Hallett's study.[34] In a dissertation on moral reform at Angola, Stephanie Gaskill considers various prisoner-run activities at Angola, including a newspaper, *The Angolite*, and various theater productions, all often touted in admiring accounts as providing opportunities for penitential rehabilitation at Angola. Gaskill argues that while "[p]opular documentaries about Angola redefine rehabilitation as a means for the prison's majority-black population to find purpose inside prison rather than prepare for life on the outside . . . [m]edia produced by incarcerated people themselves . . . reinterpret rehabilitation as a mode of structural critique as well as individual redemption."[35] Gaskill argues that there is another story to be told at Angola. "[P]eople in prison," she says, "cite scriptures, statutes, and episodes from America's long history of racial oppression to define rehabilitation as means to demand release as a legal right and call the public to self-examination and repentance. In prisoner-produced media, rehabilitation becomes a means to achieve racial justice and efface the structural racism inherent in the criminal justice system."[36] In other words, it is not just the prisoner who is in need of rehabilitation.[37]

With Dennis Childs, Stephanie Gaskill, and the prisoners they speak with and for, I seek here to connect the Angola Church to a broader

33. Bernard Harcourt, "Risk as a Proxy for Race," University of Chicago Public Law & Legal Theory Working Paper No. 323 (2010). See also Michelle Alexander, "The Newest Jim Crow," *New York Times*, opinion, November 11, 2018. https://www.nytimes.com/2018/11/08/opinion/sunday/criminal-justice-reforms-race-technology.html/ (accessed November 11, 2018).

34. For a subtle exploration of narratives of black religion and law enforcement, see Dew, *The Aliites*.

35. Stephanie Gaskill, "Moral Rehabilitation: Religion, Race, and Reform in America's Incarceration Capital," Ph.D. dissertation, University of North Carolina, 2017, iv.

36. Gaskill, "Moral Rehabilitation," 226–227.

37. Albert Woodfox, one of what are known as the Angola 3, unjustly imprisoned in solitary confinement at Angola for more than forty years, has just published a memoir. *Solitary: Unbroken by Four Decades in Solitary Confinement: My Story of Transformation and Hope* (New York: Grove Press, 2019).

history of the black church-in-law, a history that has depended in part on an insidious mutual implication between black religiosity and black criminality.

Black religiosity and black criminality

In the Hallett study of Angola, as in other sociological work in this vein, religion is rationalized—rendered modern—in order to be valorized. Religious work is carefully edited for its positive pro-social effects, translated into the secular language of social science, so that the explanation for individual change is understood as being effected through "personalist attention to inmates' needs and private pains."[38] Prisoners are enlisted in a churchstateness that will civilize them.

The stakes are high in the US right now for those who want to show that "faith works." Strong claims were made at the beginning of the faith-based initiative in the mid 1990s.[39] Efforts to document those claims continue. Deploying empirical social science to validate their conviction, scholar-advocates of such programs push back against what they take to be secularist assumptions that a range of physical, psychological, and social pathologies are best healed through secular "evidence-based" regimes of medical, psychological, and sociological intervention. Recent studies argue that various kinds of "faith" can cure disease, heal depression, and lead to the rehabilitation of criminal offenders—as well as lead to worldly success and personal happiness. Seeking to exploit recent academic critiques of secularism and secularization theories and purporting to turn the tables on skeptics and unbelievers, these researchers argue that religion can succeed where secular strategies have failed.[40] One of the most ambitious of such projects is faith-based prison ministry, both in-prison and reentry programs. This chapter seeks to set faith-based prison ministry, as an avatar of the church-in-law, very specifically in the history of religion and race

38. Hallett et al., *The Angola Prison Seminary*, 42.

39. See Sheila Suess Kennedy, *Charitable Choice at Work: Evaluating Faith-Based Job Programs in the States* (Washington, DC: Georgetown University Press, 2006).

40. There is nevertheless an irony that in their effort to offer evidence of rehabilitation, faith is arguably objectified and essentialized in a way that undermines the very claims that are being made. Reclaiming the sacred for law will require a more fundamental reorientation of our theological anthropology. See Ashe, "Beyond Nomos and Narrative"; Yelle, *Sovereignty and the Sacred*; and Carter, "Religion and the Future of Blackness," *South Atlantic Quarterly* 112 (2013): 589–611.

in the US, in what Khalil Gibran Muhammad names the "criminalization of blackness."[41]

Beginnings are hard to locate and causes multiple. While the history of the black church in the US conventionally begins in the mid-eighteenth century with the story of the creation of slave churches in the southern states,[42] *the* black church-in-law relies on a racialization of religion that has roots deep in the history of Christianity.[43] The inherent racism of Christianity, long the subject of critique by a range of voices, inside and outside of the churches, is underlined now in histories being told by a new generation of professional historians.[44] What Muhammad calls the invention of blackness has many, many progenitors. J. Kameron Carter and others would begin this history in the first days of the christian community, tracing the racialization of Christianity to the point when Christianity distinguished itself from Judaism.[45] Others would focus more recently on the early modern Atlantic world and the colonial empires that created the slave trade. Still others look very specifically at the languages and practices of Reconstruction, to the late nineteenth- and early twentieth-century US.

To say that this is a single story would be to essentialize both race and Christianity in indefensible ways, indeed to fall into the very trap illustrated in the Angola study. The beginnings of what is misnamed the Common Era are important, but I will begin here with the more proximate causes of the creation of the legal conditions that have made possible the current US iterations of the black church-in-law and their legal instrumentalization through the use and abuse of positivist social science.[46]

41. Khalil Gibran Muhammad, *The Condemnation of Blackness: Race, Crime, and the Making of Modern Urban America* (Cambridge: Harvard University Press, 2010).

42. See, e.g., Albert Raboteau, *Slave Religion: The Invisible Institution in the Antebellum South*, updated ed. (Oxford: Oxford University Press, 2004; originally published 1978).

43. For a discussion of the ways in which racism is also endemic to democracy, see Michael G. Hanchard, *The Spectre of Race: How Discrimination Haunts Western Democracy* (Princeton: Princeton University Press, 2018).

44. See, e.g., Sylvester A. Johnson, *African American Religions, 1500–2000* (Cambridge: Cambridge University Press, 2015). Importantly, these historians build on the work of Charles Long, among others. See Louis Benjamin Rolsky, "Charles H. Long and the Re-orientation of American Religious History," *Journal of the American Academy of Religion* 80 (2012): 750–774.

45. Carter, *Race*. See also Daniel Boyarin, *Border Lines: The Partition of Judaeo-Christianity* (Philadelphia: University of Pennsylvania Press, 2004); and Gil Anidjar, *Blood: A Critique of Christianity* (New York: Columbia University Press, 2014).

46. Evans, *The Burden of Black Religion*, 108ff. For a recent effort to reappraise the relationship of law to social science more generally, see Elizabeth Mertz, William K. Ford, and

Sylvester Johnson begins his history of African-American religions with a close look at the rise of Atlantic commercial ventures in the mid-fifteenth century.[47] He describes a business partnership between the Kongo and Portuguese empires and the strategic conversions to Christianity of members of the Kongo elite. This marks the beginnings of what he calls Afro-European commercialism. It also marked the beginning of religious exchanges that occurred among European christians and sub-Saharan Africans. While these early contacts were with catholic christians, competition between catholic and protestant colonizers would also characterize the ensuing centuries, as the reformations played out in the empires with a contest for souls.

It was not just that these Africans were becoming christians, it was also that the distinctiveness of black religiosity was being invented. Johnson traces the racialization of religion to European colonialist constructions of African religion as fetish religion, concluding that "[t]he earliest Portuguese accounts of Guinea highlight fetishism and idolatry as the essential elements of religion among Black people. Later, the fetish itself became the singular essence of Black religion, and it would remain the preeminent marker of Black religion and African civilization (or lack thereof) in the Western civilization."[48] The discourse of the fetish, according to Johnson, undergirded not just talk of religion but migrated into "the discourses of market capitalism and eventually the emergence of the social sciences."[49]

From the perspective of several hundred years later, Curtis Evans describes the racialization of US religion as founded in the characterization of black persons by early social science researchers as being of an assumed intellectual inferiority and a heightened capacity for feeling. Like Johnson, Evans is also interested in the emergence of the social sciences as well as the role of black intellectuals in that emergence; he tracks varied versions of an American racialized religiosity, both "romantic" and "pathologizing," in academic descriptions of black religiosity.[50] One might see in the early work of social scientists already a multiplicity in the imaginary of the caricatures of the black church that continues today, that is, the emotional

Gregory Matoesian, *Translating the Social World for Law: Linguistic Tools for a New Legal Realism* (Oxford: Oxford University Press, 2016).

47. Johnson, *African American Religions*, 13.

48. Johnson, *African American Religions*, 100. See also Raboteau's critique of Herskovits in Raboteau, *Slave Religion*, 48–60.

49. Johnson, *African American Religions*, 100. See also Lofton, *Consuming Religion*.

50. Evans, *The Burden of Black Religion*, 10.

black church of the rural south, the mainline black churches of the north, the church of the civil rights movement, and the "churches" such as the Moorish Science Temple that refused christianity.[51] As Johnson and Evans both teach, grouping these together into a single religious formation as the black church depends on a deeply embedded and depressing racial logic.

Importantly, slave conversion to protestant Christianity was a mostly relatively late development in the Atlantic slave trade. As Katharine Gerbner and others have shown, early planters in the protestant Atlantic colonies, in contrast to the catholic ones, resisted, even prohibited, christian evangelization of slaves out of fear that conversion would either lead automatically to manumission or out of fear that conversion (and the literacy enabled by it) would lead to rebellion.[52] Protestants, unlike catholics, mostly insisted on literacy as a prelude to conversion, but literacy was dangerous.

Notwithstanding biblical and other evidence that most in the early churches saw Christianity as being entirely compatible with slavery, these colonial-era protestant christians associated christian conversion with what they understood to be specifically protestant liberties, religious and political.[53] The seventeenth-century planters in the Caribbean and in North America at first practiced what Gerbner calls "Protestant Supremacy." Protestant supremacy, in the English, Dutch, and Danish colonies, was an ideology that identified protestantism with the cultural and religious superiority of slaveowners over slaves, understood to be heathens—and over catholics, both slaves and their owners. Protestant control of slaves was maintained in part through the exclusion of slaves from church membership on the ground that they were understood to be naturally primitive in their religiosity.

Colonial expansion and exploitation in North America took place in a time of rapid change back in England and Europe. Evan Haefeli argues that the usual narrative of the invention of religious toleration in the North American colonies misunderstands the causes for the relative growth of peaceable coexistence in North America. It was not so much an ideological commitment born of John Locke's and Thomas Paine's writings as a situation of chaotic political and social change in the metropole.

51. I recently had a conversation with a black colleague who does not study religion. When I asked him about his associations with the expression "the black church," he replied that his family was catholic. "The black church" for him, he said, was characterized by the emotional and expressive worship of storefront pentecostalism.

52. Gerbner, *Christian Slavery*.

53. Gerbner, *Christian Slavery*, 22.

Instability in England prevented a consistent colonial policy of religious uniformity, one that could have been administered from a distance.[54] As Gerbner tells the story, mid-seventeenth century colonial disestablishment of the church after the English Civil War and the lack in the English colonies of an imperial evangelization project cut planter churches off from political currents in London, allowing them to be controlled by the local planter elite.[55] In the Barbadian settlements, for example, parish churches were internal to the hierarchical institutionalization of slaveowners, rather than satellites of British churches. Sixteenth- and seventeenth-century protestant colonies also suffered from a massive shortage of ministers and a dearth of bishops. Protestant settlements lacked both a nationalist church ideology and the missionary orders that naturalized Catholic conversion of enslaved populations. It was the planters who invented Protestant Supremacy.

Over the course of the eighteenth century, as British politics stabilized, however, the ideology of protestant supremacy underlying the resistance to slave conversion was challenged "by missionaries, by imperial officials, and by enslaved men and women who advocated for their right to become Christians."[56] As protestant missionaries began to increase through the agency of the British Society for the Propagation of the Gospel and other mission senders, an opportunistic new teaching emerged that protestant Christianity could be reconciled with slavery. Realizing that the only way to overcome the resistance of owners was to accept chattel slavery, quaker missionaries and others, some pioneers in the movement to abolish slavery, began to teach that slavery was compatible with Christianity and that slave conversion was the duty of protestant owners. Planters were reassured that baptism would not automatically result in freedom. In other words, there was so much opposition to the missionaries' work with slaves that quakers, moravians, and anglicans invented—or rediscovered—christian slavery as a means to evangelization, as well as to enforce submission of slaves to control by their owners and to reinforce public and private order.[57] Gerbner shows that as slave conversions increased, there

54. Haefeli, "The Problem with the History of Toleration."

55. Gerbner, *Christian Slavery*.

56. Gerbner, *Christian Slavery*, 30. On eighteenth-century British colonial efforts to create legal uniformity in the empire, see Keally McBride, *Mr. Mothercountry: The Man Who Made the Rule of Law* (Oxford: Oxford University Press, 2016).

57. Albert Raboteau and Curtis Evans tell parallel stories in the antebellum south. See Raboteau, *Slave Religion*, and Evans, *The Burden of Black Religion*.

was a shift in slaveowner ideology from one of Protestant Supremacy over heathens to an ideology of white christian supremacy over black christians. The difference between owners and enslaved persons, no longer one of religion, now both being protestant christians, was expressed instead through an explicit assertion of racial superiority.[58]

Importantly, this is a legal as well as a religious story. Colonial law determined who could be a christian and on what terms. Law as well as religion became increasingly explicitly racialized. The Society for the Propagation of the Gospel pressed for laws permitting baptisms without manumission. Moravians stopped teaching literacy and permitted polygamy. As the number of free black christians increased, there was a shift in legal language from identifying planters as christian and slaves as heathen to identifying planters as white and slaves as black. Gerbner tracks this shift toward a racialized legal language in the Barbadian legislation passed between 1660 and 1725.[59] This system was most clearly the case, she says, in those plantation colonies where blacks greatly outnumbered whites, in North America as well as in the Caribbean.

One might say then that at least in the specific context of the Atlantic colonies, it was the shift from established to disestablished religion effected through the relinquishing of control of the churches by the authorities in England to the planters that created the early modern conditions for the invention of a legally licensed religious apartheid. A parallel process of disestablishment and the corresponding creation of black Christianity can be seen in the constitutional formation of the United States. It was the early capture of the churches by the planters and the ecclesiologies that resulted that set the stage for the black church in-law. That is one of the dark sides of free religion, then and now. Whether racism is or is not latent in Christianity as some have argued, it was arguably control of the churches by slaveowners that led to creation of the black church-in-law in North America and the Carribbean.

Conditions in Angola Prison in Louisiana today provide an uncanny parallel to the situation in the Atlantic colonies. Christian conversion at Angola has become a means of control through the simultaneous suppression of black religiosity in its "militant" political forms and an embrace

58. Gerbner, *Christian Slavery*, 89.

59. Gerbner, *Christian Slavery*, 85. See also John T. Noonan, Jr., *Persons and Masks of the Law: Cardozo, Holmes, Jefferson, and Wythe as Makers of the Masks* (Berkeley: University of California Press, 1976), for a discussion of the embedded racism in antebellum law.

of black prisoners as christian.[60] The racial marking of these conversions also echoes the earlier history. The emerging Atlantic black church-in-law would eventually connect the US black church-in-law to a global black church-in-law. As Sylvester Johnson says, "European trans-oceanic empire, the invasion and conquest of indigenous Americans, and the institutions for executing human trafficking of African peoples, were all enabling conditions of the christian church's transnationalism."[61] The inheritance of that history is evident today in the work of US evangelicals abroad, both black and white.[62]

The appellation "the black church" is relatively recent in US parlance, succeeding Du Bois' use of "the Negro Church."[63] Du Bois lived a long time and had a complex and changing understanding of African-American Christianity.[64] Nevertheless, what Du Bois described helped to set up the question of the political utility of the black church, as historians Barbara Savage and Curtis Evans have shown.[65] Du Bois himself described what he called the Negro Church as the continuation of a prechristian African social and political institution—the tribe—evidence of innate primitive religiosity. But while he, with other historians, sociologists, and activists, was critical in many ways of the then-current practices of African-American churches, he also saw it as a potentially exemplary institution of social uplift—perhaps the one institution that could do that. As Savage explains, "Implicit in the chorus of complaints against the church is a call for the church to be all things to all people, to be the savior institution at a time when the institutional infrastructure—economic, political, and

60. The exclusion and suppression of black nationalism did not, and does not, of course, just happen in prisons. See Pratt, *Churches and Urban Government in Detroit and New York*.

61. Johnson, "Divine Imperium and the Ecclesiastical Imaginary," 1007.

62. Stephen Selka's work shows the black church-in-law at work in the expectations of African-American religious tourism in Brazil, both for African Americans and for those whom they visit. Stephen Selka, "Morality in the Religious Marketplace: Evangelical Christianity, Candomblé, and the Struggle for Moral Distinction in Brazil," *American Ethnologist* 37, no. 2 (2010): 291–307. See also Melani McAlister on twentieth-century evangelical missions in Africa. McAlister, *The Kingdom of God Has No Borders*. David Chidester's *Wild Religion: Tracking the Sacred in South Africa* (Berkeley: University of California Press, 2012), describes parallel arrangements of politics, law, and black religiosity in South Africa.

63. Evans, *The Burden of Black Religion*, 10–11.

64. Barbara Dianne Savage, "W. E. B. Du Bois and the Negro Church," *Annals of the American Academy of Political and Social Science* 568 (March 2000): 235–250; Anthony Pinn, "Reading Du Bois Through Religion and Religious Commitment," *Journal of Religion* 94, no. 3 (July 2014): 370–382.

65. See Evans, *The Burden of Black Religion*, and Savage, "W. E. B. Du Bois and the Negro Church," 235.

social—of the African American community was seen as so very limited."[66] She describes "attempts in the 1930s to convert congregations of black people across regional and denominational lines into a mass organizing base for greater political, social, and economic power. Although unrealized at the time, this notion had such appeal precisely because of the tantalizing potential of creating a nation of black people united by religion but organized for political purposes."[67] This double bind of the black church, as the indispensable institution always falling short, arguably also underlies the view that black religion is singularly both the cause of and the solution to black criminality.

The invention of the black church closely tracks the history of the criminalization of blackness. In his dry, devastating book, Khalil Muhammad documents the post–Reconstruction era statistical racial segregation of the new social sciences and the invention of specifically black crime and criminality.[68] Notwithstanding the ongoing efforts of black and some white intellectuals beginning with Du Bois and Ida B. Wells to consider the troubles of black citizens "within the broader moral community,"[69] the production of statistics purporting to distinguish blacks as singularly dangerous was inscribed in statistical practices and in the sociology of crime. While the separate identification of white ethnics in crime statistics—as Irish or Italian or etc.—was gradually phased out as those groups were understood to become integrated—whitened, that is—crime statistics continued and continue today to separately categorize what they call black crime. Muhammad's book ends in the mid twentieth century but his conclusion points to the continued racism of the statistical reporting of crime.[70] Heather Schoenfeld details how the present carceral state is the result of specific racially motivated political decisions to expand carceral capacity.[71]

66. Savage, "W. E. B. Du Bois and the Negro Church," 245.

67. Savage, "W. E. B. Du Bois and the Negro Church," 245.

68. Muhammad, *The Condemnation of Blackness*. See also Schoenfeld, *Building the Prison State*.

69. Muhammad, *The Condemnation of Blackness*, 3, citing Orlando Patterson.

70. For a description of the ways in which risk assessment of criminal defendants purporting to predict recidivism, in its reliance on racially biased metrics of "dangerousness," ratchets up the racialization of crime, see Harcourt, "Risk as a Proxy for Race." As Harcourt explains, "Risk, today, is predominantly tied to prior criminal history, and prior criminality has become a proxy for race. The result is that decarcerating by means of risk instruments is likely to aggravate the racial disparities in our already overly racialized prisons," (237). See also Bernard E. Harcourt, *Against Prediction: Profiling, Policing, and Punishing in an Actuarial Age* (Chicago: University of Chicago Press, 2007).

71. Schoenfeld, *Building the Prison State*, 11–14.

The racialization of religion and the racialization of crime both depend on essentializing accounts of blackness. The celebratory legal narrative of religious freedom and the defining of religion in law in the US are also critically linked to racialized and criminalized religion in ways not usually marked.[72] Legal enforcement of rights to religious freedom is always about separating good religion from bad religion.[73] The same is true with black religion, as we will see in the next section. While it is common to lament a US past characterized by anti-Catholicism, anti-Mormonism, and the suppression of Native American religion, a past now believed to be largely overcome, in telling the progressive story of US religious freedom it is not common to tell the story of black religion as a story of the denial of First Amendment rights. Bad black religion is seen as singularly political and therefore usually policed as criminally dangerous, not as religion. Malcolm vs. Martin, as the shorthand today goes. Indeed, it has been difficult for courts to see black religion as religion for constitutional purposes. As Johnson and Evans detail, black religion is always double and always suspect.[74]

Prison religion

The intertwined story of black religion and black criminality can be seen in the prisoners' religious freedom rights cases. Until the 1970s, prisoners, black and white, in the US, had virtually no rights. They were, formally speaking, slaves of the state, as Dennis Childs' title announces, named as such in law.[75] Beginning in the 1950s and 1960s, however, cases on behalf of prisoners established basic rights, including a substantially conditioned right to the free exercise of religion.[76] The pioneering cases were brought by members of the Nation of Islam.[77] These cases and the other early

72. Tisa Wenger gives an account of part of this story. Tisa Wenger, *Religious Freedom: The Contested History of an American Ideal* (Durham: University of North Carolina Press, 2017).

73. Hurd, *Beyond Religious Freedom.*

74. Johnson, *African American Religions*; Evans, *The Burden of Black Religion.* See also Savage, "W. E. B. Du Bois and the Negro Church," and Pinn, "Reading Du Bois Through Religion and Religious Commitment," 370.

75. *Ruffin v. Commonwealth*, 62 Va. 790, 796 (Va. 1871).

76. *Cooper v. Pate*, 378 U.S. 546 (1964). All prisoner rights are qualified by the availability of the often conclusive claim of security needs by the prison management.

77. For an exploration of the long history of the judicial construction of Islam in the US, and the various categories into which the Nation of Islam was slotted—gang, cult, terrorist

to mid-twentieth-century cases federalizing the Bill of Rights arguably recognized religion in a new way, one mandated by the late-blooming Fourteenth Amendment and its new take on liberty.[78] For prisoners, those rights were further underlined with the passage in 2000 of the Religious Land Use and Institutionalized Persons Act (RLUIPA).[79]

But none of these developments in protections for the religious rights of prisoners changed the ongoing criminalization of blackness in the US. Indeed, Schoenfeld suggests that prisoner litigation had the unintended consequence of enhancing the conditions for the building of carceral capacity, including racialized perceptions of crime.[80] And while the Nation of Islam and other muslim groups gradually won more recognition as "legitimate" religions, in prison and out, all legal protections for the accommodation of religious practice come at a price and continue to depend on sorting out real religion from false religion, good religion from bad religion, religion from politics. Black religion has always been less visible to courts as real or as good. This has been particularly the case in prisons, where the legal establishment of a particular version of the black church is privileged—one that teaches a "prosocial gospel."

Among the steady stream of prisoner religious freedom cases that followed the initial victories was one that continues to haunt conversations about what counts as religion for legal purposes. In 1981, Frank Africa sued the State of Pennsylvania for an injunction requiring the prison in which he was incarcerated to provide him with the raw food diet he told them that his religion mandated.[81] Africa was a member of MOVE, a Philadelphia community founded in the early 1970s that was committed to the teaching of radical visionary John Africa. (In 1985, several years after this decision, the city of Philadelphia dropped a bomb on the house occu-

organization, heterodox Islam—see Khaled A. Beydoun, "Islam Incarcerated: Religious Accommodation of Prisoners Before *Holt v. Hobbs*," *University of Cincinnati Law Review* 84, no. 1 (2016): 99–151. For an account of the sharing of lawyers and legal strategies by the Nation of Islam and the Jehovah's Witnesses, see Sarah Barringer Gordon, *The Spirit of the Law: Religious Voices and the Constitution in Modern America* (Cambridge: Harvard University Press, 2010), 96–132.

78. See above at 2–3 for an explanation of the incorporation doctrine.

79. *Religious Land Use and Institutionalized Persons Act* (*RLUIPA*), Pub.L. 106–274, passed in 2000 and codified as 42 U.S.C. § 2000cc et seq.

80. Schoenfeld, *Building the Prison State*, 27.

81. *Africa v. Pennsylvania*, 662 F.2d 1025 (1981). Frank Africa did not want special food purchased for him. All he wanted was to eat the fruit and vegetables that they already had, uncooked. Their refusal highlights the ways in which internal prison regulation is about having rules not about actual cost and security risk.

pied by MOVE, causing a fire that burned down a full city block.)[82] Following a hearing, the district court, in a rather conclusory memorandum and order, found that MOVE was not a religion but that it was "merely a quasi-back-to-nature social movement of limited proportion."[83]

In his opinion in the case, Judge John Berne Hannum explained his theory of religion and why MOVE did not fit: "[T]he plaintiff's testimony revealed only that MOVE was concerned with concepts of health and a return to simplistic living. Its precepts are concerned only with a social philosophy and thus quite apart from a religion within the purview of the First Amendment. While MOVE members may respect and respond to religious concepts, these concepts are not subsumed by the MOVE ideology."[84] Religious concepts, according to the judge, must be "subsumed" by the ideology in order to make your ideology a religion. The judge concluded with the extraordinarily opaque observation that "MOVE exists, as do virtually all other organizations in our society, independent of religion and with separate and distinct purposes while still respecting and abiding by external religious principles."[85] It is hard to say what he means by external religious principles and where he imagines them to reside.

The court of appeals opinion affirming Judge Hannum's decision in *Africa* also considered at length the question of whether Frank Africa's diet was in fact religiously motivated. Although not formally precedential beyond the facts of the case, the opinion is often cited by other courts and by law professors in discussions of what counts as religion in US law. Judge Arlin Adams began his opinion for the three-judge panel that considered the appeal by summarizing the trial testimony about MOVE's teaching:

> MOVE is a "revolutionary" organization "absolutely opposed to all that is wrong." MOVE was founded, although the record does not reveal when, by

82. Characterizing MOVE is difficult by design, according to historical sociologist Robin Wagner-Pacifici. In a book analyzing the discourses of violence that contributed to the MOVE disaster in 1985, she notes "a self-conscious resistance to categorization on the part of MOVE members. Group members are insistent, in fact, that the name MOVE itself does not stand for anything." Robin Wagner-Pacifici, *Discourse and Destruction: The City of Philadelphia versus MOVE* (Chicago: University of Chicago Press, 1994), 11. In 1985, after a long period of harassment by Philadelphia police, the Philadelphia police fire-bombed the Philadelphia houses where the MOVE organization lived. John Edgar Wideman wrote a novel about it. *Philadelphia Fire* (Boston: Houghton Mifflin, 1990). The current iteration of MOVE hosts a website: http://onamove.com/ (accessed November 12, 2018).

83. 662 F.2d at 1029.

84. *Africa v. Pennsylvania*, 520 F. Supp. 967 at 970 (1981).

85. 520 F. Supp. at 970.

> John Africa, who serves as the group's revered "coordinator" and whose teachings Frank Africa and his fellow "family" members follow. MOVE has no governing body or official hierarchy; instead, because "everything is level" and "there are no ups or downs," all MOVE members, including John Africa, occupy an equivalent position within the organization. In fact, MOVE really has only "one member, one family, one body" since, according to Frank Africa, to talk to an individual MOVE "disciple" is to "talk to everybody."[86]

He further explained that "Africa testified that MOVE members participate in no distinct 'ceremonies' or 'rituals'; instead, every act of life itself is invested with religious meaning and significance."[87] He then quoted Africa directly:

> We are practicing our religious beliefs all the time: when I run, when I put information out like I am doing now, when I eat, when I breathe. All of these things are in accordance to our religious belief. . . . We don't take a date out of the week to practice our religion and leave the other days and say that we are not going to practice our religion . . . It is not a one-day thing or a once-a-week thing or a monthly thing. It doesn't have anything to do with time. Our religion is constant. It is as constant as breathing. . . . Every time a MOVE person opens their mouth, according to the way we believe, according to the way we do things, we are holding church.[88]

Testimony saturated with religious language fell on deaf ears.

Africa insisted, as do all defendants in lawsuits brought to enforce laws that circumscribe a person's religious exercise, that he had no choice about his activity. It was mandated by his church. The appellate court quotes Africa extensively: "To take away our diet is to leave me to eat nothing, for I have no choice, because when given a choice between eating poison and eating nothing, I have no choice but to eat nothing, for I can't eat other than raw. This would be suicidal and suicide is against life's ministry . . . Our religious diet is work, hard work, simple consistent unmechanized unscientific self-dependent work." He concludes: "[O]ur religious diet is family, unity, consistency, (and) uncompromising togetherness."[89] Summa-

86. 662 F. 2d at 1026.
87. 662 F. 2d at 1027.
88. 662 F. 2d at 1027.
89. 662 F. 2d at 1028.

rizing the trial testimony, appellate Judge Adams characterized MOVE as "absolutely opposed to all that is wrong," as having "one member, one family, one body," as committed to the idea that "every act of life itself is invested with religious meaning and significance," and that "our religious diet is family, unity, consistency, (and) uncompromising togetherness." Nevertheless, MOVE's ideas and practices did not meet the bar to be a religion. The extensive quotation has the double effect of giving Africa his say and taking away his voice.

After acknowledging that the Supreme Court has never defined religion for purposes of the First Amendment—and after rehearsing the difficult and delicate task that he had before him—Judge Adams adopted a definition from another lower court case, one recognizably indebted to mid-twentieth-century protestant theologies and sociologies of religion. He announced, "First, a religion addresses fundamental and ultimate questions having to do with deep and imponderable matters. Second, a religion is comprehensive in nature; it consists of a belief-system as opposed to an isolated teaching. Third, a religion often can be recognized by the presence of certain formal and external signs."[90] He then concluded, given those parameters, that MOVE was not a religion. It was not a religion, he said, because it

> does not satisfy the "ultimate" ideas criterion. Save for its preoccupation with living in accord with the dictates of nature, MOVE makes no mention of, much less places any emphasis upon, what might be classified as a fundamental concern. MOVE does not claim to be theistic: indeed it recognizes no Supreme Being and refers to no transcendental or all-controlling force. Moreover, unlike other recognized religions, with which it is to be compared for first amendment purposes, MOVE does not appear to take a position with respect to matters of personal morality, human mortality, or the meaning and purpose of life.[91]

Fatal to its classification as a religion, then, was MOVE's "preoccupation" with natural living, its nontheism, and its failure "to take a position with respect to matters of personal morality, human mortality, or the meaning and purpose of life."

Even if one accepts the judges' description of the evidence in the case

90. 662 F. 2d at 1032.
91. 662 F. 2d at 1033.

as accurate and the definition as plausible, it is difficult to fathom how his conclusion can be defended. Clearly MOVE has fundamental concerns. Its members committed to a collective life style at great personal cost. Many ended up losing their lives for their commitment. Africa's testimony is replete with concerns of morality and the meaning and purpose of life. But these facts remain invisible to the court. The Court put up a mirror to Africa in which only white religion could be seen.

The *Africa* decision continues to be cited and followed and discussed by law professors who rarely interrogate its rationality or the implicit racial bias of its conclusions.[92] Desperate for stability in a definitional field that the Supreme Court has wisely mostly avoided, *Africa* is simply accepted, along with the conscientious objector cases, *Seeger* and *Welsh*, as one of the limit cases defining religion for legal purposes.[93] Yet it is arguable that its real significance is in its capacity to illustrate the illegibility and threat to law posed by African-American religious collectivity. What law sees is that their last name is *Africa*, they perform primitivity and they are militant black environmentalists. They are the religion that is not protected by the First Amendment. The distinctions made in the opinion eerily track the history of the construction of black religion told by Sylvester Johnson and Curtis Evans. One also hears in the MOVE decisions echoes of earlier decisions on the danger of the Nation of Islam in prisons, but also of post-9/11 efforts at the legal containment of Islam.[94]

A growing body of research is documenting US government surveillance of black religion. J. Edgar Hoover's obsession with Martin Luther King, Jr., is well known.[95] A new volume of essays edited by Sylvester Johnson and Steven Weitzman surveys the FBI's surveillance of religion in the century preceding 9/11.[96] Among other things, these essays show once again the ways in which the good religion/bad religion dichotomy characterizes the governance of religion in the US more generally. As

92. *Real Alternatives, Inc. v. Sec'y of HHS*, 867 F.3d 338 (2017); *Fallon v. Mercy Catholic Med. Ctr.*, 877 F.3d 487 (2017). See also, e.g., Mark Strasser, "Free Exercise and the Definition of Religion," *Houston Law Review* 53 (2016): 909–937.

93. *United States v. Seeger*, 380 U.S. 163 (1965); *Welsh v. United States*, 398 U.S. 333 (1970).

94. Wagner-Pacifici notes the destructive effect in real time of calling MOVE members terrorists. See *Discourse and Destruction*, 134–136.

95. For thorough documentation of Hoover's surveillance of King, see the archives housed at the Martin Luther King, Jr. Research and Education Institute, https://kinginstitute.stanford.edu/encyclopedia/federal-bureau-investigation-fbi/ (accessed November 12, 2018).

96. Sylvester A. Johnson and Steven Weitzman, eds., *The FBI and Religion: Faith and National Security before and after 9/11* (Berkeley: University of California Press, 2017).

Johnson and Weitzman explain, "Hoover used his influence to promulgate a particular conception of religion, one that not only rendered progressive and pacifist christians highly suspect but also distinguished left-leaning jews from Judaism, and differentiated between authentic and mongrelized forms of Islam. Under his direction, the FBI at once defended the United States and policed the borders between true and false religion."[97] This policing took on a particular focus with respect to black religion.[98] Disestablishment arguably enables this work by blurring the line between the religious and the secular.

Rehabilitation

The flipside of the criminalization of the wrong kind of black religion is the effort to enlist the right kind in the civilizational project of moral rehabilitation. "Scholars have documented," sociologist Byron Johnson announces, "that the African-American church has been an important agency of social control and organization among black Americans."[99] This statement in an article summarizing studies purporting to show the importance of churches in reducing crime among black youth, with its rhetorical consolidation of black religious life and its careful and strategic grammatical reach back in time, similar to Michael Hallett's description of the Angola Church, carefully erases the complex and diverse history of the politics of black religion in the US and its relationship to government.[100] While secularist sociologists have offered secular explanations for any correlation observed between church attendance and various social goods, Johnson and his various collaborators have argued in the last several decades that faith, or religion, has health and social benefits that exceed secular explanations. Faith, particularly black religious faith, works, they say, accomplishing what secular agency cannot.

In Stephanie Gaskill's interviews at Angola with Burl Cain, Cain com-

97. Johnson and Weitzman, *The FBI and Religion*, 3–4. See also Dew, *The Aliites*.

98. Lerone Martin's work focuses particularly on the FBI's surveillance of black preachers. See, e.g., *"Sincerely Yours, J. Edgar Hoover": Religion and the F.B.I.* (forthcoming from Princeton University Press).

99. Byron Johnson, "The Role of African-American Churches in Reducing Crime among Black Youth," Baylor University ISR (2008).

100. See Barbara Dianne Savage, *Your Spirits Walk Beside Us: The Politics of Black Religion* (Cambridge: Harvard University Press, 2012).

mented specifically on his reading of race and religion at Angola. In apparent contrast to Hallett, he describes the black church as a thing of the past. Race had definitely been a problem in America's past, he acknowledges. But no longer. Christianity now binds them together in a colorblind present, thanks to Dr. King and President Obama. Cain, according to Gaskill, "implies that moral rehabilitation has eliminated racial tensions at Angola. 'The dynamics of it is, we have unity among ourselves,' he explains. 'We don't have racial problems; we don't have any of those kinds of things here. Just doesn't exist, and we don't have time for all that foolishness.'"[101] Gaskill explains that "[d]uring an impromptu speech at a 2006 Martin Luther King Day celebration, Cain revealed that he had had an epiphany 'in the shower' where," he said, "'God speaks to [me] the most.'" His epiphany, according to Gaskill, was that "as 'a young white man in the 60s' he 'did not appreciate Dr. King.' But this was only because he did not recognize at the time that 'King's dream was not for black people, but it was for all people.' Cain concluded, 'I had to come to Angola to appreciate the dream that Dr. King had.'"[102] As with Hallett and Johnson, the criminal justice system is for Cain where the now-whitened black church is particularly effective and visible. It is where you have to come to appreciate King's dream.

Obama's presidency too revealed the oneness of American Christianity to Cain: "'Now we have our first black president,' he concluded. 'But he doesn't look black to me, looks like American.'"[103] "King's work was done," for Cain, as Gaskill explains, because "his efforts had made it possible for the election of the first black president."[104] Indeed, for Cain, "race played a role in the past, but the Civil Rights movement erased racial discrimination, creating a colorblind society that allows for the election of Obama and the equal participation of African Americans in American society." Including prison.

But Cain understood prison religion at Angola to be distinctively southern—and black—notwithstanding his commitment to colorblindness. He told Gaskill that "the dominant religion [in the South] was Bapti-costal . . . and especially in prison, and that's the culture, because

101. The following quotations are from unpublished writing provided to me by and quoted with permission from Stephanie Gaskill. "Cain, MLK, Obama" (unpublished dissertation material, February 13, 2017), Microsoft Word file.

102. Gaskill, "Cain, MLK, Obama."

103. Gaskill, "Cain, MLK, Obama."

104. Gaskill, "Cain, MLK, Obama."

it's primarily black, about 75 percent black."[105] What bound southerners together, he thought, was that morality is to be found in religion, making religion the solution to prison violence. "From his first days as a warden," Gaskill explains, "Cain readily admitted that his emphasis on religious programming was primarily a means to ensure that prisoners served their sentences peacefully. He proudly claimed that 'spiritual commitment' among prisoners was valuable because it could be irrefutably proven to decrease violence inside penal institutions . . . 'If you can keep them over to Christianity, they're not as violent.'"[106]

Cain's challenge at Angola was how to control a large group of prisoners without any hope of release. As he explained, "'My real job is just keeping them in there . . . My first concern is custody and control, and the safety of prisoners and officers.'"[107] Christians in Angola are more peaceful, he suggests, because they can look forward to heaven, if not to their release from prison. "When we give up hope of being free here," he says, "we have to pick up and say, well, we're gonna be free when we die. So thank God we can believe in heaven."[108] This logic works for the public as well, says Cain. "Though people are 'afraid' of prisoners and 'want 'em to be punished,' nevertheless, 'they do care about their soul.' 'Nobody wants people just to go to hell,' Cain asserts. 'They want 'em to go to heaven.'"[109] The Angola Church ensures that they will go to heaven.

Stories about Angola abound. It is truly a case of an *embarras de richesses* for researchers and reporters. Indeed, there is a real danger when talking about Angola of slipping into a prurient penal tourism.[110]

Dennis Childs describes his first visit to the archives at Angola, with a first stop at the gift shop:

105. Gaskill, "Cain Black Bapti-costals" (unpublished dissertation material, February 13, 2017), Microsoft Word file.

106. Gaskill, "Cain Black Bapti-costals."

107. Gaskill, "Cain Black Bapti-costals."

108. Gaskill, "Cain Black Bapti-costals."

109. Gaskill, "Cain Black Bapti-costals."

110. For descriptions of Angola, see, among many others, Liam Kennedy, "'Today They Kill with the Chair Instead of the Tree': Forgetting and Remembering Slavery at a Plantation Prison," *Theoretical Criminology* 21, no. 2 (May 2017): 133–150; Melissa Schrift, "The Angola Prison Rodeo: Inmate Cowboys and Institutional Tourism," *Ethnology* 43, no. 4 (Fall 2004): 331–344; Melissa Schrift, "The Wildest Show in the South: The Politics and Poetics of the Angola Prison Rodeo and Inmate Arts Festival," *Southern Cultures* 14, no. 1 (Spring 2008): 22–41.

> On my way to find the staff member who was to help me locate the photographs, I walked through the gift shop, which is the first room one sees upon entering the museum site. Here, in easily the largest area within what is generally a rather small building, one can choose between an array of prison-plantation-themed objects intended to elicit chuckles and dollars from patrons, including handcuff key chains, replicas of striped shirts . . . emblazoned with the words "Angola: A Gated Community," stuffed animals in the likeness of bloodhounds.[111]

Stuffed toy bloodhounds.

You can also buy caskets at Angola. When Billy Graham died in early 2018, news stories reported that his coffin was made by Angola prisoners in a prison coffin shop started by Burl Cain.[112] Since a visit to the prison by Franklin Graham in 2005, the Graham family has given hundreds of thousands of dollars to Angola to build chapels and to support prison ministry. As the *Charlotte Observer* reported,

> The prison wanted to host Billy Graham but by the early 2000s, the evangelist was unable to make the trip. His son Franklin, though, visited several times. So did his daughter Ruth. A tour of Angola in 2005 took Franklin Graham to the woodworking shop, where he was moved by the simple dignity of the caskets and the inmates' care in building them. According to [Assistant Warden] [Gary] Young, who was on the tour that day, Franklin said his father was a "simple man with a simple message," and would want to be laid to rest in a simple casket. Franklin Graham asked Cain to have Angola carpenters make a casket for his mother, Ruth Bell Graham, and his father, and to burn the builders' names into the wood.[113]

Here we see the Angola Church as corporation, continuous in some ways with *Hobby Lobby* and with the religion of consumption described by Kathryn Lofton, the prisoners' lives branded and sold to support the prison.[114]

111. Childs, *Slaves of the* State, 99–100.

112. See, e.g., Anna Douglas, "The Story Behind Billy Graham's Casket and the Prison Inmates Who Made It," *Charlotte Observer*, March 1, 2018. https://www.charlotteobserver.com/living/religion/article202833794.html/.

113. Douglas, "The Story Behind Billy Graham's Casket."

114. Lofton, *Consuming Religion*. See discussion in conclusion.

The black church-in-law

It is not just the Grahams. What is made visible in the redemption story about the prisoners who made Billy Graham's casket is the network of evangelical christian and other religious prison ministries, including Prison Fellowship Ministry founded by Charles Colson, which have taken up the programming vacuum left by mass incarceration, underfunding, and the absence of secular alternatives.[115] Prison religion is a religion in which crime is equated with sin and rehabilitation with conversion, distracting attention from the systemic pathologies in the US criminal justice system.[116]

The church is everywhere at Angola. Until very recently, a signboard at the entrance announced that

> The light of God surrounds you,
> The love of God enfolds you,
> The power of God protects you,
> And the presence of God watches over you;
> Wherever you are, God is.

The words were attributed on the sign to Paul's Letter to the Philippians. A biblical painting of Daniel in the lions' den adorns a wall in the waiting room that adjoins the death chamber.

In 2012 Angola started a program of public passion play performances. Directed by a visiting Scottish expert on passion plays, the acting and technical work is performed by prisoners. Writer Zachary Lazar and photographer Deborah Luster attended the play in 2013. Their photographs and commentary were published in an issue of *Aperture* magazine entitled *Prison Nation*.[117] Lazar later wrote about their visit, describing the set-up for the performance:

> Upon our arrival at Angola, the crew was still building the stage sets. Three wooden crosses, bedecked with ropes, had been raised on a mound of dirt. A crowd of prisoners was standing around, chatting amid a few ranks of potted

115. Cf. Sullivan, *Prison Religion*.

116. Gaskill, "Moral Rehabilitation."

117. Deborah Luster and Zachary Lazar, "Angola Passion Play," *Aperture* (April 2018). See also Sean Patrick Farrell, "Prison Passion Play," *New York Times*, https://www.nytimes.com/video/us/100000001529143/prison-passion-play.html/.

> shrubs and a fake Roman temple made of plywood. It dawned on me that the men working with tape measures, levels, hammers, and saws on the emerging sets were not hired carpenters, but prisoners. The man standing next to me shooting with a Nikon turned out to be a prisoner who was a reporter for the prison magazine, the *Angolite*, covering the same story Luster and I were: A man who happens to be the son of God is betrayed, convicted, and sentenced to death. On the third day, he rises from the grave to save the world with a message not of retribution, but of mercy.[118]

The story is irresistible. The fusion of horizon whisks the redeemed prisoner straight to heaven, as Cain suggests. It is very difficult to find the appropriate distance from these events. Gaskill's insistence on the always conjoined religious and political motivations of the prisoners is a beginning.

Angola prison is also known for its rodeos.[119] In these rodeos, held every Sunday in October, untrained prisoners compete in rodeo events before paying public audiences. Burl Cain sells these shows as opportunities for prisoner redemption. Sociologist Melissa Schrift comments that "[m]ockery of the convict cowboy, prevalent throughout the rodeo program, is primarily through emphasis on the inmate participant's inexperience with livestock, riding, and rural life in general. Rodeo advertising repeatedly underscores participants' inexperience to embellish the sense of danger and excitement of the rodeo."[120] The rodeos are accompanied by an Inmate Arts Festival. What the rodeo program describes is, in effect, conversion by law.[121] Prisoners, like slaves before them, are healed and uplifted in their confinement, just as Hallett suggests. All of the activity at Angola—ministry, theater, journals, rodeos, picking cotton—feed an external narrative of personal redemption and rehabilitation.[122]

118. Luster and Lazar, "Angola Passion Play," 68.

119. Angola Rodeo: Louisiana State Penitentiary, http://www.angolarodeo.com/.

120. Schrift, "The Angola Prison Rodeo," 338.

121. Perhaps all conversion is conversion by law? See forum convened by Mona Oraby: *The Immanent Frame*, "Crossing and Conversion," https://tif.ssrc.org/category/exchanges/crossing-and-conversion/.

122. Photographs of prisoners working in the cotton fields at Angola are eerily timeless. Recent pictures of black men picking cotton under the supervision of white officers with shotguns on horseback seem undistinguishable from similar scenes any time in the last hundred plus years. See, for example, the video accompanying Whitney Benns, "American Slavery, Reinvented," *The Atlantic*, Sept. 21, 2015, https://www.theatlantic.com/business/archive/2015/09/prison-labor-in-america/406177/ (accessed April 12, 2019).

Conclusion

Any assessment of the religious life at Angola tends to fall into the functionalist dichotomy Curtis Evans describes so brilliantly in his intellectual history of the study of black religion. Either it is about protest or it is about accommodation. Either it is about escapism or it is about progress. Either it is about trouble-making or it is about responsibility. The narrative explaining the success of faith-based social service programs carefully narrows the religious field to one that serves this narrative. While there are arguably multiple black churches present in Angola, it is only the one that conforms its prisoners to incarceration that counts. As Gaskill explains in her review of *The Angola Seminary*, "[F]aith-based rehabilitation programs are successful in that their participants feel compelled to make recompense for their actions rather than condemning society for their plight. Those who interpret incarceration as a systemic injustice seem to be automatically excluded from the ranks of the rehabilitated."[123] They are also excluded from the statistics reported by Hallett. Gaskill reports that "[a] Catholic prison ministry volunteer at Angola told me . . . when she tried to bring a scholar of African American history to a Bible study group inside the prison the administration rejected her request, saying, 'We don't wanna talk about racism up here. We don't see people as black and white at Angola; we just see people.'"[124]

Hallett and Johnson mobilize one black church—the mythologized prophetic black church—shorn of its revolutionary ambitions and remodeled to a chastened twenty-first-century individualism, as uniquely capable of the moral uplift of black prisoners. Both they and Cain participate in the racialization of black religion arguably created in the Atlantic world of the sixteenth and seventeenth centuries described by Katharine Gerbner and by US courts over the past century of litigation by black prisoners.

There is danger from both within and without the church of stabilizing the church for purposes of capture. There is a danger in the academic study of religion as well as in law of recognizing—establishing, in American legal terms—the church, perhaps particularly the black

123. Stephanie Gaskill, "The Angola Prison Seminary," review of *The Angola Prison Seminary: Effects of Faith-Based Ministry on Identity, transformation, Desistance, and Rehabilitation*, by Michael Hallett, Joshua Hayes, Byron Johnson, Sung Joon Jang, and Grant Duwe, for Reading Religion, June 1, 2018: http://readingreligion.org/books/angola-prison-seminary.

124. Stephanie Gaskill, email message to author, May 25, 2018.

church. Disestablishment—disaggregation—of the church seems to pose a specific issue for black Americans. They both need and need to reject corporate solidarity. Yet the church, the state, and the corporation—and the academy—are all involved in the racial and religious politics of contemporary US corrections.[125]

Curtis Evans concludes his book by referring to the work of historian Marla Frederick and her refusal of the good religion/bad religion story of the black church. "Frederick argues," he says "that the accommodation and resistance paradigm fails to capture the complexity of the everyday lives of religious practitioners, especially black women . . . Assessing the function of the black church . . . has restricted the focus of the historiography of African American religion by obscuring the varied religious motives and activities of black religious persons." Such an assessment "implies a unity that is not there." "[W]e must realize that to call certain religious positions escapist or unrealistic because they failed to encourage political activity that promised relief to downtrodden groups conceals how little many people have gotten from politics."[126] Evans argues that "[n]ewer work must move beyond the black church . . . lifting the burden that has weighed so heavily on histories and interpretations of African American religion."[127] One might include the promise of the religion clauses, including disestablishment, as among those burdens.

125. Rosemary Corbett, "Freedom," in "Capitol and Secular Roundtable," *Journal of the American Academy of Religion*, forthcoming.

126. Evans, *Burden of Black Religion*, 279, citing Marla F. Frederick, *Between Sundays: Black Women and Everyday Struggles of Faith* (Berkeley: University of California Press, 2003).

127. Evans, *Burden of Black Religion*, 279–280.

CONCLUSION

The Church-in-law Otherwise

But over the course of ten years . . . I got used to conceptualizing "other Catholics" alongside Roman Catholicism.—Julie Byrne, *The Other Catholics*[1]

The church-in-law today in the US—that is, constitutionally disestablished religion under law—is widely criticized. It does not seem to be working well for anyone, inside or outside of the churches. Locating ourselves as individuals in relation to various collectives has become difficult, legally speaking. Family. Church. Nation. Political party. Planet. But the churches have a particular problem. We want them to do so many contradictory things. At the beginning of this book I suggested that what is needed is to speak back theologically to law—to refuse the secularist separation of church and state by imagining disestablishment differently. I have tried to begin that effort here: that is, to say to the courts and other institutions of US law, and to all of us, that collective religion—the church with the definite article—need not be as we/they construe it. The church-in-law's persistence suggests that the religious collective is necessary, even valuable, but that the terms of its legal status are something to argue about, not to enforce.

Political philosopher Cécile Laborde suggests that asking law to do

1. Julie Byrne, *The Other Catholics: Remaking America's Largest Religion* (New York: Columbia University Press, 2016), 3.

Artist Lorrie Payne's installation at Mother Bethel Church Museum in Philadelphia, Pennsylvania.

a better job of religion is to misunderstand liberalism's promise: "We shouldn't ask for the law to capture religion any more than we should want it to capture friendship, marriage or the arts . . . Secular law is only interested in those dimensions of religion that generate rights against others, or against the state. Secular law is not comprehensive: it does not tell you how to live—it only makes it possible for you to live under just terms with those with different gods, or none." It does this, she says, by distinguishing "'living by the will of God' and 'coercing others to live by the will of God.'" "In a liberal state," she insists, "I can live by the will of

God: preach, proselytise, organise, witness, serve, organise vibrant forms of communal life, work for justice. But what I can't do is use the formidable power of the state to coerce others to live by the will of (my) God."[2] But that is exactly the problem. What are "just terms"? The liberal state does coerce people to live by the will of its God. The church-in-law constrains the legal imagination by determining the rights of employees, access to health care, the capacity of religious communities to run their own affairs, and the administration of criminal justice.

When and how must we subordinate ourselves to the collective? Whether that collective is the state or the church? Distinguishing the religious from the secular or your God from my God will not answer that question. That has been tried.[3]

Can the church-in-law be otherwise? Or is that an anachronistic question? Are all of its avatars—the church, the state, the corporation, and the black church-in-law—just so twentieth century and so mutually contaminating? Are they all teetering on the edge of collapse? Like other modern institutions, they are attacked from without and subverted from within in a radically feverish media landscape. Is it that they are not up to the challenges of corrosive and persistent racism and misogyny, climate change, entrepreneurial war, and economic inequality? Or is it also that they are just not up to being the carriers of the leading edge of dreams of sustainability, peaceable coexistence, and justice? Is it possible to imagine law and church and economic life differently, as collective possibilities outside of a patriarchal racist and statist model or pious neoliberalism?[4]

One answer, maybe the most important one, is that the church-in-law is always also otherwise. We may just be looking in the wrong places. That is the teaching of Julie Byrne's wonderful book, *The Other Catholics*, quoted in the epigraph to this chapter.[5] The church-in-law is not exhausted by the

2. Cécile Laborde, "Response to Winnifred Fallers Sullivan" (blog post at *Syndicate* network forum on Laborde, *Liberalism's Religion*, https://syndicate.network/). In her book Laborde, while arguing that the state's meta-jurisdictional authority is the only route to just accommodation, does acknowledge the disingenouousness of some of liberalism's defenders on these grounds. See Laborde, "State Sovereignty and Freedom of Association," in *Liberalism's Religion* (Cambridge: Harvard University Press, 2017).

3. See Agrama, *Questioning Secularism*, and Cavanaugh, *Migrations of the Holy*.

4. See Katharyne Mitchell, "Religious Charity and the Spirit of Homo Economicus," *The Immanent Frame*, July 24, 2019, https://tif.ssrc.org/2019/07/24/religious-charity-and-the-spirit-of-homo-economicus/ (accessed August 11, 2019).

5. Byrne, *The Other Catholics*. See also Tracy Fessenden, *Religion Around Billie Holiday* (New Yor: NYU Press, 2018) and David Wojnarowicz, *A Fire in My Belly* https://www.youtube.com/watch?v=gHRCwQeKCuo/.

types imagined by the Court. Running beside and within and beyond each there are other churches-in-law. Other laws and other churches. Other ways of making a living. Even outlaw churches-in-law. How can those be both valued and reformed?

The church-in-law is certainly otherwise in other places with other legal arrangements. Some of those arrangements make possible a kind of clarity about the respective work of social institutions that is difficult in the US. They locate the work more explicitly. But there are always exclusions. There too, there is always the modern legal work of separating good religion from bad religion. Separation of church and state is not a social fact anywhere. It is an ideology. Robert Yelle argues that at the other end of the critique of secularism we can perhaps entertain again the importance of the sacred to our common life. He recommends that we imagine and consider adopting the work of repair that Jubilee—plenary loan forgiveness—did in the ancient world.[6]

An ecclesiology in law for our time demands both respect for the many-ness of the church, both historically and today, and humility about the reach and commitment of our own imaginations and possibilities. The image at the beginning of this chapter is a photograph I took of a sculpture by artist Lorric Payne. I encountered the two figures, beautiful renderings of rag dolls of nineteenth-century African-American women in the museum at Mother Bethel AME Church in Philadelphia. For me, these sculptures, one said to be of an enslaved woman, and the other one of a free black woman—although we don't fully have the words to describe their self-possession—give powerful and ambiguous witness to the other lives of the church, and of the church-in-law.[7]

Mother Bethel was founded in 1794 by African Americans who left St. George's Methodist Church in Philadelphia because of racial discrim-

6. Yelle, *Sovereignty and the Sacred.*

7. Hannah Garvey, research assistant for this book and a Ph.D. student at Indiana University studying African-American religion, wrote this to me about her own encounter with this image, helping me to articulate my own:

> After taking a moment to really look at the Mother Bethel image I finally get it. They are the church and the church-in-law . . . It makes the image fascinating for me in the way I think it has been fascinating for you all along . . . what about bringing them in to the conclusion and your exploration of Aretha. I see her in these faces. Open yet formed. Hands clasped in prayer or perhaps about to burst into song? And is she/Aretha/the-church in law/the child—with hands seemingly clasped though perfectly hidden behind the mother's, face upturned towards . . . the light? They are separate and yet entirely entangled. They are two and the same.

ination; it is often spoken of as one of the first African-American-led churches. During an impromptu visit to the church, we were shown around the sanctuary and invited to come back to worship by a minister of the church. We then descended to the crypt. The crypt holds the remains of the Rev. Richard Allen and his wife, Sarah Allen, founders of the African Methodist Episcopal denomination, as well as a small museum about their lives and the life of the church.[8]

The two sculptures inhabit an old-fashioned museum case, wooden with glass windows. But they don't seem to really belong there. Their bright liveliness stands out in the rather staid museumness of the rest of the basement. Confined yet honored, separated and yet together, the two women call you out. Their presence reminds us of the often-overlooked women preachers of the AME church and of other denominations—of church ladies—of women generally in many churches—of otherwise churches-in-law.[9]

With this invocation of other churches-in-law in mind, the other catholics and the women of Mother Bethel, we might ask again, is it constitutional for the US Supreme Court to use the definite article in speaking of church? What would it take for us to acknowledge the church-in-law in the US as otherwise?

As I completed this book, the most recent pronouncement on religion by the US Supreme Court was its 2018 decision in *Masterpiece Cakeshop v. Colorado Civil Rights Commission*.[10] News stories and most legal commentators have described the result in that decision as narrow and doctrinally uninteresting. They have seen it as legally minimalist, even cowardly—as having avoided the hard issues.[11] There were both anxious and

8. The website can be found at https://www.motherbethel.org/content.php?cid=8.

9. Jarena Lee (1783–1864), the first woman licensed to preach by the Rev. Richard Allen, wrote an autobiography. See, Jarena Lee, "The Life and Religious Experience of Jarena Lee," in *Sisters of the Spirit: Three Black Women's Autobiographies of the Nineteenth Century*, ed. William L. Andrews, (Bloomington: Indiana University Press, 1986), 25–48. Thank you to Hannah Garvey for this reference.

10. *Masterpiece Cakeshop, Ltd. v. Colorado Civil Rights Commission*, 584 U.S. ___ (2018). The discussion of this case in this chapter is an extension of an argument I began in two previous pieces, both published online: "Is Masterpiece Cakeshop a Church?" *The Immanent Frame*, https://tif.ssrc.org/2018/06/08/is-masterpiece-cakeshop-a-church/, and "No Cake; No Reservations," for Syndicate Network forum on Kathryn Lofton, *Consuming Religion* https://syndicate.network/symposia/theology/consuming-religion/ (accessed August 11, 2019).

11. See, e.g., Linda Greenhouse, "The Supreme Court Is Showing an Instinct for Self-Preservation, at Least Until Next Year's Election," *New York Times*, June 20, 2019, and Mark

angry dissenters from the minimalist line, each insisting that the *Masterpiece Cakeshop* decision is indeed significant and significantly destructive of LGBT rights.[12] But whatever the decision can be read to signal for the future of religious exemptions and for LGBT rights under the Constitution, the five opinions in the case do provide some more clues as to what the justices—and perhaps the rest of us—think counts as religion today for the purposes of the First Amendment—of where, that is, the church-in-law may be found today in the US. On that question, I would argue, there is actually wide agreement, not only among those in the Court's majority, but also among the dissenters and the legal commenters.

The situation that gave rise to the *Masterpiece Cakeshop* case was deceptively simple, scripted, one might say, for contestation in the Supreme Court. In July 2012, Charlie Craig and David Mullins, together with Craig's mother, Deborah Munn, approached Jack Phillips, the baker/owner of Masterpiece Cakeshop, a bakery in Lakewood, Colorado, to order a wedding cake for Craig and Mullins' wedding. Phillips told them that he could not bake the wedding cake because of his "religious opposition" to same-sex marriage. By refusing service to Craig and Mullins, Phillips triggered application of the Colorado Anti-Discrimination Act, an act that prohibits discrimination on the basis of sexual orientation in public accommodations. By using the word "religious" to modify his opposition, Phillips invoked by reference what he took to be a right to noncompliance with that act afforded him under the "free exercise of religion" clause of the First Amendment to the US Constitution.

A hearing was held before the Colorado Civil Rights Commission.

Strasser, "Masterpiece of Misdirection?" *Washington & Lee Law Review* 76 (2019): 963–1010. Such an avoidance may continue to be the Court's most successful strategy in these cases, susceptible as they are to culture wars reductionism. The court seems usually to be able to assemble a consensus only in a cautious incrementalism. During its October 2018 term, the Court had before it a case challenging the constitutionality of a World War I memorial in the shape of a cross. *The American Legion v. American Humanist Association*, No. 17-1717. The cross is now owned and maintained by the state of Maryland although originally it was built on private land by the American Legion. As predicted, the Court's decision (June 20, 2019) in favor of letting the cross remain emphasized the respect that should be shown to those who died for their country, suggesting also that the cross had been secularized by its history. For a discussion of the logic of patriotic sacrifice and the role private military contractors have played in displacing—and reinforcing—that logic, see Mateo Taussig-Rubbo, "Outsourcing Sacrifice: The Labor of Private Military Contractors," *Yale Journal of Law & Humanities* 21 (2009): 103–166.

12. See, e.g., David S. Cohen, "Silence of the Liberals: When Supreme Court Justices Fail to Speak Up for LGBT Rights," *University of Richmond Law Review* 53 (2019): 1085–1147.

Phillips was found to have violated the act. He appealed to the Colorado Court of Appeals, which upheld the decision of the commission.[13] Phillips then petitioned the US Supreme Court to hear the case. Certiorari was granted in June 2017. The Supreme Court reversed in a 7–2 decision, the opinion for the majority written by Justice Anthony Kennedy.

The legal issues in the case took a new turn in the high court. Rather than directly address the legality of Phillips' action under the act, as the commission and the court of appeals had, Kennedy shifted focus to the hearing process, asking whether the commission itself had violated the Constitution. A majority of the Supreme Court found that hostile public comments made by some members of the commission about Phillips' refusal, and about the presumed reasons for his refusal, effectively denied Phillips the neutral treatment to which he was entitled under the First Amendment free exercise clause.

Comparing the commission's treatment of Phillips unfavorably to its treatment of defendants in other similar cases before the commission, the Court also cited statements by individual commissioners that the Court described as hostile to Phillips. One such comment, echoing Cécile Laborde, was this one by one of the commissioners: "Freedom of religion and religion has been used to justify all kinds of discrimination throughout history, whether it be slavery, whether it be the holocaust, whether it be—I mean, we—we can list hundreds of situations where freedom of religion has been used to justify discrimination. And to me it is one of the most despicable pieces of rhetoric that people can use to—to use their religion to hurt others."[14] Kennedy concluded that, taken together, the evidence revealed the commission's failure to meet the constitutional requirement that "these disputes must be resolved with tolerance, without undue disrespect to sincere religious beliefs, and without subjecting gay persons to indignities when they seek goods and services in an open market."[15] In this case, he said, it was a failure to accord respect to sincere religious beliefs that proved fatal to the legality of the commission's decision.

Creation of this wedding cake proved to be hedged around by a thicket of legal rights and obligations at the local, state, and federal levels, not to mention nonstate normative orders, religious and otherwise. Imagining

13. *Mullins v. Masterpiece Cakeshop*, 370 P.3d 272 (Colorado 2015).
14. 584 U.S. at 1729.
15. 584 U.S. at 1732.

that bakeshop and that encounter now, after the decision, one can see that the air was thick with law. Where was the church-in-law?

Both the Colorado commission and the justices of the US Supreme Court accepted without any discussion that Phillips' refusal to bake the cake was religiously motivated. Their ready acceptance resonates with the deference the Court gave to the plaintiffs' assertions about the basis of their views on contraception in *Hobby Lobby*; it is also consistent with current tautological legal practice in the United States and in many other countries, that is, that a sincere (i.e., nonfraudulent) representation that one's refusal to obey the law is founded in religious belief sufficiently proves the presence of religion and triggers the relevant protective law, without further proof. Litigants today, at least white christian litigants refusing to conform to the law, are not usually asked to offer any evidence that anyone else has such a belief or that their belief is attached to a community, found in a text, or otherwise formalized or institutionalized.[16] The religiousness or not of their belief is not measured according to any specific conception of or history of religion. It is enough that they believe it to be so.

Many secular courts today say that they do not feel competent to decide what should count as religion, so they now usually limit themselves to testing sincerity—although sincerity is also rarely subject to actual proof. Perhaps the judges feel that even were they better informed, religion is simply unsusceptible to rational proof. This narrowing of judicial cognitive capacity when it comes to thinking about religion is then often excused in the US as a constitutionally mandated compulsion to refrain from assessing the presence or not of religion.[17] Yet giving a pass to such self-serving representations permits these courts to continue to privilege one group of religious persons in the law, giving them exemptions from compliance without addressing either the resulting necessary establishment of a corporeal sovereign church-in-law or the fuzzy border between religion and nonreligion mobilized to support such distinctions. There is a kind of conspiracy in these cases between left and right to refrain from investigation into the exclusions effected by the sincerity standard.

We religion scholars should not be so constrained, in my view. Bypass-

16. It is otherwise at the border, where those seeking asylum on the basis of religious persecution are catechized by border agents testing the orthodoxy of their responses. See Elizabeth Shakman Hurd, "Border Religion," in *At Home and Abroad*, ed. Elizabeth Shakman Hurd and Winnifred Fallers Sullivan. Forthcoming.

17. See Sullivan, *Prison Religion*, 149.

ing the cautious squeamishness and unholy alliance between left and right that we see in the courts when it comes to religion in law today, let us weigh in where angels fear to tread. Where do we see the religion in this case and what kind of religion is it? Where is the church-in-law and can it be otherwise?

Jack Phillips is described by Justice Kennedy as "a devout Christian." Kennedy says of Phillips that

> [h]e has explained that his "main goal in life is to be obedient to" Jesus Christ and Christ's "teachings in all aspects of his life." And he seeks to "honor God through his work at Masterpiece Cakeshop." One of Phillips' religious beliefs is that "God's intention for marriage from the beginning of history is that it is and should be the union of one man and one woman." To Phillips, creating a wedding cake for a same-sex wedding would be equivalent to participating in a celebration that is contrary to his own most deeply held beliefs.[18]

That is all. That is what qualifies Phillips for constitutional attention under the First Amendment.

What do we know about Phillips' religion from this? We are told that he believes that his whole life should reflect fidelity to the teachings of Jesus. Justice Kennedy describes him as holding deeply held beliefs. Virtually all christians (perhaps a strong majority of Americans) would affirm that they believe—or that they fervently wish—that their whole lives should reflect fidelity to the teachings of Jesus. Presumably, that would not be enough to qualify a person for exemption from any law that interfered with what they regard themselves as obligated to do as christians. Presumably there would have to be at least an imagined credible link between a larger christian community—and a longer tradition of normative guidance—with respect to the activity in question. Presumably the church—a church—would have to be at least lurking in the shadows underwriting the nonnegotiability of such a claim.

In the joint appendix filed in the Court by the parties, an affidavit included by Phillips simply stated that "I believe that God created Adam and Eve, and that God's intention for marriage is that it should be the union of one man and one woman."[19] Some version of a belief in divine

18. 584 U.S. at 1724.
19. Joint Appendix *Masterpiece Cakeshop* at 157.

creative participation in life on this earth is perhaps fundamental across many religious traditions. God's intention with respect to marriage is a little less clear, given the presence of polygamy in the biblical text and in communities of christians and others throughout the last couple of thousand years. Is it enough that Phillips himself joins creation to heterosexual marriage? Does he thereby become a church? Do he and his bakeshop become *the* church?

What more has been required for such hands-off treatment by the court? If we look to the religion claims in past cases, before the sincerity test was standardized, we see that George Reynolds, in the famed nineteenth-century mormon polygamy case, said he would be damned if he did not practice plural marriage, such marriages being specifically mandated by his church's teaching in imitation of the biblical patriarchs.[20] The Court in *Reynolds* made a careful, if bigoted, analysis of mormon religious teaching. The Court, and the US government more broadly, understood itself to be at war with the church itself.[21] In the end, after further litigation, Congress revoked the charter of the Church of Jesus Christ of Latter-Day Saints in order to underline the federal government's displeasure with its teachings in a decision curiously titled *The Late Church of Jesus Christ of Latter-Day Saints v. U.S.*[22] Late? Made late, rather, by the US government. Thick versions of the church-in-law were very much in evidence in these mormon cases. State law, federal law, . . . and mormon law. And reports of the church's demise were greatly exaggerated.

The amish families in the 1972 *Yoder* case, appealing from their convictions for noncompliance with mandatory schooling laws in Wisconsin, said categorically that sending their children to high school would destroy the amish religious community.[23] The Supreme Court basically accepted that prediction. Supported with extensive evidence by academic experts on the history and sociology of the Amish church, and references to Henry David Thoreau, Chief Justice Warren Burger reported lovingly and at length on the history of the Amish way of life and of the threat that attending high school would pose to that way of life. In 1990 Alfred Smith and Galen Black said that ingesting peyote was a sacramental mandate, central to the weekly worship of their community, the Native American Church;

20. *Reynolds v. US*, 98 U.S. 145 (1879).
21. See Gordon, *The Mormon Question*.
22. *The Late Church of Jesus Christ of Latter-Day Saints v. U.S.*, 136 U.S. 1 (1890).
23. *Wisconsin v. Yoder*, 406 U.S. 205 (1972).

the Court decided against them.[24] Dissenting justices in the *Smith* case rehearsed the history of peyote use in the Native American Church and speculated about the church's benefits for remediating Native American alcoholism.

The Court no longer traffics in such amateur reporting on religious communal practice in free exercise cases, at least with respect to abortion and same-sex marriage. It no longer engages the church-in-law directly. Religion today has become standardized and formatted for the purposes of laws protecting religious freedom, reduced to a matter of individual sincere and usually devout belief—about sex and reproduction.[25] These cases have become predictable performances of conventionalized positions on social issues. It has become impossible for the Court to talk about religious stuff with any seriousness. Indeed, one could argue that the Court actually dodges the real challenges posed by religious freedom claims by focusing on respect and neutrality.[26]

One might see the Court's refusal to confront the possibility of a constitutional violation at the heart of the encounter in Masterpiece Cakeshop as profoundly cowardly, parallel to the cowardice revealed in Robert Cover's reading of the Court's 1982 *Bob Jones University* decision. Cover saw the Court in that decision as deflecting the racial discrimination question at issue by deciding the case on narrow statutory, rather than constitutional, grounds.[27]

What makes this Colorado baker and his beliefs so obviously deserving of special treatment? Is social prejudice what freedom of conscience—or of the church—should protect? Phillips was not asked to testify to the importance—or religiousness—of his beliefs, beyond the bare assertion that they were his. The unexceptional religiousness of his objection was apparently obvious to the Court. He was not espousing polygamy or ingesting controlled substances—or claiming sanctuary. He did not claim

24. *Employment Division v. Smith*, 494 U.S. 872 (1990).

25. See Sarah Imhoff, "Belief," in *Religion, Law, USA*, ed. Isaac Weiner and Joshua Dubler (New York: New York University Press, 2019). The Court's 1981 opinion in *Thomas v. Review Board*, 450 U.S. 707 (1981), importantly foreshadows this shift to the sincerity of individual belief. Thomas, a Jehovah's Witness, objected to participating in the production of armaments and was found to have a right to such an accommodation, notwithstanding that his belief was idiosyncratic within in his own religious community.

26. There are interesting other legal questions raised in the dissent by Justice Ginsburg in the *Masterpiece Cakeshop* case about the inadequacy of the evidence adduced by the majority to prove hostility on the part of the commissioners. She suggests that the majority's effort to avoid the constitutional question was somewhat disingenuous, but she too focuses on discrimination, not on religion.

27. See above discussion of Cover at 55–56.

a right granted by an English king at Runnymede. His last name was not Africa. He was simply expressing a common bias using religious language. According to the Court, Phillips is "devout." He believes that God intends marriage to be restricted to one man and one woman, and he believes that it would be wrong for him to sell a cake he created to a same-sex couple for their wedding. Together those elements make his refusal obviously religious to the court and to many others today. How do they know? How do we know? They seem to be grasping at straws. In *Masterpiece Cakeshop* and in other recent free exercise and RFRA cases, litigants are often described as "devout" as well as sincere.[28] Does this imply that the Constitution only protects devoutly religious people, not just ordinary religious people?

Maybe the Court is trying to signal that these particular religious people really cannot help themselves. "Here I stand. I can do no other," in the reported words of Martin Luther. Devoutness implies more than usual attention to religious matters. It implies, perhaps, an unusual piety. There is, on the one hand, the diffuse and pervasive religiousness of Americans. And then there are people who really care, whose religion is hardcore, who deserve respect for that reason alone. They are the ones left behind, perhaps, by larger social shifts. Is this then a plea for compassion for at least some of those compelled to outlawry by their convictions—a way to walk back from the Court's much-criticized decision in *Smith*, which effectively eliminated constitutional exemptions for reasons of religious conscience?

Like the owners of *Hobby Lobby*, Phillips, in the words of moral theology, apparently believes that he will be complicit with evil if he takes actions to enable what he takes to be sinful activity.[29] The Court does not inquire into whether his views on either marriage or on the possible complicity with evil of cake-baking are the teaching of the church. It is enough that he believes it—and that they believe him to be devout—and that he would suffer by losing his business if required to do it. He becomes thereby the church-in-law.

In the Vietnam-era conscientious objector cases, the Court faced a

28. See, e.g., *Holt* and *Hobby Lobby*, in which nearly identical words describe the litigants' religion. *Holt v. Hobbs*, 574 U.S. ___ (2015); *Hobby Lobby*, 573 U.S. at 700.

29. In his own words, he says that "I believe it is also very clear that Bible commands me to flee from sin and not to participate or encourage it in any way." Joint Appendix at 159. See Cathleen Kaveny, *Ethics at the Edges of Law: Christian Moralists and American Legal Thought* (Oxford: Oxford University Press, 2018), for a thorough examination of the argument from complicity.

similar challenge from individualized religious conviction; availability of the longstanding statutory exemption for conscientious objectors to war was gradually expanded beyond members of the historically pacifist churches to which the exemption was originally limited.[30] It was quite clear initially that exemption from the draft was limited to the amish and their like. But slowly, other positions on war were pressed. Did one's conviction have to stem from belief in a supreme being? Could one be only philosophically opposed to war, without making an explicitly religious reference? Could one object only to a particular war, as opposed to all war? Could one be a catholic and be a conscientious objector, arguing on the basis of just war teaching? The contentiousness of the politics around the Vietnam War intensified those questions and put pressure on law's capacity to fairly accommodate minorities and dissenters through exemptions founded in religious reasons. The specific narrative of persecution and martyrdom supporting anabaptist opposition to war gave way to a wider range of narratives, increasingly focused on the psychological burden to the individual, not of the historic commitment of a minority religious community.

A parallel situation is developing today around issues of reproductive rights and sexual morality. No longer confined to a recognizable and bounded community such as the catholic hospital or school, beliefs float free of historical institutional definition—available to shore up new churches-in-law.

Also supporting this new jurisprudence is the assumption that conservative views about sex are properly understood to be religious while liberal ones are secular. No explanation needs to be given as to why a particular view with respect to sex or reproduction is religious. Yet as discussed above in chapter three concerning the *Hobby Lobby* decision, historians such as R. Marie Griffith and Joan Wallach Scott, have shown that this alignment is very recent and is based in a distorted view of the historical evidence.[31] Issues of sex and reproduction have not historically always been positioned as central to church teaching in the way they are today. The theology of complicity has been much contested. The sexual identity of customers has not always been understood to disqualify commerce with those whose actions are judged sinful. More importantly, secu-

30. *United States v. Seeger*, 380 U.S. 163 (1965); *Welsh v. United States*, 398 U.S. 333 (1970). Winnifred Fallers Sullivan, "'The Conscience of Contemporary Man': Reflections on *U.S. v. Seeger* and *Dignitatis Humanae*," *U.S. Catholic Historian* 24 (Winter 2006): 107–123.

31. See Scott, *Sex and Secularism*; Griffith, *Moral Combat*.

lar people are not and have not necessarily been less biased and judgmental about reproductive rights and same-sex marriage than religious people. The record is very mixed.[32]

While he did not need to reach the issue because the case was decided on other grounds, Justice Kennedy did speculate as to the proper scope of constitutionally mandated accommodation to such discriminatory practices against gay couples. He conceded that accommodation of beliefs in opposition to same-sex marriage could get out of hand, resulting in serious discrimination against the LGBT community, so, after dealing with the commission's lack of neutrality, Kennedy speculated that any exemption be limited to clergy. And the church appeared once more.

Kennedy assumed that everyone would agree that clergy are a special case. "When it comes to weddings," he said, "it can be assumed that a member of the clergy who objects to gay marriage on moral and religious grounds could not be compelled to perform the ceremony without denial of his or her right to the free exercise of religion. This refusal would be well understood in our constitutional order as an exercise of religion, an exercise that gay persons could recognize and accept without serious diminishment to their own dignity and worth."[33] On the other hand, to extend a well-understood clerical privilege, a familiar feature of the church-in-law, to others involved in providing services for weddings might create a social stigma parallel to that of Jim Crow laws. As he explained, "[I]f that exception were not confined, then a long list of persons who provide goods and services for marriages and weddings might refuse to do so for gay persons, thus resulting in a community-wide stigma inconsistent with the history and dynamics of civil rights laws that ensure equal access to goods, services, and public accommodations."[34]

Well, yes. Exactly. Religious bias, like racial discrimination, cannot be confined by limiting the parties exempted to clergy, especially perhaps with respect to weddings. Everyone is involved. The clerical privilege he mobilizes is hopelessly out of date. Read the wedding columns in the newspaper. Professional clergy are increasingly rare at weddings and many today are living under a cloud of accusations. Instead, there are mail-order ministers, friends, family, and wedding planners—and bakers. They are the

32. See *The Immanent Frame* discussion of "Sex, Secularism, and 'Femonationalism,'" https://tif.ssrc.org/category/exchanges/sex-secularism-femonationalism/, May 18–July 29, 2018.

33. 584 U.S. at 1727.

34. 584 U.S. at 1727.

celebrants. Religion in the US doesn't work in that hierarchically church-y way, as Justice Thurgood Marshall noted. Kennedy is misinformed.

Phillips does not mention clergy. In the opinions in *Masterpiece Cakeshop*, Phillips' religious objection to baking for those he would very likely name as sinners appears entirely individual, unconnected to any theological tradition or any religious community. And yet, like the owners of Conestoga and Hobby Lobby, it could be argued that he does belong to a church. He belongs to the web of consumption that Kathryn Lofton describes with Durkheimian intensity in *Consuming Religion*. He belongs to the wedding-industrial complex.[35]

The Colorado Civil Rights Act explicitly exempts churches, synagogues, and mosques from its strictures against discrimination.[36] Religion is naturally discriminatory, they seem to concede, but like Justice Kennedy, they want such discrimination to be confined to houses of worship. Many of Phillips' critics argue that if he does not want to serve everyone, then he should go into another line of work. Religion does not belong in a shop, they say, as they said about Hobby Lobby. This criticism reveals again a real misunderstanding of American religious life. Religion and commerce have always mixed in the United States.[37] Hobby Lobby and the Masterpiece Cakeshop are not doing something new in mixing business and God. Religion in the workplace is one way in which Americans as workers and as consumers have practiced disestablished religion and today is one way in which they are refusing the privatization of religion. Many Americans are finding church at work and through their consumption practices. There is a sense in which they are reclaiming public religion.

Lofton argues that our lives as consumers have become even more devoutly religious under late capitalism.[38] Linking a serious engagement with the great thinkers on religion, on the one hand, with astonishingly complex readings of a varied range of US cultural phenomena—the office cubicle, cleanliness, parenting, the Kardashians, Goldman Sachs, Herman

35. Lofton, *Consuming Religion*.

36. "It is a discriminatory practice and unlawful for a person, directly or indirectly, to refuse, withhold from, or deny to an individual or a group, because of disability, race, creed, color, sex, sexual orientation, marital status, national origin, or ancestry, the full and equal enjoyment of the goods, services, facilities, privileges, advantages, or accommodations of a place of public accommodation." Colorado Revised Statutes §24-34-601(2)(a) (2017). The act defines "public accommodation" broadly to include any "place of business engaged in any sales to the public and any place offering services . . . to the public," but excludes "a church, synagogue, mosque, or other place that is principally used for religious purposes." §24-34-601(1)

37. See above at 109–110.

38. Lofton, *Consuming Religion*.

Miller, 9/11, the internet—on the other, she figures the US marketplace as religious. On this theory, one might argue that the gay couple and their guests in this case are also consuming their religion through the buying of a custom wedding cake.

Lofton urges us to stop consuming religion and commit ourselves to making religion "do something different." Can we do that? Can the church-in-law be made to do something different?[39]

What if we entertain the possibility that Masterpiece Cakeshop could be a different kind of church-in-law, a church and a law defined by a public practice of collaborative justice? The shop is a place where Jack Phillips says he honors God through his craft.[40] It is a place where Charlie Craig and David Mullins sought to acquire ritual food for a religious event. A coffee shop is a place of worship and fellowship today, one might say. Could we then say back to Phillips that Jesus ate with sinners? Or that all are sinners? Or "judge not that ye be not judged"? Or that hospitality and table fellowship have been virtues in many traditions? *And then listen to his response.* Is all that can be done is, first, to isolate and segregate devout religious people, and then, either vilify them or treat them with kid gloves? By focusing on alternative or even outlaw churches-in-law, rather than on consuming religion, can we reimagine our common life without denying the awe-ful power of the collective and our responsibility to reform it?

The *Masterpiece Cakeshop* decision was announced on Monday, June 4, 2018. On Friday, June 8, Anthony Bourdain, chef and food journalist, was found dead in his hotel room in Strasbourg, France, apparently by suicide. On June 9, 2018, religion scholar Courtney Bender drew attention to the link between these two events in a tweet responding to my June 8 blog post on the *Masterpiece Cakeshop* decision. She wrote: "Spent my day playing out various versions of what might have transpired if Anthony Bourdain had taken *No Reservations* to Masterpiece Cakeshop."[41]

39. Or perhaps it will be forced to? I write this as the Roman Catholic Church undergoes massive reconstruction, in part to disentangle itself from its pretensions to sovereignty, as described above in chapter one. See Massimo Faggioli, "Abuse Crisis: Shifting Boundaries Between Church and State," *The Immanent Frame*, February 5, 2019, https://tif.ssrc.org/2019/02/05/abuse-crisis-shifting-boundaries-between-church-and-state/.

40. "I desire to honor God through my work at Masterpiece Cakeshop, Inc." Joint Appendix at 157. Other would-be litigants have continued to enter Phillips' shop seeking cakes. See op-ed by Jack Phillips, "Can I Just Be a Cake Artist Again?," *Denver Post*, https://www.denverpost.com/2019/03/08/jack-phillips-can-i-just-be-a-cake-artist-again/.

41. Courtney Bender, (@achtungbender), Twitter, June 9, 2018, 3:14p.m., https://twitter.com/achtungbender/status/1005573766024450048.

Still from "Hanoi," Parts Unknown, produced by CNN, September 2016.

Immediately what came to my mind was Bourdain seated in the shop with the baker and his customers—on plastic chairs. A transposition, in other words, of the well-known video of Bourdain and Barack Obama eating at a noodle shop in Saigon, filmed for an episode of Bourdain's *Parts Unknown*.[42]

As they eat and drink their beer, Obama and Bourdain speak of their common conviction that, in Obama's words, "People everywhere are pretty much the same." Around them Saigonese are eating their noodles. A couple. A family. Presumably the secret service detail. All on plastic chairs. If we imagine Bourdain as the minister of this church—they are convened to speak of peace—and, importantly, to eat together in public.

I do not want to speak for her but I will take it that Courtney Bender was suggesting that rather than regarding the cake decision as revealing the truth about religion and about our unbridgeable predicament, that is, that religious people are defined by their disdain for LGBT folks and that we are implacably divided between those who do and those who do not favor same-sex marriage, we might rather imagine another truth, one argued for by Bourdain in his travel and food programs. Instead of the tight jurisdictional focus on the opposition between Phillips and Craig and Mullins, trapped as they are into consuming their religion, we might consider a broader community that encompasses all three.

42. Anthony Bourdain, "Hanoi," *Parts Unknown*, season 8, episode 1 (aired September 24, 2016), CNN.

"Barack Obama, Jack Phillips, and Anthony Bourdain," drawing by Kay Read.

No cake. Just noodles. And beer. Or, as imagined in religion scholar Kay Read's drawing, coffee and muffins. No reservations.[43]

We need, as Benjamin Berger argues, to change our legal aesthetics.[44] In this other world that he imagines, we could live the hospitality and table fellowship that all religions teach. We could see a cakeshop as a church-in-law, a place, in Lofton's words, "within the precarious challenge of encounter."[45] In this scenario, Phillips' evident gift for baking would be in service of this other community.

But no wedding cakes.

What if, inspired by the work of radical empathy taught by Hillel Gray,[46] we listened to Phillips instead of hating on him?

Another image by a Bloomington artist.

Bourdain and Obama are, of course, a part of the very celebrity world of consumption Lofton describes. We all are. Community is a fragile matter.

43. See Kay Read, "To Eat and Be Eaten: Mesoamerican Human Sacrifice and Ecological Webs," *The Wiley-Blackwell Companion to Material Religion*, ed. Vasudha Narayanan (Oxford, UK: Wiley-Blackwell, 2019).

44. Berger, *Law's Religion*.

45. Lofton, *Consuming Religion*, 293.

46. "Empathy and the Religious 'Enemy,'" http://www.miamioh.edu/cas/academics/departments/comp-religion/research/empathy/index.html/ (accessed April 13, 2019).

Image by Rose Harding, artist based in Bloomington, Indiana.

I borrow the scene imagined by Bender, and illustrated by artist and religion scholar Kay Read and artist Rose Harding, offering it as what James Boyd White calls "an act of hope."[47] Perhaps as a gesture toward an ethic of care, as described by Mariana Valverde, following Judith Butler's reading of *Antigone*.[48]

Masterpiece Cakeshop was litigated as a free exercise case, but in many ways it is more interesting as an establishment clause case. What is problematic about allowing Phillips to deny service to Craig and Mullins as a matter of right is that Phillips' prejudice is allowed to constitute the church-in-law. It has become a place where equal protection law does not reach.

Disestablishment is usually thought of as something that happened at the beginning of our history as a country, setting us free as religious people. Disestablishmentarianism holds out the utopian promise of a country at once filled with religion and in which no one's religious life is constrained by law. The First Amendment was ratified and the government was disabled from passing a law "respecting an establishment of religion."

47. White, *Acts of Hope*.
48. Valverde, *Chronotopes of Law*, 120–122.

It might make more sense to think of disestablishment as a project—not one of purification, which is impossible—but of realizing a distinctively American church-in-law. All of the European churches that crossed the Atlantic began a process of disestablishment from the geographically bound theologies they left behind. They became mobile and dangerously free, free of law, cooperating with genocide and enslavement—but also available for new possibilities for justice.

Perhaps, following *New York Times* Wesley Morris, we should imagine Aretha Franklin, rather than Anthony Bourdain, in the cakeshop? Morris' cry in his bereavement honors *her* as church . . . and state.

> Despite the world's bereavement over her death, despite her having been less a household name and more a spiritual resident of our *actual home*, despite giving us soundtracks for loneliness, for lovemaking, for joy, for church, cookouts and bars, despite the induction ceremonies, medals and honorary degrees, despite her having been the only Aretha most of us have ever heard of, is it possible that we've taken her for granted, that in failing to make her president, a saint or her own country, we still might not have paid her *enough* respect?

"We still have not paid her enough respect." How might we do that? J. Kameron Carter argues for another we, an us found in a rejection of the we made by white supremacy and an embrace of blackness as sacred.[49] Perhaps she could help us do that. Together with Marie Ashe, and Pussy Riot and the lay orthodox who tried to make a new church, and the ladies of Mother Bethel, and Anthony Bourdain. As well as Cheryl Perich, the Greens, the Hahns, and the prisoners at Angola. The bakeshop would be crowded but it might make a beginning.

In his 2009 homily to the Roman Catholic Church in Paris, Giorgio Agamben urges the church to understand itself as living not in the chronological time of "the juridification and commodification of human relations"—or what might be called in the US the legal/penal modernization/rationalization/bureaucratization of religion—that characterizes a church in which salvation history is permanently deferred, nor in the apocalyptic time of imminent crises, but in a messianic time conscious of the end but not collapsing into it, suspended in tension, already but not yet.[50]

49. Carter, *Black Rapture*. See also Su'ad Abdul Khabeer, *Muslim Cool: Race, Religion, and Hip Hop in the United States* (New York: New York University Press, 2016).

50. Giorgio Agamben, *The Church and the Kingdom*, trans. Leland de la Durantaye (Chicago: Seagull Books, 2012). See also Esmeir, *Juridical Humanity*.

Acknowledgments

I am very grateful to Alan Thomas and Kyle Wagner at the University of Chicago Press for their patient support of this project and to the American Bar Foundation for the year's residence as a visiting fellow which allowed me to complete it.

I began to think through the church-in-law as a result of invitations to give lectures at Princeton University and at the Center for the Study of Religion at the University of California–Berkeley. Sorting out what I intuited and how to explain it—to myself and to the mixed audiences I encountered in Berkeley and in Princeton—across fields and cultures—gave me a start. Writing the religion and law of this book has been more difficult. I am grateful to the many who have helped me to do that. Many, many thanks to friends and colleagues who have read part or all of the manuscript and who have provided both encouragement and honest critique. Good friends indeed: Joe Bartzel, Courtney Bender, Spencer Dew, Alessandro Ferrari, Constance Furey, Hannah Garvey, Evan Haefeli, Cooper Harriss, Beth Hurd, Fred Konefsky, Rick Nance, Jothie Rajah, Noah Salomon, Steve Selka, Susan Shapiro, Barry Sullivan, and James Boyd White. Thanks also to the anonymous reviewers for the press who read carefully and commented thoroughly on the manuscript. I have incurred many intellectual debts over the last several decades of working on these questions. I apologize to those who I have not named here or in the footnotes. I am nevertheless grateful for your teaching.

Thank you to Indiana University graduate students Hannah Garvey and Matt Graham for help in the preparation of the manuscript for submission.

The Department of Religious Studies at Indiana University has been a nurturing and stimulating intellectual community in which to do this work. I feel very lucky to be in that company.

Bibliography

Legal Cases

Africa v. Pennsylvania, 662 F.2d 1025 (1981).

American Legion v. American Humanist Association, No. 17-1717.

Americans United v. Prison Fellowship, 555 F. Supp. 2d 988 (S.D. Iowa 2008).

Bryce v. Episcopal Church, 289 F.3d 648, 655–57 (10th Cir. 2002).

Burwell v. Hobby Lobby, 573 U.S. ___ (2014).

Canea Catholic Church v. Greece, European Court of Human Rights (143/1996/762/963).

Cantwell v. Connecticut, 310 U.S. 296 (1940).

Citizens United v. Federal Election Commission, 558 U.S. 310 (2010).

Combs v. Cent. Tex. Annual Conference, 173 F.3d 343, 345–50 (5th Cir. 1999).

Cooper v. Pate, 378 U.S. 546 (1964).

EEOC v. Catholic Univ. of Am., 83 F.3d 455, 460–63, 317 U.S. App. D.C. 343 (D.C. Cir. 1996).

EEOC v. Hosanna-Tabor Evangelical Lutheran Church & Sch., 582 F. Supp. 2d 881(2008).

EEOC v. Hosanna-Tabor Evangelical Lutheran Church, 597 F.3d 769, 776 (2011).

EEOC v. Roman Catholic Diocese, 213 F.3d 795, 800–01 (4th Cir. 2000).

Employment Division v. Smith, 494 U.S. 872 (1990).

Erie v. Tompkins, 304 U.S. 64 (1938).

Everson v. Board of Education, 330 U.S. 1 (1947).

Fallon v. Mercy Catholic Med. Ctr., 877 F.3d 487 (2017).

Fratello v. Archdiocese of N.Y., 863 F.3d 190, 198 (2017).

Free Church of Scotland v. Overtoun, [1904] AC 515.

Freedom from Religion Found. Inc. v. Lew, 983 F. Supp. 2d 1051(2013).

Freedom from Religion Foundation v. Lew, 773 F.3d 815 (2014).

Gaylor v. Mnuchin, Nos. 18-1277 & 18-1280 (2019).

Gellington v. Christian Methodist Episcopal Church, Inc., 203 F.3d 1299, 1301–04 (11th Cir. 2000).

Hollins v. Methodist Healthcare, Inc., 474 F.3d 223, 225–27 (6th Cir. 2007).

Hosanna-Tabor Evangelical Lutheran Church and School v. EEOC, 565 U.S. 171 (2012).

Kedroff v. St. Nicholas Cathedral of Russian Orthodox Church, 344 U.S. 94 (1952).

Masterpiece Cakeshop, Ltd. v. Colorado Civil Rights Commission, 584 U.S. ___(2018).

McCollum v. Board of Education, 333 U.S. 203 (1948).

Mullins v. Masterpiece Cakeshop, 370 P.3d 272 (Colorado 2015).

Natal v. Christian & Missionary Alliance, 878 F.2d 1575, 1578 (1st Cir. 1989).

Petruska v. Gannon Univ., 462 F.3d 294, 303–07 (3d. Cir. 2006).

Pfeil v. St. Matthews Evangelical Lutheran Church of the Unaltered Augsburg Confession, 877 N.W.2d 528 (Minn. 2016).

Ponce v. Roman Catholic Church, 210 US 296 (1904).

R(E) v. The Governing Body of JFS, [2009] UKSC 15.

Real Alternatives, Inc. v. Sec'y of HHS, 867 F.3d 338 (2017).

Reynolds v. US, 98 U.S. 145 (1879).

Ruffin v. Commonwealth, 62 Va. 790, 796 (Va. 1871).

Scharon v. St. Luke's Episcopal Presbyterian Hosp., 929 F.2d 360, 362–63 (8th Cir. 1991).

Schleicher v. Salvation Army, 518 F.3d 472, 475–76 (7th Cir. 2008).

Serbian E. Orthodox Diocese v. Milivojevich, 426 U.S. 696 (1976).

St. Martin Evangelical Lutheran Church v. South Dakota, 451 U.S. 772 (1981).

Trinity Lutheran Church of Columbia, Inc. v. Comer, 582 U.S. ___ (2017).

Trustees of Dartmouth College v. Woodward, 17 U.S. 518 (1819).

Wallace v. Jaffree, 472 U.S. 38, 91–113, 113 (1985).

Watson v. Jones, 80 U.S. (13 Wall.) 679 (1871).

Werft v. Desert Sw. Annual Conference, 377 F.3d 1099, 1100–04 (9th Cir. 2004).

Wisconsin v. Yoder, 406 U.S. 205 (1972).

Zelman v. Simmons-Harris, 536 U.S. 639 (2002).

Briefs

Burwell v. Hobby Lobby, 573 U.S. ___ (2014), Amicus Curiae Brief of Corporate and Criminal Law Professors in Support of Petitioners.

Burwell v. Hobby Lobby, 573 U.S. ___ (2014), Brief of the Christian Booksellers Association et al.

Hosanna-Tabor Evangelical Lutheran Church and School v. EEOC, 565 U.S. 171 (2012), Brief Amici Curiae of Professor Eugene Volokh et al.

Hosanna-Tabor Evangelical Lutheran Church and School v. EEOC, 565 U.S. 171 (2012), Brief for the Petitioner.

Hosanna-Tabor Evangelical Lutheran Church and School v. EEOC, 565 U.S. 171 (2012), Brief of the Lutheran Church–Missouri Synod As Amicus Curiae in Support of Petitioner.

Constitutions, Statutes, Rules

U.S. Const. art. I, §10.
U.S. Const. amend. I, § 1.
U.S. Const. amend. XIV § 1.
26 U.S.C. §107.
26 U.S.C. §5000A(f)(2); §§4980H(a), (c)(2).
42 U.S.C. §§ 2000cc et seq.
42 U.S.C. §§ 2000e et seq.
42 U.S.C. §§2000bb–1(a),(b).
42 U.S.C. § 12113(d).
45 CFR §147.131(a).
45 CFR §147.131(b).
27 Fed. Sent. R. 237
77 Fed. Reg. 8725.
78 Fed. Reg. 39874 (2013).
H.R. Rep. No. 485 part 2, 101st Cong., 2d Sess. 76–77 (1990).
Missouri Const. art. I, §7.
Virginia Const. art. IV, § 59.
Northwest Ordinance of 1787. art. VI, 1 Stat. 51 n.(a).

Books, Articles, and Films

Agamben, Giorgio. *The Kingdom and the Glory: For a Theological Genealogy of Economy and Government.* Translated by Lorenzo Chiesa with Matteo Mandarini. Stanford: Stanford University Press, 2011.

———. *The Church and the Kingdom.* Translated by Leland de la Durantaye. Chicago: Seagull Books 2012.

Agrama, Hussein Ali. *Questioning Secularism: Islam, Sovereignty, and the Rule of Law in Egypt.* Chicago: University of Chicago Press, 2012.

Alexander, Michelle. "The Newest Jim Crow" (opinion). *New York Times*, November 11, 2018. https://www.nytimes.com/2018/11/08/opinion/sunday/criminal-justice-reforms-race-technology.html/. Accessed November 11, 2018.

Ambasciano, Leonardo, and Thomas J. Coleman. "History as a Canceled Problem? Hilbert Lists, du Bois-Reymond's Enigmas, and the Scientific Study of Religion." *Journal of the American Academy of Religion* 87 (2019): 366–400.

Anidjar, Gil. *Blood: A Critique of Christianity.* New York: Columbia University Press, 2014.

Årsheim, Helge. "Imagine There's No Religion—and No State Church Too?: The Curious Tale of How the State of Norway Left a Religion and Established a Church." *Religion Going Public.* http://religiongoingpublic.com/archive/2017/imagine-theres-no-religion-and-no-state-church-too/. Accessed August 25, 2018.

Asad, Talal. *Formations of the Secular: Christianity, Islam, Modernity.* Stanford: Stanford University Press, 2003.

Ashe, Marie. "Beyond Nomos and Narrative: Unconverted Antinomianism in the Work of Susan Howe." *Yale Journal of Law and Feminism* 18, no. 1 (2006): 5–59.

Balkin, Jack M., and Sanford Levinson. "The Dangerous Thirteenth Amendment." *Columbia Law Review* 112, no. 7 (November 2012): 1459–1499.

Barkan, Joshua. *Corporate Sovereignty: Law and Government under Capitalism.* Minneapolis: University of Minnesota Press, 2013.

Bartzel, Joe. "Between Riot and Reconciliation: History, Narrative, and the Ferguson Commission on the Path to Freedom, Justice, and Equality." Ph.D. dissertation, Indiana University. Forthcoming.

Bellafonte, Gina. "Why Should Religion Be a Bar to Vaccines?" *New York Times*, April 14, 2019.

Bender, Courtney. "The Power of Pluralist Thinking." In *The Politics of Religious Freedom*, edited by Winnifred Fallers Sullivan, Elizabeth Shakman Hurd, Saba Mahmood, and Peter Danchin, 66–77. Chicago: University of Chicago Press, 2016.

Benns, Whitney. "American Slavery, Reinvented." *The Atlantic*, September 21, 2015, https://www.theatlantic.com/business/archive/2015/09/prison-labor-in-america/406177/. Accessed April 12, 2019.

Benton, Lauren, and Richard J. Ross, eds. *Legal Pluralism and Empires: 1500–1850.* New York: New York University Press, 2013.

Berger, Benjamin L. *Law's Religion: Religious Difference and the Claims of Constitutionalism.* Toronto: University of Toronto Press, 2015.

Bernstein, Elizabeth, and Janet Jakobsen. "Sex, Secularism, and Religious Influence in US Politics." *Third World Quarterly* 31, no. 6 (September 2010): 1023–1039.

Beydoun, Khaled A. "Islam Incarcerated: Religious Accommodation of Prisoners Before *Holt v. Hobbs." University of Cincinnati Law Review* 84, no. 1 (2016): 99–151.

Black, Antony, ed. *Community in Historical Perspective.* A translation of selections from Otto von Gierke, *Das Deutsche Genossenschaftrecht* (The German Law of Fellowship). Translated by Mary Fisher. Cambridge: Cambridge University Press, 1990.

Blair, Margaret M. "Corporate Personhood and the Corporate Persona." *University of Illinois Law Review* 3 (2013): 785–820.

Blair, Margaret M., and Elizabeth Pollman. "The Supreme Court's View of Corporate Rights: Two Centuries of Evolution and Controversy." In *Corporations and American Democracy*, ed. Naomi R. Lamoreaux and William J. Novak, 245–285. Cambridge: Harvard University Press, 2017.

Bonner, Jeremy. "What Is Truth? Ecclesiology, Law, and the Historian Expert Witness in Twenty-First Century America." Ecclesiastical History Society, Summer Conference, Cambridge, July 24, 2018.

Bonner, Robert. "How Dartmouth College Commemorated the Bicentennial of the Dartmouth College Case," HistPhil forum, https://histphil.org/2019/07/16/how-dartmouth-college-commemorated-the-bicentennial-of-the-dartmouth-college-case/.

Boyarin, Daniel. *Border Lines: The Partition of Judaeo-Christianity*. Philadelphia: University of Pennsylvania Press, 2004.

Brown, Ronald. "The Black Church in a Post-Church Federation Era," Preface to Henry Pratt, *Churches and Urban Government in Detroit and New York*. Detroit: Wayne State University Press, 2004.

Brunson, Rod K., Anthony A. Braga, David M. Hureau, and Kashea Pegram. "We Trust You, But Not *That* Much: Examining Police–Black Clergy Partnerships to Reduce Youth Violence." *Justice Quarterly* 32, no. 6 (2015): 1006–1036.

Byrne, Julie. *The Other Catholics: Remaking America's Largest Religion*. New York: Columbia University Press, 2016.

Caldwell, Melissa. "Sacred Spaces and Civic Action: Topographies of Pluralism in Russia." *Religion and Society*. Forthcoming.

Carrington, Paul, and Paul H. Haagen. "Contract and Jurisdiction" *Supreme Court Review* 1996: 331–402.

Carter, J. Kameron. *Black Rapture*. Forthcoming 2020.

———. *Race: A Theological Account.* Oxford: Oxford University Press, 2008.

———. "Religion and the Future of Blackness." *South Atlantic Quarterly* 112 (2013): 589–611.

Cavanagh, Edward. "A Company with Sovereignty and Subjects of Its Own? The Case of the Hudson's Bay Company, 1670–1763." *Canadian Journal of Law and Society* 26 (2011): 25–50.

Cavanaugh, William. *Migrations of the Holy: God, State, and the Political Meaning of the Church.* Grand Rapids, MI: Eerdmans, 2011.

Chemerinsky, Erwin. *Constitutional Law: Principles and Policies.* 4th ed. New York: Wolters Kluwer, 2011.

———. "The Parsonage Exemption Violates the Establishment Clause and Should Be Declared Unconstitutional." *Whittier Law Review* 24 (2003): 707.

Chidester, David. *Wild Religion: Tracking the Sacred in South Africa*. Berkeley: University of California Press, 2012.

Childs, Dennis. *Slaves of the State: Black Incarceration from the Chain Gang to the Penitentiary*. Minneapolis: University of Minnesota Press, 2015.

Chodorow, Adam. "The Parsonage Exemption." *UC Davis Law Review* 51 (2018): 849–910.

Cohen, David S. "Silence of the Liberals: When Supreme Court Justices Fail to Speak Up for LGBT Rights." *University of Richmond Law Review* 53 (2019): 1085–1147.

Cone, James H. *The Cross and the Lynching Tree.* Maryknoll, NY: Orbis Books, 2011.

Cooper, Melinda. *Family Values: Between Neoliberalism and New Social Conservatism.* Cambridge, MA: MIT Press, 2017.

Corbett, Rosemary "Freedom," in "Capitol and Secular Roundtable," *Journal of the American Academy of Religion*, forthcoming.

Cover, Robert M. "The Supreme Court, 1982 Term—Foreword: Nomos and Narrative" (1983). Faculty Scholarship Series. Paper 2705. http://digitalcommons.law.yale.edu/fss_papers/2705.

Crawley, Ashon T. "The Sound Made Flesh." *NPR Music.* August 19, 2018, https://www.npr.org/2018/08/19/639680162/sound-made-flesh-inventive-force-aretha-franklin-gospel/.

Cressler, Matthew. *Authentically Black and Truly Catholic: The Rise of Black Catholicism in the Great Migration.* New York: New York University Press, 2017.

Dale, Elizabeth. "Spelunking, or, Some Meditations on the New Presentism." In *The Oxford Handbook of Legal History*, edited by Markus D. Dubber and Chris Tomlins, 312–321. Oxford: Oxford University Press, 2018.

Dane, Perry. "Master Metaphors and Double-Coding in the Encounters of Religion and State." *San Diego Law Review* 53, no. 1 (Winter 2016): 53–104.

Demerath, N. J., III, Peter Dobkin Hall, Terry Schmidt, and Rhys H. Williams, eds. *Sacred Companies: Organizational Aspects of Religion and Religious Aspects of Organizations.* Oxford: Oxford University Press, 1998.

Dew, Spencer. *The Aliites: Race and Law in the Religions of Noble Drew Ali.* Chicago: University of Chicago Press, 2019.

Douglas, Anna. "The Story Behind Billy Graham's Casket and the Prison Inmates Who Made It." *Charlotte Observer,* March 1, 2018. https://www.charlotteobserver.com/living/religion/article202833794.html/.

During, Simon. *Against Democracy: Literary Experience in the Era of Emancipation.* New York: Fordham Press, 2012.

Durkheim, Émile. *The Elementary Forms of Religious Life.* Oxford: Oxford University Press, 2008.

Edgar, John. *Philadelphia Fire*. Boston: Houghton Mifflin, 1990.

Ellman, Ira Mark. "Driven from the Tribunal: Judicial Resolution of Internal Church Disputes." *California Law Review* 69, no. 5 (September 1981): 1378–1444.

Engelke, Matthew. *A Problem of Presence: Beyond Scripture in an African Church.* Berkeley: University of California Press, 2007.

Esmeir, Samera. *Juridical Humanity: A Colonial History*. Stanford: Stanford University Press, 2012.

Eusebius. *The History of the Church*. Translated by Jeremy M. Schott. Oakland: University of California Press, 2019.

Evans, Curtis J. *The Burden of Black Religion*. Oxford: Oxford University Press, 2008.

Farrell, Sean Patrick. "Prison Passion Play." *New York Times*. May 5, 2012. https://www.nytimes.com/video/us/100000001529143/prison-passion-play.html.

Ferencz, Nicholas. *American Orthodoxy and Parish Congregationalism*. Piscataway, NJ: Gorgias Press, 2006.

Figgis, John Neville. *Churches in the Modern State*. London: Longmans Green, 1914.

Foucault, Michel. *Security, Territory, Population: Lectures at the College de France, 1977–1978*. Translated by Graham Burchell. Edited by Michel Sennelart. New York: Picador, 2007.

Funk, Kellen. "Church Corporations and the Conflict of Laws in Antebellum America." *Journal of Law and Religion* 32, no. 2 (July 2017): 263–284. https://doi.org/10.1017/jlr.2017.31.

———. "Shall These Bones Live?: Property, Pluralism, and the Constitution of Evangelical Reform." *Law & Social Inquiry* 41, no. 3 (Summer 2016): 742–774.

Garland, David. *The Culture of Control: Crime and Social Order in Contemporary Society*. Chicago: University of Chicago Press, 2001.

Garnett, Richard W. "The Story of *Kedroff v. St Nicholas Cathedral*." *Journal of Supreme Court History* 38, no. 1 (2013): 80–93.

Gaskill, Stephanie. "Moral Rehabilitation: Religion, Race, and Reform in America's Incarceration Capital." Ph.D. dissertation, University of North Carolina, 2017.

———."Cain Black Bapticostals." Unpublished dissertation material, May 26, 2018. Microsoft Word file.

———."Cain, MLK, Obama." Unpublished dissertation material, May 26, 2018. Microsoft Word file.

———. "The Angola Prison Seminary." Review of *The Angola Prison Seminary: Effects of Faith-Based Ministry on Identity, transformation, Desistance, and Rehabilitation*. By Michael Hallett, Joshua Hayes, Byron Johnson, Sung Joon Jang, and Grant Duwe, for Reading Religion, June 1, 2018: http://readingreligion.org/books/angola-prison-seminary.

Gerbner, Katherine. *Christian Slavery: Conversion and Race in the Protestant Atlantic World*. Philadelphia: University of Pennsylvania Press, 2018.

Girard, René. *Violence and the Sacred*. New York: W. W. Norton, 1979.

Gordon, Sarah Barringer. "The First Disestablishment: Limits on Church Power and Property before the Civil War." *University of Pennsylvania Law Review* 162, no. 2 (January 2014): 307–372.

———. *The Mormon Question: Polygamy and Constitutional Conflict in 19th Century America*. Chapel Hill: University of North Carolina Press, 2002.

———. *The Spirit of the Law: Religious Voices and the Constitution in Modern America*. Cambridge, MA: Belknap Press, 2010.

Grabenstein, J. D. "What the World's Religions Teach, Applied to Vaccines and Immune Globulins." *Vaccine* 31 (2013): 2011–2023.

Grant, Bruce. "New Moscow Monuments, or, States of Innocence" *American Ethnologist* 28, no. 2 (2001): 332–362.

Green, Steven K. *The Second Disestablishment: Church and State in Nineteenth-Century America*. Oxford: Oxford University Press, 2010.

Greenawalt, Kent. *Religion and the Constitution*. Vol. 2: *Establishment and Fairness*. Princeton: Princeton University Press, 2008.

Griffith, R. Marie. *Moral Combat: How Sex Divided American Christians and Fractured American Politics.* New York: Basic Books, 2017.

Gum, Kathryn Lin, and Lerone Martin. "American Religion and the Rise of Internal Security: A Prologue." In *The FBI and Religion: Faith and National Security before and after 9/11*, edited by Sylvester A. Johnson and Steven Weitzman, 17–31. Berkeley: University of California Press, 2017.

Haefeli, Evan, ed., *Against Popery: Anti-Catholicism and the British-American World*. Charlottesville: University of Virginia Press, forthcoming 2020.

———. *English Tolerance and Overseas Expansion Between Renaissance and Early Enlightenment, 1497–1688.* University of Chicago Press. Forthcoming.

———. "A Home, Made Abroad: American Religion from Colonies to Civil War." In *At Home and Abroad,* edited by Elizabeth Shakman Hurd and Winnifred Fallers Sullivan (forthcoming).

———. "The Problem with the History of Toleration." In *Politics of Religious Freedom*, ed. Winnifred Fallers Sullivan, Elizabeth Shakman Hurd, Saba Mahmood, and Peter Danchin. Chicago: University of Chicago Press, 2015.

Hallett, Michael, Joshua Hays, Byron Johnson, Sung Joon Jang, and Grant Duwe. *The Angola Prison Seminary: Effects of Faith-Based Ministry on Identity Transformation, Desistance, and Rehabilitation*. New York: Routledge, 2018.

Hamburger, Philip. *Separation of Church and State.* Cambridge: Harvard University Press, 2002.

Hanchard, Michael G. *The Spectre of Race: How Discrimination Haunts Western Democracy*. Princeton: Princeton University Press, 2018.

Harcourt, Bernard E. *Against Prediction: Profiling, Policing, and Punishing in an Actuarial Age*. Chicago: University of Chicago Press, 2007.

———. "Risk as a Proxy for Race." University of Chicago Public Law & Legal Theory Working Paper No. 323 (2010).

Hartog, Hendrik. *The Trouble with Minna: A Case of Slavery and Emancipation in the Antebellum North*. Chapel Hill: University of North Carolina Press, 2016.

Heim, Irene. *The Semantics of Definite and Indefinite Noun Phrases.* New York: Garland Publishers, 1988.

Herman, Edward S., and Noam Chomsky. *Manufacturing Consent: The Political Economy of the Mass Media.* New York: Pantheon, 1988.

Himes, Chester. *Yesterday Will Make You Cry.* New York: W. W. Norton and Company, 1998.

Hindmarsh, Bruce. "Is Evangelical Ecclesiology an Oxymoron? A Historical Perspective." *International Journal for the Study of the Christian Church* 7(2007): 302–322.

Hoeper, Jeffery D., and James H. Pickering. *Poetry: An Introduction.* New York: Macmillan, 1990.

Hooker, Richard. *Of the Lawes of Ecclesiasticall Politie.* London: Da Capo Press, 1594.

Horwitz, Paul. "Freedom of the Church Without Romance." *Journal of Contemporary Legal Issues* 21, no. 1 (2013): 59–132.

Howard, A. E. Dick. *Magna Carta: Text and Commentary.* Charlottesville: University Press of Virginia, 1998.

———. *The Road from Runnymede: Magna Carta and Constitutionalism in America.* Charlottesville: University of Virginia Press, 1968.

Howe, Mark DeWolfe. "Foreword: Political Theory and the Nature of Liberty." *Harvard Law Review* 67 (1953): 91–179.

———. *The Garden and the Wilderness: Religion and Government in American Constitutional History*. Chicago: University of Chicago Press, 1967.

Hurd, Elizabeth Shakman. *Beyond Religious Freedom: The New Global Politics of Religion*. Princeton: Princeton University Press, 2015.

———. "Border Religion." In *At Home and Abroad*, ed. Elizabeth Shakman Hurd and Winnifred Fallers Sullivan. Forthcoming.

Hurd, Elizabeth Shakman, and Winnifred Fallers Sullivan, eds. *At Home and Abroad*. Forthcoming.

Hurst, James Willard. *The Legitimacy of the Business Corporation in the Law of the United States, 1780–1970*. Charlottesville: University Press of Virginia, 1971.

Imhoff, Sarah. "Belief." In *Religion, Law, USA*, edited by Isaac Weiner and Joshua Dubler. New York: New York University Press, 2019.

Inazu, John D. "The Freedom of the Church (Revised Standard Version)." *Journal of Contemporary Legal Issues* 21, no. 1 (2013): 335–368.

Jakobsen, Janet R., and Ann Pellegrini. *Love the Sin: Sexual Regulation and the Limits of Religious Tolerance.* Boston: Beacon Press, 2004.

Jay, Nancy. *Throughout Your Generations Forever: Sacrifice, Religion and Paternity*. Chicago: University of Chicago Press, 1992.

Johnson, Byron. "The Role of African-American Churches in Reducing Crime Among Black Youth." Baylor University ISR Report 2008. https://www.baylor.edu/content/services/document.php/24230.pdf.

Johnson, Elizabeth A. *She Who Is: The Mystery of God in Feminist Theological Discourse*. New York: Crossroad Publishing, 1992.

Johnson, Paul Christopher, Pamela Klassen, and Winnifred Fallers Sullivan. *Ekklesia: Three Inquiries in Church and State.* Chicago: University of Chicago Press, 2018.

Johnson, Sylvester A. *African American Religions, 1500–2000.* Cambridge: Cambridge University Press, 2015.

———. "Divine Imperium and the Ecclesiastical Imaginary: Church History, Transnationalism, and the Rationality of Empire." *Church History* 83, no. 4 (December 2014): 1003–1008.

Johnson, Sylvester A., and Steven Weitzman, eds. *The FBI and Religion: Faith and National Security before and after 9/11* (Berkeley: University of California Press, 2017).

Ludin, Sara. "The Reformation Suits: Litigation as Constitution-Making in a German Imperial Court, 1521–1555." Ph.D. dissertation, University of California at Berkeley, 2019.

Kantorowicz, Ernst H. *The King's Two Bodies: A Study in Medieval Political Theology.* Princeton: Princeton University Press, 1957.

Kaveny, M. Cathleen. "Complicity with Evil." *Criterion* (2003): 20–29.

———. *Ethics at the Edges of Law: Christian Moralists and American Legal Thought.* Oxford: Oxford University Press, 2018.

Kennedy, Liam. "'Today They Kill with the Chair Instead of the Tree': Forgetting and Remembering Slavery at a Plantation Prison." *Theoretical Criminology* 21, no. 2 (May 2017): 133–150.

Kennedy, Sheila Suess. *Charitable Choice at Work: Evaluating Faith-Based Job Programs in the States*. Washington, DC: Georgetown University Press, 2006.

Kessler, Amalia. *Inventing American Exceptionalism: The Origins of American Adversarial Legal Culture, 1800–1877*. New Haven: Yale University Press, 2017.

Khabeer, Su'ad Abdul. *Muslim Cool: Race, Religion, and Hip Hop in the United States*. New York: New York University Press, 2016.

Kirk, Nicole C. *Wanamaker's Temple: The Business of Religion in an Iconic Department Store*. New York: New York University Press, 2018.

Koppelman, Andrew. "The Freedom of the Church in the Modern Era: 'Freedom of the Church' and the Authority of the State." *Journal of Contemporary Legal Issues* 21 (2013): 145.

Laborde, Cecile. *Liberalism's Religion.* Cambridge: Harvard University Press, 2017.

———. "Response to Winnifred Fallers Sullivan." Blog post at *Syndicate* network forum on Laborde, *Liberalism's Religion*, https://syndicate.network/.

Lamoreaux, Naomi R., and William J. Novak, eds. *Corporations and American Democracy*. Cambridge: Harvard University Press, 2017.

LaRue, Lewis. *Constitutional Law as Fiction: Narrative in the Rhetoric of Authority.* University Park: Pennsylvania State University Press, 1995.

Laski, Harold Joseph. "The Pluralistic State." *Philosophical Review* 28 (November 1919): 562–575.

Latour, Bruno. *An Inquiry into Modes of Existence: An Anthropology of the Moderns.* Translated by Catherine Porter. Cambridge, MA: Harvard University Press, 2013.

———. *The Making of Law: An Ethnography of the Conseil d'État.* Cambridge, UK: Polity Press, 2010.

———. *Rejoicing: Or the Torments of Religious Speech*. Cambridge, UK: Polity Press, 2013.

Latour, Bruno, and Steve Woolgar. *Laboratory Life: The Construction of Scientific Facts*. Princeton, NJ: Princeton University Press, 1986.

Laycock, Douglas. "Formal, Substantive, and Disaggregated Neutrality Toward Religion." *DePaul Law Review* 39 (1990): 993–1018.

Lee, Jarena. "The Life and Religious Experience of Jarena Lee." In *Sisters of the Spirit: Three Black Women's Autobiographies of the Nineteenth Century*, edited by William L. Andrews, 25–48. Bloomington: Indiana University Press, 1986.

Levene, Nancy. *Powers of Distinction: On Religion and Modernity.* Chicago: University of Chicago Press, 2017.

Levy, Jonathan, "From Fiscal Triangle to Passing Through: Rise of the Nonprofit Corporation." In *Corporations and American Democracy*, edited by Naomi R. Lamoreaux and William J. Novak, 213–244. Cambridge: Harvard University Press, 2017.

Lofton, Kathryn. *Consuming Religion.* Chicago: University of Chicago Press, 2017.

Loisy, Alfred. *The Gospel and the Church*. Eugene, OR: Wipf & Stock Publishers, 2001.

Long, Charles H. *Significations: Signs, Symbols, and Images in the Interpretation of Religion*. Minneapolis: Fortress Press, 1986.

Lubac, Henri de. *Corpus Mysticum: The Eucharist and the Church in the Middle Ages.* Translated by Gemma Simmonds with Richard Price and Christopher Stephens. South Bend: University of Notre Dame Press, 2006.

Lupu, Ira C., and Robert W. Tuttle. "The Mystery of Unanimity in *Hosanna-Tabor Evangelical Lutheran Church & School v. EEOC*." *Lewis & Clark Law Review* 20 (2017): 1265–1315.

Luster, Deborah, and Zachary Lazar. "Angola Passion Play." *Aperture* (April 2018).

Luther, Martin. *On the Councils and the Church* (1539). In *Luther's Works*. Vol. 41. Edited by Eric W. Gritsch. Minneapolis: Fortress Press, 1966.

MacCulloch, Diarmaid. *Thomas Cromwell: A Revolutionary Life*. New York: Viking, 2018.

Maffly-Kipp, Laurie. "The Burdens of Church History." *Church History* 82 (2013): 353–367.

Mahmood, Saba. *Religious Difference in a Secular Age: A Minority Report.* Princeton: Princeton University Press, 2016.

Maier, Pauline. "The Revolutionary Origins of the American Corporation." *William and Mary Quarterly* 50 (1993): 51–84.

Maitland, Frederic William. *State, Trust, and Corporation*. Edited by David Runciman and Magnus Ryan. Cambridge: Cambridge University Press, 2003.

Martin, Lerone. *"Sincerely Yours, J. Edgar Hoover": Religion and the F.B.I.* Under contract with Princeton University Press.

Marty, Martin E. *The Public Church: Mainline, Evangelical, Catholic*. Eugene, OR: Wipf & Stock Publishers, 1981.

Massey, Calvin. "Church Schisms, Church Property, and Civil Authority." *St. John's Law Review* 84, no. 2 (Winter 2010): 23–62.

Masuzawa, Tomoko. "The University and the Advent of the Academic Secular: The State's Management of Public Instruction." In *After Secular Law*, ed. Winnifred Fallers Sullivan, Mateo Taussig-Rubbo, and Robert Yelle, 119–139. Palo Alto: Stanford University Press, 2011.

McAlister, Melani. *The Kingdom of God Has No Borders: A Global History of American Evangelicals*. Oxford: Oxford University Press, 2018.

McBride, Keally. *Mr. Mothercountry: The Man Who Invented the Rule of Law*. Oxford: Oxford University Press, 2016.

McConnell, Michael W. "Reflections on *Hosanna-Tabor*." *Harvard Journal of Law & Public Policy* 35, no. 3 (June 2012): 821–837.

McConnell, Michael W., and Luke W. Goodrich. "On Resolving Church Property Disputes." *Arizona Law Review* 58, no. 2 (2016): 307–358.

McGarvie, Mark. "The Dartmouth College Case, the Contract Clause, and the Creation of the Private Sector." HistPhil forum, https://histphil.org/2019/07/23/the-dartmouth-college-case-the-contract-clause-and-the-creation-of-the-private-sector/.

Mead, Sidney E. *The Lively Experiment*. Eugene, OR: Wipf & Stock Publishers, 2007.

Meltzer, Françoise. *For Fear of the Fire: Joan of Arc and the Limits of Subjectivity*. Chicago: University of Chicago Press, 2001.

Mertz, Elizabeth, William K. Ford, and Gregory Matoesian. *Translating the Social World for Law: Linguistic Tools for a New Legal Realism*. Oxford: Oxford University Press, 2016.

Moreton, Bethany. *To Serve God and Wal-Mart: The Making of Christian Free Enterprise*. Cambridge: Harvard University Press, 2010.

Morris, Norval. *The Future of Imprisonment*. Chicago: University of Chicago Press, 1974.

Morris, Wesley. "Aretha Franklin Had Power. Did We Truly Respect It?" *New York Times*. August 16, 2018. https://www.nytimes.com/2018/08/16/arts/music/respect-aretha-franklin-death.html.

Morrison, Toni. *Beloved*. New York: Vintage Books, 1987.

Muhammad, Khalil Gibran. *The Condemnation of Blackness: Race, Crime, and the Making of Modern Urban America*. Cambridge: Harvard University Press, 2010.

Mullen, Lincoln. *The Chance of Salvation: A History of Conversion in America*. Cambridge: Harvard University Press, 2017.

Murray, John Courtney. *We Hold These Truths: Catholic Reflections on the American Proposition*. New York: Sheed and Ward, 1960.

Nederman, C.J. "The Liberty of the Church and the Road to Runnymede: John of Salisbury and the Intellectual Foundations of the Magna Carta." *Political Science and Politics* 43, no. 3 (July 2010): 457–461.

Nelson, William E. *The Fourteenth Amendment: From Political Principle to Judicial Doctrine*. Cambridge: Harvard University Press, 1998.

Nicholls, David. *The Pluralist State: The Political Ideas of J. N. Figgis and His Contemporaries*. Oxford: St Anthony's Press, 1975.

Noll, Mark A. *The Scandal of the Evangelical Mind*. Grand Rapids, MI: Eerdmans, 1994.

Noonan, John T., Jr. *Persons and Masks of the Law: Cardozo, Holmes, Jefferson, and Wythe as Makers of the Masks.* Berkeley: University of California Press, 1976.

O'Brien, F. William. *Justice Reed and the First Amendment: The Religion Clauses*. Washington, DC: Georgetown University Press, 1958.

O'Brien, John. *Literature Incorporated: The Cultural Unconscious of the Business Corporation, 1650–1850*. Chicago: University of Chicago Press, 2016.

Oraby, Mona. "The Difference That Affiliation Makes: Religious Conversion, Minorities, and the Rule of Law." Ph.D. dissertation, Northwestern University, 2017.

Osiek, Carolyn. "The Bride of Christ (Ephesians 5:22–33): A Problematic Wedding." *Biblical Theology* 32, no. 1 (Spring 2002): 29–39.

Peterson, Erik. *Theological Tractates*. Translated by Michael J. Hollerich. Stanford: Stanford University Press, 2011.

Peterson, Farah. "Monuments and Memory: How the Law Writes American History." Sherman Emerging Scholar Lecture Series, Warwick Center, University of North Carolina, Wilmington. October 17, 2018

Peterson, Merrill D., and Robert C. Vaughn, eds. *The Virginia Statute for Religious Freedom: Its Evolution and Consequences in American History*. New York: Cambridge University Press, 1988.

Pinn, Anthony B. *The Black Church in the Post–Civil Rights Era*. Maryknoll, NY: Orbis, 2002.

———. *The End of God-Talk: An African American Humanist Theology*. Oxford: Oxford University Press, 2012.

———. "Reading Du Bois Through Religion and Religious Commitment." *Journal of Religion* 94, no. 3 (July 2014): 370–382.

Pratt, Henry. *Churches and Urban Government in Detroit and New York*. Detroit: Wayne State University Press, 2004.

Raboteau, Albert. *Slave Religion: The Invisible Institution in the Antebellum South*. Updated ed. Oxford: Oxford University Press, 2004; originally published 1978.

Rajah, Jothie. *Authoritarian Rule of Law: Legislation, Discourse, and Legitimacy in Singapore.* Cambridge: Cambridge University Press, 2014.

Read, Kay. "To Eat and Be Eaten: Mesoamerican Human Sacrifice and Ecological Webs." In *The Wiley-Blackwell Companion to Material Religion*, edited by Vasudha Narayanan. Oxford, UK: Wiley-Blackwell, 2019.

Richland, J. B. "Jurisdiction: Grounding Law in Language." *Annual Review of Anthropology* 42 (2013): 209–226.

Rideau, Wilbert, and Billy Sinclair. "Prisoner Litigation: How it Began in Louisiana." *Louisiana Law Review* 45 (1985): 1061–1076.

Ridgeway, James. "The Overseer." *Mother Jones* 36, no. 4 (July/August 2011): 44–51.

Rivers, Julian. *The Law of Organized Religions: Between Establishment and Secularism*. Oxford: Oxford University Press, 2010.

Rolsky, Louis Benjamin. "Charles H. Long and the Re-orientation of American Religious History." *Journal of the American Academy of Religion* 80 (2012): 750–774.

Rose, Gillian. *Love's Work: A Reckoning with Life*. New York: Schocken Books, 1997.

———. *Mourning Becomes the Law: Philosophy and Representation*. Cambridge: Cambridge University Press, 1996.

Rowe, Nina. *The Jew, the Cathedral, and the Medieval City: Synagoga and Ecclesia in the Thirteenth Century*. Cambridge: Cambridge University Press, 2011.

Sager, Lawrence G. "Why Churches (and Possibly, the Tarpon Bay Women's Blue Water Fishing Club) Can Discriminate." In *The Rise of Corporate Religious Liberty*, edited by Micah Schwartzman, Chad Flanders, and Zoe Robinson, 77–102. New York: Oxford University Press, 2016.

Salomon, Noah. *For Love of the Prophet: An Ethnography of Sudan's Islamic State*. Princeton: Princeton University Press, 2016.

Sandoz, Ellis, ed. *The Roots of Liberty: Magna Carta, Ancient Constitution, and the Anglo-American Tradition of Rule of Law*. Indianapolis: Liberty Fund, 2008.

Santner, Eric L. *The Royal Remains: The People's Two Bodies and the Endgames of Sovereignty*. Chicago: University of Chicago Press, 2011.

Sarkisian, Aram. "The Cross Between Hammer and Sickle: Russian Orthodox Christians in the United States, 1908–1928." Ph.D. dissertation, Northwestern University, 2019.

Satz, Meridith. "Comment: Re-interpreting the Parsonage Exclusion: Constitutional Challenges and the Agency Response in the Wake of *Freedom From Religion Foundation, Inc. v. Lew*." *Administrative Law Review* 67, no. 4 (Fall 2016): 751–772.

Savage, Barbara Dianne. "W. E. B. Du Bois and the Negro Church." *Annals of the American Academy of Political and Social Science* 568 (March 2000): 235–250.

———. *Your Spirits Walk Beside Us: The Politics of Black Religion*. Cambridge: Harvard University Press, 2008.

Schneider, David. *American Kinship: A Cultural Account*. Chicago: University of Chicago Press, 1968.

Schoenfeld, Heather. *Building the Prison State: Race and the Politics of Mass Incarceration*. Chicago: University of Chicago Press, 2018.

Schragger, Richard, and Micah Schwartzman. "Against Religious Institutionalism." *Virginia Law Review* 99:5 (September 2013): 917–985.

Schrift, Melissa. "The Angola Prison Rodeo: Inmate Cowboys and Institutional Tourism." *Ethnology* 43, no. 4 (Fall 2004): 331–344.

———. "The Wildest Show in the South: The Politics and Poetics of the Angola Prison Rodeo and Inmate Arts Festival." *Southern Cultures* 14, no. 1 (Spring 2008): 22–41.

Scott, Joan W. *Sex and Secularism*. Princeton: Princeton University Press, 2017.

Selka, Stephen. "Morality in the Religious Marketplace: Evangelical Christianity, Candomblé, and the Struggle for Moral Distinction in Brazil." *American Ethnologist* 37, no. 2 (2010): 291–307.

Serritella, James, ed. *Religious Organizations in the United States: A Study of Identity, Liberty, and the Law.* Durham, NC: Carolina Academic Press, 2006.

Sexton, Jason. "Greystone Chapel: Finding Freedom in Folsom Prison's Walls." *Boom: A Journal of California* 6/2 (Summer 2016): 104–111.

———. "Redeemed on the Inside: Radical Accounts of *Ecclesia* Incarcerate." *Ecclesial Practices* 5/2 (2018): 172–190.

———. "Toward a Theology of California's *Ecclesia* Incarcerate." *Theology* 118 (2015): 83–91.

Shevzov, Vera. *Russian Orthodoxy on the Eve of the Revolution*. Oxford: Oxford University Press, 2004.

———. "Women on the Fault Lines of Faith: Pussy Riot and the Insider/Outsider Challenge to Post-Soviet Orthodoxy." *Religion & Gender* 4 (2014): 121–144.

Sideris, Lisa. *Consecrating Science: Wonder, Knowledge, and the Natural World.* Berkeley: University of California Press, 2017.

Smith, James K. A. *Awaiting the King; Reforming Public Theology.* Grand Rapids, MI: Baker Academic, 2017.

Smith, Jonathan Z. *Map Is Not Territory: Studies in the History of Religions.* Chicago: University of Chicago Press, 1993.

———. *To Take Place: Toward Theory in Ritual.* Chicago: University of Chicago Press, 1987.

———. "The Wobbling Pivot." *Journal of Religion*, 52:2 (April 1972): 134–149.

Sorett, Josef. "A Fantastic Church?: Literature, Politics, and the Afterlives of Afro-Protestantism." *Public Culture* 29, no. 1 (January 2017): 17–26.

Sparrow, James T., William J. Novak, and Stephen W. Sawyer. eds. *Boundaries of the State in US History*. Chicago: University of Chicago Press, 2015.

Stack, Jonathon, and Liz Garbus. *The Farm: Angola, USA.* Highest Common Denominator Media Group, 2009.

Stackhouse, John G., Jr., ed. *Evangelical Ecclesiology: Reality or Illusion?* Grand Rapids, MI: Baker Academic, 2002.

Stern, Philip J. "The English East India Company and the Modern Corporation: Legacies, Lessons, and Limitations." *Seattle University Law Review* 39, no. 2 (Winter 2016): 423–446.

Stoddard, Brad. "The New Prison Reformers: Florida's Faith-Based Prisons and the Politics of Religious Pluralism." Ph.D. dissertation, Florida State University, 2015.

Strasser, Mark. "Free Exercise and the Definition of Religion." *Houston Law Review* 53 (2016): 909–937.

———. "Masterpiece of Misdirection?" *Washington & Lee Law Review* 76 (2019): 963–1010.

Sullivan, Winnifred Fallers. "'The Conscience of Contemporary Man': Reflections on *U.S. v. Seeger* and *Dignitatis Humanae*." *U.S. Catholic Historian* 24 (Winter 2006): 107–123.

Sullivan, Winnifred Fallers. *Impossibility of Religious Freedom*. Princeton: Princeton University Press, 2005.

———. *A Ministry of Presence: Chaplaincy, Spiritual Care, and the Law.* Chicago: University of Chicago Press, 2014.

———. *Prison Religion: Faith-Based Reform and the Constitution.* Princeton: Princeton University Press, 2009.

———. Review of Christopher J. Scalia and Edward Whelan, eds., *Scalia Speaks: Reflections on Law, Faith, and Life Well Lived. Commonweal* 2018 (June 1): 33–34.

Sullivan, Winnifred Fallers. "The World *Smith* Made." *Politics of Religious Freedom*, ed. Winnifred Fallers Sullivan, Elizabeth Shakman Hurd, Saba Mahmood, and Peter Danchin, 231–239. Chicago: University of Chicago Press, 2015.

Sullivan, Winnifred Fallers, and Elizabeth Shakman Hurd, eds. *America Is Hard to See.* Forthcoming.

Sullivan, Winnifred Fallers, Elizabeth Shakman Hurd, Saba Mahmood, and Peter Danchin, eds. *Politics of Religious Freedom*. Chicago: University of Chicago Press, 2015.

Taussig-Rubbo, Mateo. "Outsourcing Sacrifice: The Labor of Private Military Contractors." *Yale Journal of Law & Humanities* 21 (2009): 103–166.

Tocqueville, Alexis de. *Democracy in America*. Translated by George Lawrence. New York: Anchor Press, 1969.

Tomlins, Christopher L. and Bruce H. Mann, eds. *The Many Legalities of Early America*. Chapel Hill: University of North Carolina Press, 2001.

Turner, Henry S. *The Corporate Commonwealth: Pluralism and Political Fictions in England, 1516–1651*. Chicago: University of Chicago Press, 2016.

Valverde, Mariana. *Chronotopes of Law: Jurisdiction, Scale, and Governance*. Milton Park, UK: Routledge, 2015.

van der Veer, Peter. *The Modern Spirit of Asia*. Princeton: Princeton University Press, 2014.

Wagner-Pacifici, Robin. *Discourse and Destruction: The City of Philadelphia versus MOVE*. Chicago: University of Chicago Press, 1994.

Weber, Max, *The Protestant Ethic and the Spirit of Capitalism*. Translated by Talcott Parsons. London: G. Allen & Unwin, Ltd., 1930.

Weissbrod, Carol. *The Boundaries of Utopia*. New York: Random House, 1980.

Weisenfeld, Judith. *New World A-Coming: Black Religion and Racial Identity During the Great Migration*. New York: New York University Press, 2016.

Wenger, Tisa. *Religious Freedom: The Contested History of an American Ideal.* Durham: University of North Carolina Press, 2017.

White, James Boyd. *Acts of Hope: Creating Authority in Literature, Law, and Politics*. Chicago: University of Chicago Press, 1995.

———. *Justice as Translation: An Essay in Cultural and Legal Criticism*. Chicago: University of Chicago Press, 1990.

———. *The Legal Imagination: Studies in the Nature of Legal Thought and Expression*. 45th anniversary ed. New York: Wolters Kluwer, 2018.

———. "What's Wrong with Our Talk about Race? On History, Particularity, and Affirmative Action." *Michigan Law Review* 100 (2002): 1927–1953.

Wideman, John Edgar. *Philadelphia Fire.* Boston: Houghton Mifflin, 1990.

Winters, Joseph. *Hope Draped in Black: Race, Melancholy, and the Agony of Progress.* Durham: Duke University Press, 2016.

Woodfox, Albert. *Solitary: Unbroken by Four Decades in Solitary Confinement: My Story of Transformation and Hope*. New York: Grove Press, 2019.

Wuthnow, Robert. *Inventing American Religion: Polls, Surveys, and the Tenuous Quest for a Nation's Faith*. Oxford: Oxford University Press, 2015.

Yelle, Robert A. *Sovereignty and the Sacred: Secularism and the Political Economy of Religion*. Chicago: University of Chicago Press, 2018.

e-publications

"Anthony Bourdain: No Reservations." Season 7. Travel Channel. February–December 2011. https://www.travelchannel.com/shows/anthony-bourdain

Årsheim, Helge. *Religion Going Public* (blog). http://religiongoingpublic.com/archive/2017/imagine-theres-no-religion-and-no-state-church-too

"Advanced Article Usage." Englishpage.com. https://www.englishpage.com/articles/advanced-articles.htm.

Barry, A. L. "What about the Ordination of Women to the Pastoral Office?" https://www.cph.org/p-194-what-about-ordination-of-women-to-the-pastoral-office-tract-pack-of-25.aspx/.

Bourdain, Anthony. "Hanoi." *Parts Unknown*. Season 8, episode 1 (aired September 24, 2016), CNN.

"Catechism of the Catholic Church." The Holy See. http://www.vatican.va/archive/ENG0015/_INDEX.HTM (accessed October 22, 2018).

"Church, Doctrine of." Global Anabaptist Mennonite Encyclopedia Online. https://gameo.org/index.php?title=Church,_Doctrine_of.

"Crossing and Conversion." *The Immanent Frame*. https://tif.ssrc.org/category/exchanges/crossing-and-conversion/.

"Dignitatis Humanae." The Holy See. http://www.vatican.va/archive/hist_councils/ii_vatican_council/documents/vat-ii_decl_19651207_dignitatis-humanae_en.html (accessed October 22, 2018).

"Documents of the Second Vatican Council." The Holy See. http://www.vatican.va/archive/hist_councils/ii_vatican_council/index.htm (accessed October 22, 2018).

Heider, George C. "What's the *supreme* question in *Hosanna-Tabor v. EEOC*?" *The Immanent Frame.* https://tif.ssrc.org/2011/10/27/the-supreme-question-in-hosanna-tabor-v-eeoc/ (accessed November 7, 2017).

"Keystone Mennonite Fellowship." Global Anabaptist Mennonite Encyclopedia Online. https://gameo.org/index.php?title=Keystone_Mennonite_Fellowship.

"Sex, Secularism, and 'Femonationalism.'" *The Immanent Frame.* https://tif.ssrc.org/category/exchanges/sex-secularism-femonationalism/

Sullivan, Winnifred Fallers. "Is Masterpiece Cake Shop a Church?" *The Immanent Frame.* https://tif.ssrc.org/2018/06/08/is-masterpiece-cakeshop-a-church/.

Websites

Angola Rodeo: Louisiana State Penitentiary. http://www.angolarodeo.com/.

IRS FAQ. https://www.irs.gov/help-resources/tools-faqs/faqs-for-individuals/frequently-asked-tax-questions-answers/interest-dividends-other-types-of-income/ministers-compensation-housing-allowance/ministers-compensation-housing-allowance.

"Ministers Compensation and Housing Allowance." October, 2018. IRS Website. https://www.irs.gov/help-resources/tools-faqs/faqs-for-individuals/frequently-asked-tax-questions-answers/interest-dividends-other-types-of-income/ministers-compensation-housing-allowance/ministers-compensation-housing-allowance

MOVE. http://onamove.com/.

Museum of the Bible. https://www.museumofthebible.org/.

Oklevueha: Native American Church. https://nativeamericanchurches.org/native-american-church-first-nation-history/ (accessed October 20, 2018).

Supreme Court of the United States. "Oral Argument—Audio." https://www.supremecourt.gov/oral_arguments/audio/2011/10-553/.

"Tax Information for Churches and Religious Organizations." IRS Website. Accessed October 20, 2018. https://www.irs.gov/charities-non-profits/churches-religious-organizations.

Index